ROMEO
AND JULIET

The RSC Shakespeare

Edited by Jonathan Bate and Eric Rasmussen

Chief Associate Editors: Héloïse Sénéchal and Jan Sewell

Associate Editors: Trey Jansen, Eleanor Lowe, Lucy Munro,
Dee Anna Phares

Romeo and Juliet

Textual editing: Eric Rasmussen

Introduction and Shakespeare's Career in the Theater: Jonathan Bate

Commentary: Héloïse Sénéchal

Scene-by-Scene Analysis: Esmé Miskimmin

In Performance: Karin Brown (RSC stagings), Jan Sewell (overview)

The Director's Cut: Michael Attenborough

Playing Romeo: David Tennant

Playing Juliet: Alexandra Gilbreath

(interviews by Jonathan Bate and Kevin Wright)

Editorial Advisory Board

The RSC Shakespeare

William Shakespeare

ROMEO
AND JULIET

Edited by Jonathan Bate and Eric Rasmussen

Introduction by Jonathan Bate

The Modern Library
New York

CONTENTS

Introduction   vii
  "A Pair of Star-crossed Lovers"   vii
  "The Fearful Passage of their Death-marked Love"   ix
  "These Violent Delights have Violent Ends"   xi

About the Text   xvi

Key Facts   xxiii

Romeo and Juliet   1

Textual Notes   115

Scene-by-Scene Analysis   118

***Romeo and Juliet* in Performance: The RSC and Beyond**   130
  Four Centuries of *Romeo and Juliet*: An Overview   130
  At the RSC   141
  The Director's Cut: Interview with Michael Attenborough   157
  David Tennant on Playing Romeo   166
  Alexandra Gilbreath on Playing Juliet   173

Shakespeare's Career in the Theater   180
  Beginnings   180
  Playhouses   182
  The Ensemble at Work   186
  The King's Man   191

Shakespeare's Works: A Chronology   194

Further Reading and Viewing   197

References   200

Acknowledgments and Picture Credits   204

INTRODUCTION

"A PAIR OF STAR-CROSSED LOVERS"

In *Romeo and Juliet*, Shakespeare invented the idea of the teenager in love. Many of his characters—the thin and anguished Hamlet, the fat and jolly Falstaff, the sexy Cleopatra, the aged King Lear—have associations even for people who have never seen or read his plays, but none more so than Romeo and Juliet. All around the world, the pairing of the names is synonymous with the idea of being young and in love. "Juliet's balcony" has long been a tourist destination in Verona, even though she is a fictional character and there is no balcony in Shakespeare's play (in the original text she appears at her "window"; it was only in the theater of David Garrick a century and a half after the play was written that the balcony was introduced as part of the set design). Innumerable allusions in popular culture and song attest to the couple's status as archetypes of young love—"We were both young when I first saw you . . . I'm standing there / On a balcony in summer air" (Taylor Swift, "Love Story"). When this song was performed at the 2008 Country Music Awards it was accompanied by couples in eighteenth-century costume re-enacting the ball from *Romeo and Juliet*, including the sequence in which the lovers link hands. At the end of the song a handsome Romeo in breeches appeared beside Ms. Swift, the answer to every teenage girl's dream.

"The process or condition of growing up; the growing age of human beings; the period which extends from childhood to manhood or womanhood; youth; ordinarily considered as extending from 14 to 25 in males, and from 12 to 21 in females." Thus the *Oxford English Dictionary*'s definition of "adolescence." Around the beginning of the Second World War, the new word "teenager" was coined for this phase of human life, but the idea that there was a distinct period between childhood and adulthood has a long history.

In ancient Greece, Aristotle divided life into youth, middle age, and old age. In ancient Rome, Ovid's *Metamorphoses* included a sustained comparison between the four seasons and the passage of human life under the auspices of Time, the devourer of all things. In early Christianity, St. Chrysostom developed a six-fold division: infant, child, adolescent, young man, man of gravitas, old man. He suggested that each age had its own particular earthly miseries. Later writers, anticipating the famous speech by Jaques in Shakespeare's *As You Like It*, added one further age of man (decrepitude, extreme old age, or "second childhood"). The elegance of the "seven ages" was their correspondence to the quasi-magical properties of the number seven. God may have created everything in six days, but there was also the seventh day on which he rested. Both biblical and classical writers often ordered things in sevens, as with Jacob's prediction to Pharaoh of seven fat years, then seven lean ones. It was therefore widely believed that human life went in seven-year cycles.

Sixteenth-century writers typically proposed the following pattern: the first age is infancy (from Latin *infans*, meaning "unable to speak"), then comes childhood, which lasts to the age of seven, then youth, which lasts till fourteen, then adolescence, lasting from fourteen to twenty-eight and characterized as the reign of "concupiscence," which meant bodily and especially sexual appetite. Then comes virility or "man's estate," which continues until the completion of the forty-ninth year. Old age sets in at fifty and lasts until death, if you are a believer in the six ages, or until decrepitude, if you prefer seven.

Consider the Old Shepherd's entrance line in *The Winter's Tale*: "I would there were no age between ten and three-and-twenty, or that youth would sleep out the rest, for there is nothing in the between but getting wenches with child, wronging the ancientry, stealing, fighting." This suggests that Shakespeare, like many of his contemporaries, lumped together "youth" and "adolescence" into a single age of sexual indulgence, riot and high spirits, lasting fourteen years. This is where he locates Romeo and Juliet, along with the other young male blades in the play. Juliet, crucially, is on the threshold of her fourteenth birthday. Romeo's age is not specified but he has clearly not reached that stage in the mid-twenties when a young male matures fully into "man's estate."

Tragedy is traditionally focused on the undoing of heroes of extreme masculinity or on powerful rulers who climb to the top of

Fortune's wheel, then tumble to catastrophe. There was a long tradition of poetry about doomed lovers, but to make a pair of adolescents into tragic heroes in a stage play was an extraordinary innovation on Shakespeare's part.

"THE FEARFUL PASSAGE OF THEIR DEATH-MARKED LOVE"

The Irish poet W. B. Yeats remarked in a letter that only two subjects can be of any lasting interest to a serious and studious mind: sex and the dead. He was not thinking about *Romeo and Juliet* at the time, but the play is both seriously and playfully interested in the connection between the drive whose end is the creation of new life and the confrontation that ends in the extinction of life. The same ardent, youthful energy that impels Romeo to Juliet's bed leads him to fight with hot-blooded Tybalt. Death is the consequence of both the rivalry between the male gangs and the sexual attraction between Juliet and Romeo.

The play contains some of Shakespeare's most beautiful poetry, including such well-loved lines as "a rose / By any other word would smell as sweet" and "But, soft, what light through yonder window breaks? / It is the east, and Juliet is the sun." Yet it also contains some of his most raucous bawdy wordplay. Seconds before Romeo identifies Juliet with the rising sun, Mercutio makes a baser comparison: "O, that she were / An open arse and thou a pop'rin pear!" The image depends on the resemblance of the fruit known as a medlar to the female genitals and the Poperinghe species of pear to those of the male. Mercutio's ribbing of Romeo also puns on "to meddle" and "pop it in," both meaning to have sex, and on "O" as a sign of the vagina. The juxtaposition of such matter to Romeo's glorious aria on the transformative effect of love at first sight is typical of Shakespeare's unsentimental robustness. Youthful as the lovers are, Juliet especially, this is a very grown-up play, which recognizes that love and sex are inseparable.

The verbal sparring between Romeo and Mercutio at the beginning of Act 2 scene 3 repays close attention. Mercutio begins by mocking "the numbers that Petrarch flowed in," that is to say the idealizing language of courtly poetry in the sonneteering tradition of the Italian Renaissance master Petrarch writing in praise of his

Laura. As the banter unfolds, it becomes more and more obscene. Love poetry is said to be "drivelling." A lover may use spiritual language, but his purpose is distinctly bodily: "to hide his bauble in a hole." "Stop there, stop there," replies Romeo, as if playing the part of the censor outraged at the explicitness of the sexual reference. But Mercutio is on a roll: "Thou desirest me to stop in my tale against the hair." As so often with Shakespeare, multiple puns are at work: "tale" plays on "tail," a slang term for the male sex organ, while "against the hair" is both a phrase meaning "against my wish" and an allusion to pubic hair. The exchange continues with further puns on erection and flaccidity, "whole" and a woman's "hole," "occupy" as slang for having sex and "gear" as sexual equipment.

Shakespeare is rigorously honest about the paradox of being in love and making love. The same experience is both intensely spiritual and unashamedly down and dirty. The language of the play is often profane, but just as frequently it is sacred. Petrarchan love poetry is parodied, especially by Mercutio, but it is also gloriously indulged in, even woven into the dramatic action by means of the interlocking lines, hands and lips of Romeo and Juliet at the ball. The following sequence, which imitates Petrarch in treating love as a quasi-religious phenomenon, is actually written as a sonnet shared between the two characters:

ROMEO   If I profane with my unworthiest hand
     This holy shrine, the gentle sin is this:
     My lips, two blushing pilgrims, ready stand
     To smooth that rough touch with a tender kiss.
JULIET   Good pilgrim, you do wrong your hand too much,
     Which mannerly devotion shows in this,
     For saints have hands that pilgrims' hands do touch,
     And palm to palm is holy palmers' kiss.
ROMEO   Have not saints lips, and holy palmers too?
JULIET   Ay, pilgrim, lips that they must use in prayer.
ROMEO   O, then, dear saint, let lips do what hands do:
     They pray, grant thou, lest faith turn to despair.
JULIET   Saints do not move, though grant for prayers' sake.
ROMEO   Then move not, while my prayer's effect I take.

And as the sonnet is consummated in the rhyming couplet, he kisses her.

Romeo himself has some rapid growing up to do along the way. At the beginning of the play, he is in love with Rosaline. Or rather, he is in love with the idea of being in love. We never actually see Rosaline: she exists solely as the idealized love object of Romeo. She is nothing more than a literary type, the beautiful but unavailable mistress of the sonnet tradition that goes back to Petrarch. The Petrarchan lover thrives on artifice and paradox. The fire in his heart is dependent on his lady's icy maidenhood—"Feather of lead, bright smoke, cold fire, sick health, / Still-waking sleep that is not what it is!" As the Friar recognizes, this is mere "doting," not true loving. And so long as Mercutio is around, the bubble of poetic language keeps on being pricked—is it not just a matter of rhyming "love" with "dove"?

Romeo still poeticizes on seeing Juliet, though he speaks in richly textured imagery instead of the banal oxymorons inspired by Rosaline: "It seems she hangs upon the cheek of night / As a rich jewel in an Ethiope's ear." Romeo and Juliet weave their sonnet when they meet at the Capulet ball, but over the next few scenes their language evolves into something more fluid and more natural. You can hear Shakespeare growing as a poet even as you see the love between Juliet and Romeo growing from infatuation at first sight to the conviction that each has found the other's soul mate. Love is a chemistry that begins from a physiological transformation—Romeo is "bewitchèd by the charm of looks"—but it becomes a discovery of the very core of a human being: "Can I go forward when my heart is here? / Turn back, dull earth, and find thy centre out."

"THESE VIOLENT DELIGHTS HAVE VIOLENT ENDS"

Shakespeare often thought in pairs. Give him an idea and he is equally interested in its opposite. Sometimes he will handle similar material in successive works, trying it out as comedy in one case and tragedy in the other. In 1593–94, the theaters were closed due to a severe outbreak of plague in London. During this time, Shakespeare wrote a pair of narrative poems on the subject of erotic desire: the playful *Venus and Adonis* and the mournful *Rape of Lucrece*. Both were based on stories by the Roman poet Ovid, Shakespeare's prime precursor in the art of quick changes and sudden contradictions.

Within a year or so of the theaters reopening, he wrote his most Ovidian play, *A Midsummer Night's Dream*, that wonder-filled anatomy of love in which "quick bright things come to confusion" and "everything seems double," until out of dream and illusion there grows "something of great constancy." *Dream* turns on comedy's ancient plot of young people finding true love in the face of parental opposition. In the final act, the opposite ending of the same story is invoked: Bottom and his friends perform Ovid's story of Pyramus and Thisbe, a pair of lovers from rival households who lose their lives in a tragedy of bad timing and misapprehension. Though played in the style of parody, the "very tragical mirth" of Pyramus and Thisbe is a reminder that, in the matter of love, all does not necessarily end well.

So it is that, like *Venus* and *Lucrece*, *A Midsummer Night's Dream* and *Romeo and Juliet* are companion pieces. As *Dream* is a comedy darkened by something of the night, so *Romeo* is a tragedy that keeps surprising us with flashes of comedy. The shock of Juliet's apparent death is heightened by proximity to the cheerful bustle of the wedding preparations and the comic dialogue of Clown and Musicians. Equally, Shakespeare takes character types from the comic tradition— the tyrannical father, the bawdy servant, the meddling friar, the witty and cynical friend—and transforms them into such complex, many-layered beings as Old Capulet, the Nurse, and Mercutio.

The spirit of the play is fundamentally Ovidian, although the story is closely based on a different source, an Italian Renaissance novella that was mediated to Shakespeare via a drearily written poem called *The Tragicall Historye of Romeus and Juliet*. As in Ovid's *Metamorphoses*, "violent delights have violent ends": intense passions lead to dramatic transformations, the bright flame of young love is swiftly and cruelly snuffed out, but something of constancy endures at the close. Ovid's Pyramus and Thisbe meet by an ancient tomb outside the city. They fall to earth in death, but their love is symbolically remembered in the ripening of the blood-dark mulberry. A couplet of Friar Laurence's neatly sums up the structure of feeling that underlies this and so many other of Ovid's transformations: "The earth that's nature's mother is her tomb: / What is her burying grave, that is her womb."

Taken as a whole, the Friar's soliloquy cuts to the quick of Shakespeare's double vision. It is structured around the rhetorical figure of oxymoron, the paradox whereby opposites are held together. Not only womb and tomb, but also day and night, herbs and flowers that are simultaneously poisonous and medicinal, virtue and vice, God's grace and our own desires: "such opposèd kings encamp them still / In man as well as herbs."

In Peter Quince's staging of Pyramus and Thisbe, Snout memorably plays the part of the Wall that divides the households of the two lovers. *Romeo and Juliet* begins with Sampson, a servant of the house of Capulet, bragging of how he will thrust the Montague maids up against a wall. That is to say, having beaten up the rival men, he will have their women: sex is a matter of taking, not giving. Sampson boasts the biblical name of a man capable of bringing walls tumbling down, but what actually happens is that Romeo lightly o'erleaps the orchard wall—like Ovid's Hercules entering the fabulous gardens of the Hesperides—and moves the action into a new key. The lovers give themselves to each other and, though they are then taken in death, the wall of division crumbles away. The memory of Romeo and Juliet binds together the houses of Montague and Capulet, drawing a line under their ancient grudge.

The great Romantic critic and essayist William Hazlitt read Shakespeare as profoundly as he meditated upon love. "Romeo is Hamlet in love," he said. For Hazlitt, falling in love is like coming home to your dreams: "We have never before seen anything to come up to our newly discovered goddess, but she is what we have been all our lives looking for. The idol we fall down before and worship is an image familiar to our minds. It has been present to our waking thoughts, it has haunted us in our dreams." But what also haunts the lover—remember the teasing paradoxes of *A Midsummer Night's Dream*—is the suspicion that it might all be a dream. Mercutio spins a tale of how love is but the mischief of Queen Mab, midwife of illusion. Romeo blesses the night, but then acknowledges his fear that "Being in night, all this is but a dream, / Too flattering-sweet to be substantial."

Juliet has to deal with another fear. For a girl in Shakespeare's time, chastity was a priceless commodity. To lose her virtue without the prospect of marriage would be to lose herself. In the speech that begins "Thou know'st the mask of night is on my face," Juliet reveals quite remarkable self-understanding. She is acutely aware that in love the stakes for a woman are far higher than they are for a man. Here Shakespeare's poetic language becomes the vehicle of both argument and emotion. The artifice of rhyme is replaced by blank verse that moves with the suppleness of thought itself.

In the original production, the lines would have been spoken by a young male actor of perhaps around the same thirteen years of age as the character of Juliet. By highlighting extreme youthfulness (in the source, Juliet is sixteen), Shakespeare makes a bold implicit claim for his poetic drama. Both actor and character are speaking with maturity far beyond their years: such, the dramatist implies, is the metamorphic potency of the mingled fire and powder of love and art. Though younger than Romeo, Juliet is more knowing. She senses the danger in his talk of idolatry. In the soaring love duet that is their final scene together before Romeo's exile, she wills the song to be that of the nightingale rather than the lark because she knows that the break of day will mean the end of their night of love and the dawn of a harsh reality in which she will be reduced to the status of a bargaining chip in the negotiations between Verona's powerful families.

According to the social code of the time, it was the duty of the young to obey the old. Marriage was a matter not of love, but of the consolidation and perpetuation of wealth and status. Arthur Brooke, author of the *Tragicall Historye of Romeus and Juliet* which Shakespeare had before him as he wrote, told his readers that the moral of the story was that young lovers who submit to erotic desire, neglecting the authority and advice of parents and listening instead to drunken gossips and superstitious friars, will come to a deservedly sticky end. Shakespeare's play, by contrast, glories in the energy of youth. It does not seek to advance a moral or to condemn what Juliet calls the "disobedient opposition" of child to parent. The drama offers instead the tragic paradox that the heat in the blood that animates the star-crossed lovers is the same ardor that leads young men to scrap in the street and to kill out of loyalty to their friends. The kinship of love and revenge, the perpetual war between the generations: Shakespeare was to return to this territory in later plays such as *Hamlet* and *King Lear*.

It is sometimes said that *Romeo and Juliet* is a lesser work than these "mature" tragedies because its catastrophe is provoked by fate rather than the actions of the characters themselves. Shakespeare does impose an artistic shape upon the plot through the device of the Chorus, with its emphasis on events being written in the stars. But the misadventure that provokes the disastrous ending is not merely a piece of bad luck: the reason Romeo does not get Friar Laurence's crucial letter is that Friar John is detained for fear that he might have been infected with plague. Plague was an everyday reality in Shakespeare's London. Puritan preachers may have proclaimed it as a judgment sent by an angry God, but that is not how it would have seemed to Shakespeare's original audience. Everybody in the theater would have known families whose future had been blighted by plague.

Parents are supposed to die before their children, the old before the young. With plague, it is not always like that. The tragic irony of *Romeo and Juliet* is that the houses of both Capulet and Montague escape the plague, yet still the children die first. The final scene takes place in an ancestral tomb, but those who lie dead are the flower of a city's youth—Mercutio, Tybalt, Paris, Juliet and her Romeo.

ABOUT THE TEXT

Shakespeare endures through history. He illuminates later times as well as his own. He helps us to understand the human condition. But he cannot do this without a good text of the plays. Without editions there would be no Shakespeare. That is why every twenty years or so throughout the last three centuries there has been a major new edition of his complete works. One aspect of editing is the process of keeping the texts up-to-date—modernizing the spelling, punctuation, and typography (though not, of course, the actual words), providing explanatory notes in the light of changing educational practices (a generation ago, most of Shakespeare's classical and biblical allusions could be assumed to be generally understood, but now they can't).

But because Shakespeare did not personally oversee the publication of his plays, editors also have to make decisions about the relative authority of the early printed editions. Half of the sum of his plays only appeared posthumously, in the elaborately produced First Folio text of 1623, the original "Complete Works" prepared for the press by Shakespeare's fellow actors, the people who knew the plays better than anyone else. The other half had appeared in print in his lifetime, in the more compact and cheaper form of "Quarto" editions, some of which reproduced good-quality texts, others of which were to a greater or lesser degree garbled and error-strewn. In the case of a few plays there are hundreds of differences between the Quarto and Folio editions, some of them far from trivial.

If you look at printers' handbooks from the age of Shakespeare, you quickly discover that one of the first rules was that, whenever possible, compositors were recommended to set their type from existing printed books rather than manuscripts. This was the age before mechanical typesetting, where each individual letter had to be picked out by hand from the compositor's case and placed on a stick (upside down and back to front) before being laid on the press. It was an age of murky rushlight and of manuscripts written in a secretary hand that had dozens of different, hard-to-decipher forms. Printers' lives were a lot easier when they were reprinting existing books rather than struggling with handwritten copy. Easily the quickest way to have created the First Folio would have been simply to reprint those eighteen plays that had already appeared in Quarto and only work from manuscript on the other eighteen.

But that is not what happened. Whenever Quartos were used, playhouse "promptbooks" were also consulted and stage directions copied in from them. And in the case of several major plays where a reasonably well-printed Quarto was available, the Folio printers were instructed to work from an alternative, playhouse-derived manuscript. This meant that the whole process of producing the first complete Shakespeare took months, even years, longer than it might have done. But for the men overseeing the project, John Hemings and Henry Condell, friends and fellow actors who had been remembered in Shakespeare's will, the additional labor and cost were worth the effort for the sake of producing an edition that was close to the practice of the theater. They wanted all the plays in print so that people could, as they wrote in their prefatory address to the reader, "read him and again and again," but they also wanted "the great variety of readers" to work from texts that were close to the theater life for which Shakespeare originally intended them. For this reason, the *RSC Shakespeare*, in both *Complete Works* and individual volumes, uses the Folio as base text wherever possible. Significant Quarto variants are, however, noted in the Textual Notes.

Romeo and Juliet is one of the plays where the Folio text was printed from a Quarto, though with reference to a playhouse manuscript, which provided some additional stage directions. Most modern editors use the Second Quarto as their copy text, but import stage directions, act divisions and some corrections from Folio. Our Folio-led editorial practice follows the reverse procedure, using Folio as copy text, but deploying the Second Quarto as a "control text" that offers assistance in the correction and identification of compositors' errors in the Folio, of which there are many (as a result of large parts of this play having been set in type by the least experienced of the Folio compositors).

The 1622 Fourth Quarto of *Romeo and Juliet* was based on the 1609 Third Quarto, but a printing house editor consulted the (very different, often defective, but sometimes illuminating) 1597 First Quarto and, as a result, introduced a number of highly intelligent corrections and emendations. This fact makes us question the usual editorial assumption that earlier texts are to be preferred to later ones. The traditional notion of fidelity to Shakespeare's first Quartos (or first good-quality Quartos), on the grounds that they represent the texts closest to "what the author wrote," is sometimes more an ideal than a reality. Early Quartos have errors too. And later Quartos made good corrections as well as introducing new errors. In the case of *Romeo and Juliet*, modern editors say that they are editing the Second Quarto (the first good-quality Quarto), but since there are many errors in the Second Quarto and since the Fourth Quarto makes excellent corrections and conjectural emendations in the face of those errors (partly by means of judicious use of the "bad" or "short" or "copied by the ear" First Quarto), the reality of modern editions of *Romeo and Juliet* is that they are closer to the Fourth than the Second Quarto. Folio *Romeo and Juliet* was printed from a marked-up copy of the Third Quarto, often corrected similarly to the Fourth Quarto's correction of the Second. If supposedly Second Quarto–derived editions are actually closer to the Fourth Quarto and Folio is also close to the Fourth Quarto, though independent from it, then there need be no intrinsic objection to our beginning from Folio, though restoring Second (and occasionally First) Quarto readings where Folio is manifestly in error. The lesson of textual transmission is the same as that of the theater: the Shakespearean text was mobile in its own time and remains ever mobile. Each time one of the plays is performed, whatever the "copy text," the words will be slightly different, thanks to the tricks of actors' memories. So, too, each time the play is edited, there will be dozens of differences of punctuation, emendation and interpretation. Textual mobility is an essential part of Shakespeare's evolving creative afterlife.

The following notes highlight various aspects of the editorial process and indicate conventions used in the text of this edition:

Lists of Parts are supplied in the First Folio for only six plays, not including *Romeo and Juliet*, so the list here is editorially supplied. Capitals indicate that part of the name which is used for speech headings in the script (thus "MONTAGUE, Romeo's father").

Locations are provided by the Folio for only two plays. Eighteenth-century editors, working in an age of elaborately realistic stage sets, were the first to provide detailed locations. Given that Shakespeare wrote for a bare stage and often imprecise sense of place, we have relegated locations to the explanatory notes at the foot of the page, where they are given at the beginning of each scene where the imaginary location is different from the one before. The whole of *Romeo and Juliet* takes place in locations in and around Verona, a city in Veneto in northern Italy, with the exception of Act 5 Scene 1, which is located in Mantua, the capital of nearby Lombardy, to which Romeo has been exiled.

Act and Scene Divisions were provided in the Folio in a much more thoroughgoing way than in the Quartos. Sometimes, however, they were erroneous or omitted; corrections and additions supplied by editorial tradition are indicated by square brackets. Five-act division is based on a classical model, and act breaks provided the opportunity to replace the candles in the indoor Blackfriars playhouse which the King's Men used after 1608, but Shakespeare did not necessarily think in terms of a five-part structure of dramatic composition. The Folio convention is that a scene ends when the stage is empty. Nowadays, partly under the influence of film, we tend to consider a scene to be a dramatic unit that ends with either a change of imaginary location or a significant passage of time within the narrative. Shakespeare's fluidity of composition accords well with this convention, so in addition to act and scene numbers we provide a *running scene* count in the right margin at the beginning of each new scene, in the typeface used for editorial directions. Where there is a scene break caused by a momentary bare stage, but the location does not change and extra time does not pass, we use the convention *running scene continues*. There is inevitably a degree of editorial judgment in making such calls, but the system is very valuable in suggesting the pace of the plays.

Speakers' Names are often inconsistent in Folio. We have regularized speech headings, but retained an element of deliberate inconsistency in entry directions, in order to give the flavor of Folio.

Verse is indicated by lines that do not run to the right margin and by capitalization of each line. The Folio printers sometimes set verse as prose, and vice versa (either out of misunderstanding or for reasons of space). We have silently corrected in such cases, although in some instances there is ambiguity, in which case we have leaned toward the preservation of Folio layout. Folio sometimes uses contraction ("turnd" rather than "turned") to indicate whether or not the final "-ed" of a past participle is sounded, an area where there is variation for the sake of the five-beat iambic pentameter rhythm. We use the convention of a grave accent to indicate sounding (thus "turnèd" would be two syllables), but would urge actors not to overstress. In cases where one speaker ends with a verse half-line and the next begins with the other half of the pentameter, editors since the late eighteenth century have indented the second line. We have abandoned this convention, since the Folio does not use it, and nor did actors' cues in the Shakespearean theater. An exception is made when the second speaker actively interrupts or completes the first speaker's sentence.

Spelling is modernized, but older forms are occasionally maintained where necessary for rhythm or aural effect.

Punctuation in Shakespeare's time was as much rhetorical as grammatical. "Colon" was originally a term for a unit of thought in an argument. The semicolon was a new unit of punctuation (some of the Quartos lack them altogether). We have modernized punctuation throughout, but have given more weight to Folio punctuation than many editors, since, though not Shakespearean, it reflects the usage of his period. In particular, we have used the colon far more than many editors: it is exceptionally useful as a way of indicating how many Shakespearean speeches unfold clause by clause in a developing argument that gives the illusion of enacting the process of thinking in the moment. We have also kept in mind the origin of punctuation in classical times as a way of assisting the actor and orator: the comma suggests the briefest of pauses for breath, the colon a middling one and a full stop or period a longer pause. Semicolons, by contrast, belong to an era of punctuation that was only just coming in during Shakespeare's time and that is coming to an end now: we have accordingly only used them where they occur in our copy texts (and not always then). Dashes are sometimes used for parenthetical interjections where the Folio has brackets. They are also used for interruptions and changes in train of thought. Where a change of addressee occurs within a speech, we have used a dash preceded by a full stop (or occasionally another form of punctuation). Often the identity of the respective addressees is obvious from the context. When it is not, this has been indicated in a marginal stage direction.

Entrances and Exits are fairly thorough in Folio, which has accordingly been followed as faithfully as possible. Where characters are omitted or corrections are necessary, this is indicated by square brackets (e.g. "[*and Attendants*]"). *Exit* is sometimes silently normalized to *Exeunt* and *Manet* anglicized to "remains." We trust Folio positioning of entrances and exits to a greater degree than most editors.

Editorial Stage Directions such as stage business, asides, indications of addressee and of characters' position on the gallery stage are only used sparingly in Folio. Other editions mingle directions of this kind with original Folio and Quarto directions, sometimes marking them by means of square brackets. We have sought to distinguish what could be described as *directorial* interventions of this kind from Folio-style directions (either original or supplied) by placing them in the right margin in a different typeface. There is a degree of subjectivity about which directions are of which kind, but the procedure is intended as a reminder to the reader and the actor that Shakespearean stage directions are often dependent upon editorial inference alone and are not set in stone. We also depart from editorial tradition in sometimes admitting uncertainty and thus printing permissive stage directions, such as an **Aside?** (often a line may be equally effective as an aside or a direct address—it is for each production or reading to make its own decision) or a *may exit* or a piece of business placed between arrows to indicate that it may occur at various different moments within a scene.

Line Numbers in the left margin are editorial, for reference and to key the explanatory and textual notes.

Explanatory Notes at the foot of each page explain allusions and gloss obsolete and difficult words, confusing phraseology, occasional major textual cruces, and so on. Particular attention is given to nonstandard usage, bawdy innuendo and technical terms (e.g. legal and military language). Where more than one sense is given, commas indicate shades of related meaning, slashes alternative or double meanings.

Textual Notes at the end of the play indicate major departures from the Folio. They take the following form: the reading of our text is given in bold and its source given after an equals sign, with "Q1" indicating that it derives from the First Quarto of 1597, "Q2" that it derives from the Second Quarto of 1599, "Q1/Q2" a reading in which the First and Second Quartos agree, "Q3" that it derives from the Third Quarto of 1609, "Q4" from the Fourth Quarto of 1622, "F" from the First Folio of 1623, "F2" a reading from the Second Folio of 1632, and "Ed" one that derives from the subsequent editorial tradition. The rejected Folio ("F") reading is then given. So, for example, "**1.4.68 maid** = Q1. F = man" indicates that at Act 1 Scene 4 line 68, we have adopted the First Quarto's "maid" because the First Folio's "man" is not a defensible reading.

KEY FACTS

MAJOR PARTS: (*with percentage of lines/number of speeches/scenes on stage*) Romeo (20%/163/14), Juliet (18%/118/11), Friar Laurence (11%/55/7), Nurse (9%/90/11), Capulet (9%/51/9), Mercutio (8%/62/4), Benvolio (5%/64/7), Lady Capulet (4%/45/10), Escalus (3%/16/3), Paris (2%/23/5), Montague (1%/10/3).

LINGUISTIC MEDIUM: 90% verse, 10% prose.

DATE: 1595–96. Includes part for Will Kempe, who joined the Lord Chamberlain's Men in 1594; published 1597, with assignment to "Lord Hunsdon's Men" (the name of Shakespeare's company from July 1596 to April 1597); astrological allusions and earthquake reference may suggest composition in 1595–96; close links with *A Midsummer Night's Dream*.

SOURCES: Based on Arthur Brooke's long narrative poem *The Tragicall Historye of Romeus and Juliet* (1562), which was itself based on an Italian novella by Matteo Bandello (1554, possibly known to Shakespeare via William Painter's English translation in his 1567 *Palace of Pleasure*). Shakespeare's alterations to Brooke include considerable expansion of the roles of the Nurse and Mercutio.

TEXT: The First Quarto (1597) is poorly printed, so has traditionally been assumed to be an orally reconstructed or "reported" text, though this assumption was challenged in the late twentieth century; it seems to have had a playhouse origin. The Second Quarto (1599) is longer and better printed, justifying its title-page claim "Newly corrected, augmented, and amended"; it is generally thought to have been derived from Shakespeare's manuscript. A Third Quarto (1609) reprinted the Second, and a Fourth (1622) reprinted the Third, but with intelligent corrections, some of them deriving from consultation of the First Quarto. The 1623 First Folio text was printed from the Third Quarto, though introducing its own intelligent corrections and additional stage directions, but also many new errors as a result of its being printed almost entirely by "Compositor E," by far the least competent of the workmen who set the Folio into print. Modern editions are traditionally based on the Second Quarto, but we respect the intentions of the Folio, seeking to retain the innovations of its original editor while eliminating what we judge to be its compositorial errors by means of emendation from the Second Quarto (and occasionally the other Quartos). The Folio lacks the Prologue, an omission we highlight by enclosing the lines within asterisks. Folio follows the Second Quarto in including a number of repeated lines (e.g. the description of dawn at the end of Act 2 Scene 1 and the beginning of Act 2 Scene 2); the likeliest explanation on each of the three occasions when this occurs is that the first of the duplicated passages represents authorial "first thoughts" intended for deletion: these lines are retained in our text but are indicated by enclosure within double solidi (// //).

THE TRAGEDY OF
ROMEO AND JULIET

LIST OF PARTS

CHORUS

ROMEO

MONTAGUE, Romeo's father

LADY MONTAGUE, Romeo's mother

BENVOLIO, Montague's nephew

ABRAHAM, Montague's servingman

BALTHASAR, Romeo's man

JULIET

CAPULET, Juliet's father

LADY CAPULET, Juliet's mother

NURSE to Juliet

TYBALT, Capulet's nephew

SECOND CAPULET

Petruchio

PETER
SAMPSON } servingmen to the Capulets
GREGORY

MUSICIANS

SERVINGMEN

PRINCE Escalus of Verona

MERCUTIO
PARIS } his kinsmen

PAGE to Paris

Mercutio's Page

FRIAR LAURENCE

FRIAR JOHN

APOTHECARY

OFFICER

CITIZENS

CONSTABLE

WATCHMEN

Prologue

[Enter Chorus]

›CHORUS   Two households, both alike in dignity,
    In fair Verona, where we lay our scene,
From ancient grudge break to new mutiny,
    Where civil blood makes civil hands unclean.
5 From forth the fatal loins of these two foes
    A pair of star-crossed lovers take their life,
Whose misadventured piteous overthrows;
    Doth with their death bury their parents' strife.
The fearful passage of their death-marked love;
10   And the continuance of their parents' rage,
Which, but their children's end, nought could remove,
    Is now the two hours' traffic of our stage;
The which if you with patient ears attend,
What here shall miss, our toil shall strive to mend.*

                        [Exit]

Act 1 Scene 1

Enter Sampson and Gregory with swords and bucklers, of the House of Capulet

SAMPSON   Gregory, o'my word, we'll not carry coals.

GREGORY   No, for then we should be colliers.

SAMPSON   I mean, if we be in choler, we'll draw.

Prologue 1 CHORUS this speech which did not appear in the First Folio is from the Quarto editions of the play; it is written in the form of a sonnet **1 dignity** social status/worth **2 Verona** city in northern Italy **3 ancient** long-standing **mutiny** discord **4 civil** of citizens (plays on the sense of "civilized") **5 fatal** fateful/deadly **6 star-crossed** thwarted by fate (the malign influence of a star or planet) **take their life** derive life (with sinister play on the sense of "commit suicide") **7 misadventured** unfortunate **9 fearful** frightened/fearsome **passage** progress/passing (playing on the sense of "death") **11 but** but for **12 traffic** business **14 miss** be found wanting, be unsuccessful **1.1 *Location: a public place in Verona* bucklers** small round shields **1 carry coals** submit to indignity or insult **2 colliers** those who carry coal for sale (a dirty profession and one often associated with cheating) **3 in choler** angry (puns on "collier") **draw** i.e. our swords (puns on the sense of "carry, haul")

GREGORY   Ay, while you live, draw your neck out o'th'collar.

5   SAMPSON   I strike quickly, being moved.

GREGORY   But thou art not quickly moved to strike.

SAMPSON   A dog of the house of Montague moves me.

GREGORY   To move is to stir; and to be valiant is to stand: therefore, if thou art moved, thou runn'st away.

10   SAMPSON   A dog of that house shall move me to stand. I will take the wall of any man or maid of Montague's.

GREGORY   That shows thee a weak slave, for the weakest goes to the wall.

SAMPSON   True, and therefore women being the weaker
15   vessels are ever thrust to the wall: therefore I will push Montague's men from the wall, and thrust his maids to the wall.

GREGORY   The quarrel is between our masters and us their men.

20   SAMPSON   'Tis all one, I will show myself a tyrant: when I have fought with the men, I will be civil with the maids, and cut off their heads.

GREGORY   The heads of the maids?

SAMPSON   Ay, the heads of the maids, or their maidenheads,
25   take it in what sense thou wilt.

GREGORY   They must take it in sense that feel it.

SAMPSON   Me they shall feel while I am able to stand, and 'tis known I am a pretty piece of flesh.

---

4 draw . . . o'th'collar withdraw your neck from the hangman's noose (**collar** puns on **colliers** and **choler**)   **5 strike** attack (plays on the sense of "have sex")   **moved** provoked (plays on the sense of "sexually aroused")   **8 move . . . stir** in addition to "be provoked/become sexually aroused," both verbs also now signify "move physically, displace oneself"   **valiant** courageous/firm physically   **stand** stand firm/get an erection   **11 take the wall** take the side of the road nearest the wall (forcing anyone else to walk in the gutter that ran down the center of an Elizabethan street)   **12 slave** rogue   **goes . . . wall** are always forced to submit (a proverbial expression)   **15 thrust . . . wall** i.e. for sex   **19 men** male servants, i.e. not women   **20 one** the same thing   **24 maidenheads** virginities   **26 take** understand/receive sexually   **sense** meaning/physical feeling   **27 stand** remain upright/have an erection **28 pretty . . . flesh** fine fellow/man with a fine penis

GREGORY   'Tis well thou art not fish: if thou hadst, thou hadst

30   been poor John. Draw thy tool, here comes of the house of

the Montagues.

Enter two other Servingmen [Abraham and Balthasar]   *Sampson draws*

SAMPSON   My naked weapon is out. Quarrel, I will back thee.

GREGORY   How, turn thy back and run?

SAMPSON   Fear me not.

35   GREGORY   No, marry, I fear thee!

SAMPSON   Let us take the law of our sides: let them begin.

GREGORY   I will frown as I pass by, and let them   *Frowns*

take it as they list.

SAMPSON   Nay, as they dare. I will bite my thumb   *Bites his thumb*

40   at them, which is a disgrace to them if they bear it.

ABRAHAM   Do you bite your thumb at us, sir?

SAMPSON   I do bite my thumb, sir.

ABRAHAM   Do you bite your thumb at us, sir?

SAMPSON   Is the law of our side, if I say ay?   *Aside*

45   GREGORY   No.

SAMPSON   No, sir, I do not bite my thumb at you, sir, but I bite

my thumb, sir.

GREGORY   Do you quarrel, sir?

ABRAHAM   Quarrel sir? No, sir.

50   SAMPSON   If you do, sir, I am for you. I serve as good a man as

you.

ABRAHAM   No better?

SAMPSON   Well, sir.

Enter Benvolio

GREGORY   Say 'better'— here comes one of my   *Aside*

55   master's kinsmen.

SAMPSON   Yes, better.

ABRAHAM   You lie.

---

29 fish i.e. the opposite of **flesh** (meat)/a woman or a vagina   **30 poor John** salted hake, a
poor type of food/sexually inadequate, the possessor of a shriveled penis   **tool** sword/penis
32 naked weapon continues the phallic wordplay   **33 How** what   **34 Fear** doubt (possibly,
Gregory then shifts the sense to an incredulous "be afraid of")   **35 marry** by the Virgin Mary
36 of on   **38 list** please   **39 bite my thumb** an offensive gesture signifying threat or defiance

SAMPSON   Draw, if you be men. Gregory, remember thy
        swashing blow.   *They fight*
60 BENVOLIO   Part, fools! Put up your swords, you   *Draws and*
        know not what you do.   *parts them*

Enter Tybalt

TYBALT   What, art thou drawn among these heartless
        hinds?
        Turn thee, Benvolio, look upon thy death.   *Draws*
BENVOLIO   I do but keep the peace. Put up thy sword,
65   Or manage it to part these men with me.
TYBALT   What, drawn, and talk of peace? I hate the word,
        As I hate hell, all Montagues, and thee.
        Have at thee, coward!   *Fight*

Enter three or four Citizens with clubs

OFFICER   Clubs, bills and partisans! Strike! Beat them down!
70   Down with the Capulets! Down with the Montagues!

Enter Old Capulet in his gown, and his Wife

CAPULET   What noise is this? Give me my long sword, ho!
LADY CAPULET   A crutch, a crutch! Why call you for a sword?
CAPULET   My sword, I say! Old Montague is come,
        And flourishes his blade in spite of me.

Enter Old Montague and his Wife

75 MONTAGUE   Thou villain Capulet!— Hold me not, let me go.
LADY MONTAGUE   Thou shalt not stir a foot to seek a foe.

Enter Prince Escalus with his train

PRINCE   Rebellious subjects, enemies to peace,
        Profaners of this neighbour-stainèd steel—
        Will they not hear?— What, ho! You men, you beasts,
80   That quench the fire of your pernicious rage
        With purple fountains issuing from your veins:

---

59 **swashing** a particular stroke in fencing/slashing with great force   62 **heartless hinds**
cowardly menials, with a pun on "hartless hinds"—i.e. female deer (**hinds**) without
males (harts)   65 **manage** use   69 **Clubs . . . partisans** rallying cry used to summon
armed apprentices   **bills and partisans** long-handled weapons with blades at the end
gown dressing-gown   71 **long sword** heavy, old-fashioned sword with a long blade
74 **in spite of** out of spite/malice for   *train* retinue   78 **Profaners . . . steel** you who defile
your swords by staining them with your fellow citizens' blood   80 **pernicious** destructive

On pain of torture, from those bloody hands
Throw your mistempered weapons to the ground,
And hear the sentence of your movèd prince.

85   Three civil broils, bred of an airy word,
By thee, Old Capulet, and Montague,
Have thrice disturbed the quiet of our streets,
And made Verona's ancient citizens
Cast by their grave beseeming ornaments

90   To wield Old partisans, in hands as old,
Cankered with peace, to part your cankered hate:
If ever you disturb our streets again,
Your lives shall pay the forfeit of the peace.
For this time, all the rest depart away:

95   You Capulet, shall go along with me,
And, Montague, come you this afternoon,
To know our further pleasure in this case,
To old Freetown, our common judgement-place.
Once more, on pain of death, all men depart.

Exeunt. [Montague, Lady Montague and Benvolio remain]

100   MONTAGUE   Who set this ancient quarrel new abroach?
Speak, nephew, were you by when it began?

BENVOLIO   Here were the servants of your adversary,
And yours, close fighting ere I did approach:
I drew to part them: in the instant came

105   The fiery Tybalt, with his sword prepared,
Which, as he breathed defiance to my ears,
He swung about his head and cut the winds,
Who nothing hurt withal hissed him in scorn:
While we were interchanging thrusts and blows,

83 **mistempered** disordered/created for wrongful purposes/wrongly tempered (i.e. made hard)
with blood instead of water   84 **movèd** angry   88 **ancient** aged/venerable   89 **grave
beseeming ornaments** dignified and seemly accessories/the trappings appropriate to dignified
old age   91 **Cankered** corroded, rusted (with disuse)   **cankered** malignant, infected with
evil   93 **pay . . . peace** be the price for breaching the peace   97 **pleasure** intentions,
resolution   100 **new abroach** newly in motion   101 **by** nearby, present   103 **ere** before
105 **prepared** i.e. drawn   108 **withal** thereby

110 Came more and more, and fought on part and part,
Till the prince came, who parted either part.

LADY MONTAGUE   O, where is Romeo? Saw you him today?
Right glad am I he was not at this fray.

BENVOLIO   Madam, an hour before the worshipped sun
115 Peered forth the golden window of the east,
A troubled mind drave me to walk abroad,
Where, underneath the grove of sycamore
That westward rooteth from the city side,
So early walking did I see your son:
120 Towards him I made, but he was ware of me
And stole into the covert of the wood:
I, measuring his affections by my own,
Which then most sought where most might not be found,
Being one too many by my weary self,
125 Pursued my humour, not pursuing his,
And gladly shunned who gladly fled from me.

MONTAGUE   Many a morning hath he there been seen,
With tears augmenting the fresh morning's dew,
Adding to clouds more clouds with his deep sighs,
130 But all so soon as the all-cheering sun
Should in the farthest east begin to draw
The shady curtains from Aurora's bed,
Away from light steals home my heavy son,
And private in his chamber pens himself,
135 Shuts up his windows, locks fair daylight out
And makes himself an artificial night:
Black and portentous must this humour prove,
Unless good counsel may the cause remove.

---

110 **part and part** one side and the other   115 **forth** from forth   116 **drave** drove
abroad out, away from home   118 **westward . . . side** grows on the west side of the city
120 **ware** aware/wary   121 **covert** shelter/hiding place   122 **affections** emotions/
inclinations   123 **then . . . found** were chiefly concerned to find a place of solitude
125 **humour** mood   126 **who** he who   132 **Aurora** goddess of the dawn   133 **heavy**
sorrowful (plays on the sense of "weighty," generating a play on **light**—i.e. "bright/not
weighty")   **son** puns on **sun**   137 **Black** black/gloomy/deadly   **humour** includes the sense
of "bodily fluid thought to affect mood," in this case the **black** bile that caused melancholy

BENVOLIO	My noble uncle, do you know the cause?
140 MONTAGUE	I neither know it nor can learn of him.
BENVOLIO	Have you importuned him by any means?
MONTAGUE	Both by myself and many other friends,

But he, his own affections' counsellor,
Is to himself — I will not say how true —
145 But to himself so secret and so close,
So far from sounding and discovery,
As is the bud bit with an envious worm,
Ere he can spread his sweet leaves to the air,
Or dedicate his beauty to the same.
150 Could we but learn from whence his sorrows grow,
We would as willingly give cure as know.

Enter Romeo

BENVOLIO	See, where he comes. So please you, step aside,

I'll know his grievance, or be much denied.

MONTAGUE	I would thou wert so happy by thy stay

155 To hear true shrift.— Come, madam, let's away.

Exeunt [Montague and Lady Montague]

BENVOLIO	Good morrow, cousin.
ROMEO	Is the day so young?
BENVOLIO	But new struck nine.
ROMEO	Ay me, sad hours seem long.

160 Was that my father that went hence so fast?

BENVOLIO	It was. What sadness lengthens Romeo's hours?
ROMEO	Not having that, which, having, makes them short.
BENVOLIO	In love?
ROMEO	Out—
165 BENVOLIO	Of love?
ROMEO	Out of her favour where I am in love.

---

140 of it of   141 importuned . . . means urged him to tell you by every means possible
144 true honest/constant/dependable   145 close secretive, shut up from view
146 sounding having his thoughts fathomed   147 envious malicious   worm cankerworm,
the plant-destroying grub   154 I . . . stay I hope that by remaining here you will be fortunate
enough   155 shrift confession   156 cousin a general term for a relative or close friend

BENVOLIO   Alas that love, so gentle in his view,
Should be so tyrannous and rough in proof!

ROMEO   Alas that love, whose view is muffled still,
170   Should, without eyes, see pathways to his will!
Where shall we dine? O me! What fray was here?
Yet tell me not, for I have heard it all.
Here's much to do with hate, but more with love:
Why, then, O brawling love, O loving hate,
175   O anything of nothing first create!
O heavy lightness, serious vanity,
Misshapen chaos of well-seeming forms,
Feather of lead, bright smoke, cold fire, sick health,
Still-waking sleep that is not what it is!
180   This love feel I, that feel no love in this.
Dost thou not laugh?

BENVOLIO   No, coz, I rather weep.

ROMEO   Good heart, at what?

BENVOLIO   At thy good heart's oppression.

185   **ROMEO**   Why, such is love's transgression.
Griefs of mine own lie heavy in my breast,
Which thou wilt propagate, to have it pressed
With more of thine: this love that thou hast shown
Doth add more grief to too much of mine own.
190   Love is a smoke made with the fume of sighs,
Being purged, a fire sparkling in lovers' eyes,
Being vexed, a sea nourished with loving tears.
What is it else? A madness most discreet,
A choking gall and a preserving sweet.
195   Farewell, my coz.

---

167 **view** appearance (Romeo's reply shifts the sense to "sight")   168 **proof** practice,
experience   169 **muffled** Cupid, the Roman god of love, was traditionally depicted as being
blind or blindfolded   **still** always   175 **create** created   176 **vanity** trifles, foolishness
177 **well-seeming** apparently orderly   179 **Still-waking** ever wakeful   187 **propagate**
increase, multiply (perhaps with connotations of sexual reproduction, picked up in **pressed**
which can refer to the pressing of one body on another during sex)   188 **love** i.e. concern
for me   191 **purged** purified, rid of **smoke**   192 **vexed** tormented, afflicted   193 **discreet**
discerning, prudent   194 **gall** bitterness/poison   195 **coz** cousin

BENVOLIO	Soft, I will go along,
	An if you leave me so, you do me wrong.
ROMEO	Tut, I have lost myself, I am not here:
	This is not Romeo, he's some other where.

200   BENVOLIO   Tell me in sadness, who is that you love.

ROMEO   What, shall I groan and tell thee?

BENVOLIO   Groan? Why, no. But sadly tell me who.

ROMEO   A sick man in sadness makes his will:

A word ill-urged to one that is so ill.

205   In sadness, cousin, I do love a woman.

BENVOLIO   I aimed so near, when I supposed you loved.

ROMEO   A right good mark-man! And she's fair I love.

BENVOLIO   A right fair mark, fair coz, is soonest hit.

ROMEO   Well, in that hit you miss: she'll not be hit

210   With Cupid's arrow, she hath Dian's wit,

And in strong proof of chastity well armed,

From love's weak childish bow she lives uncharmed.

She will not stay the siege of loving terms,

Nor bide th'encounter of assailing eyes,

215   Nor ope her lap to saint-seducing gold:

O, she is rich in beauty, only poor

That when she dies with beauty dies her store.

BENVOLIO   Then she hath sworn that she will still live chaste?

ROMEO   She hath, and in that sparing makes huge waste,

220   For beauty starved with her severity

---

196 Soft wait a moment   **197 An if** if   **200 sadness** seriousness (Romeo's response plays
on the sense of "sorrow")   **is that** is it that   **206 aimed so near** i.e. guessed as much
207 mark-man marksman   **208 fair mark** unobstructed target/attractive vagina   **hit** plays
on the sense of "copulated with"   **210 Cupid's arrow** playing on phallic connotations
Dian's wit the wisdom and ingenuity of Diana, huntress and Roman goddess of chastity
(**wit** may play on a sense of "genitals")   **211 proof** proven impenetrability/armor
212 love's i.e. Cupid's, who was traditionally depicted as a young boy   **uncharmed** resistant to
Cupid's spells/unsubdued (some editors emend to the First Quarto's "unharmed")
213 stay endure   **214 bide** undergo, suffer   **encounter** assault/sexual engagement
215 ope . . . gold a reference to Danae, whom Jove, Roman king of the gods, seduced in the
form of a shower of gold   **lap** vagina   **217 That . . . store** i.e. when she dies unmarried, her
beauty will die for ever as she has had no children   **store** wealth/stock/potential to reproduce
218 still always   **219 sparing** thrift, economy   **waste** puns on "waist," generating the
paradoxical image of a pregnant belly resulting from chastity   **220 starved** killed off

Cuts beauty off from all posterity.
She is too fair, too wise, wisely too fair,
To merit bliss by making me despair.
She hath forsworn to love, and in that vow
225 Do I live dead that live to tell it now.

BENVOLIO   Be ruled by me, forget to think of her.

ROMEO   O, teach me how I should forget to think.

BENVOLIO   By giving liberty unto thine eyes:
Examine other beauties.

230 ROMEO   'Tis the way
To call hers exquisite, in question more:
These happy masks that kiss fair ladies' brows
Being black puts us in mind they hide the fair.
He that is strucken blind cannot forget
235 The precious treasure of his eyesight lost:
Show me a mistress that is passing fair,
What doth her beauty serve, but as a note
Where I may read who passed that passing fair?
Farewell, thou canst not teach me to forget.

240 BENVOLIO   I'll pay that doctrine, or else die in debt.   *Exeunt*

[Act 1 Scene 2]

Enter Capulet, County Paris and the Clown [a Servingman]

CAPULET   Montague is bound as well as I,
In penalty alike, and 'tis not hard, I think,
For men so old as we to keep the peace.

---

222 fair beautiful/just   **223 merit . . . despair** deserve heaven (through her chastity) by
casting me into despair (with its attendant risks of damnation)   **despair** spiritual
hopelessness (thought to precede suicide)   **224 forsworn to** abandoned, repudiated
230 'Tis . . . more that would only lead me to reflect on her exquisite beauty even more (to "call
in question" means "to consider or examine")   **232 happy** fortunate   **masks** worn by ladies
to protect their fashionably pale complexions from the sun   **234 strucken** struck
236 passing surpassingly, exceedingly   **237 note** marginal note/sign/reminder   **238 passed**
surpassed   **240 pay that doctrine** i.e. give you that lesson   **1.2 Location: *a public place in
Verona   County*** Count   ***Clown*** a rustic, comic character   **1 bound** formally required (to
keep the peace)

PARIS   Of honourable reckoning are you both,
5   And pity 'tis you lived at odds so long.
    But now, my lord, what say you to my suit?
CAPULET   But saying o'er what I have said before:
    My child is yet a stranger in the world,
    She hath not seen the change of fourteen years,
10   Let two more summers wither in their pride,
    Ere we may think her ripe to be a bride.
PARIS   Younger than she are happy mothers made.
CAPULET   And too soon marred are those so early made.
    Earth hath swallowed all my hopes but she:
15   She's the hopeful lady of my earth.
    But woo her, gentle Paris, get her heart:
    My will to her consent is but a part;
    An she agree, within her scope of choice
    Lies my consent and fair according voice.
20   This night I hold an old accustomed feast,
    Whereto I have invited many a guest,
    Such as I love, and you among the store,
    One more, most welcome, makes my number more.
    At my poor house look to behold this night
25   Earth-treading stars that make dark heaven light.
    Such comfort as do lusty young men feel
    When well-apparelled April on the heel
    Of limping winter treads, even such delight
    Among fresh fennel buds shall you this night
30   Inherit at my house: hear all, all see,
    And like her most whose merit most shall be,

---

4 reckoning estimation, reputation   **6 suit** request/courtship   **7 saying o'er** repeating
9 change passage   **10 pride** prime, fullest flowering (may play on the sense of "sexual
desire/tumescence")   **13 marred** damaged (puns on "married")   **made** puns on "maid"
14 Earth . . . she i.e. his other children are dead and buried   **15 hopeful** promising/expectant
earth world/body, from which she has sprung/land, which she will inherit   **16 gentle** noble
18 An if   **19 according** agreeing   **20 old accustomed** traditional   **22 store** plentiful
company   **26 comfort** enjoyment, pleasure   **lusty** lively/lustful   **27 well-apparelled** finely
dressed   **29 fennel** a fragrant herb with yellow flowers, sometimes associated with love
30 Inherit possess

Which one more view, of many mine being one,
May stand in number, though in reck'ning none.
Come, go with me.— Go, sirrah, trudge about   *To Servingman*
35   Through fair Verona, find those persons out   *Gives a list*
Whose names are written there and to them say,
My house and welcome on their pleasure stay.

Exeunt [Capulet and Paris]

SERVINGMAN   Find them out whose names are written. Here it is
written that the shoemaker should meddle with his yard,
40   and the tailor with his last, the fisher with his pencil, and the
painter with his nets. But I am sent to find those persons
whose names are here writ, and can never find what names
the writing person hath here writ — I must to the learnèd —
in good time.

Enter Benvolio and Romeo

45   BENVOLIO   Tut, man, one fire burns out another's burning,
One pain is lessened by another's anguish:
Turn giddy, and be holp by backward turning:
One desperate grief cures with another's languish:
Take thou some new infection to thy eye,
50   And the rank poison of the old will die.

ROMEO   Your plaintain leaf is excellent for that.

BENVOLIO   For what, I pray thee?

ROMEO   For your broken shin.

---

32 Which . . . none "which being the case, you may find that when you have viewed the ladies more thoroughly, my daughter, being but one among a number of them, may make up part of the group, but be found to be worthy of no real consideration"; some editors emend "one more view" to the Fourth Quarto's "on more view"   **33 reck'ning** estimation/consideration/ counting up   **34 sirrah** sir, often used to address a social inferior   **37 stay** wait   **38 it . . . nets** in assigning the wrong tools to each tradesman, the Servingman, who cannot read, suggests that it is pointless for him to have been given the task of identifying those who appear on a written list; his words parody a passage from John Lyly's *Euphues, the Anatomy of Wit*
39 meddle concern himself/interfere/have sex   **yard** measuring rod used by a **tailor**/penis
40 last wooden model of the foot, used by a **shoemaker** to mould shoes upon/penis   **pencil** paintbrush/penis   **44 in good time** I must do this promptly/here comes help just at the right moment   **45 another's** i.e. another fire's   **47 holp** helped   **backward turning** turning in the reverse direction   **48 another's languish** i.e. the languishing caused by another **grief**
51 plaintain herb used to ease minor cuts or bruises   **53 broken** grazed

BENVOLIO   Why, Romeo, art thou mad?

55   ROMEO   Not mad, but bound more than a madman is:
Shut up in prison, kept without my food,
Whipped and tormented and— Good e'en, good fellow.

SERVINGMAN   God gi' good e'en. I pray, sir, can you read?

ROMEO   Ay, mine own fortune in my misery.

60   SERVINGMAN   Perhaps you have learned it without book: but, I
pray, can you read anything you see?

ROMEO   Ay, if I know the letters and the language.

SERVINGMAN   Ye say honestly, rest you merry!

ROMEO   Stay, fellow, I can read.

He reads the letter

65   'Signior Martino and his wife and daughters, County
Anselme and his beauteous sisters, the lady widow of
Utruvio, Signior Placentio and his lovely nieces, Mercutio
and his brother Valentine, mine uncle Capulet, his wife and
daughters, my fair niece Rosaline, Livia, Signior Valentio

70   and his cousin Tybalt, Lucio and the lively Helena.' A fair
assembly: whither should they come?

SERVINGMAN   Up.

ROMEO   Whither? To supper?

SERVINGMAN   To our house.

75   ROMEO   Whose house?

SERVINGMAN   My master's.

ROMEO   Indeed, I should have asked you that before.

SERVINGMAN   Now I'll tell you without asking: my master is the
great rich Capulet, and if you be not of the house of

80   Montagues, I pray come and crush a cup of wine. Rest you
merry.   *Exit*

BENVOLIO   At this same ancient feast of Capulet's
Sups the fair Rosaline whom thou so loves,
With all the admired beauties of Verona:

---

55 bound . . . madman conventional treatments for madness included tying up the sufferer
and confining him in darkness   **57 e'en** evening (used for any time after noon)
58 gi' give you   **60 without book** by heart   **63 rest you merry** i.e. goodbye (the Servingman
understands Romeo to imply that he cannot read)   **71 whither** where   **80 crush** drink
82 ancient long-established

85   Go thither, and with unattainted eye,
       Compare her face with some that I shall show,
       And I will make thee think thy swan a crow.

ROMEO   When the devout religion of mine eye
       Maintains such falsehood, then turn tears to fire,
90   And these, who often drowned could never die,
       Transparent heretics, be burnt for liars.
       One fairer than my love! The all-seeing sun
       Ne'er saw her match since first the world begun.

BENVOLIO   Tut, you saw her fair, none else being by,
95   Herself poised with herself in either eye:
       But in that crystal scales let there be weighed
       Your lady's love against some other maid
       That I will show you shining at this feast,
       And she shall scant show well that now seems best.

100 ROMEO   I'll go along, no such sight to be shown,
       But to rejoice in splendour of mine own.   [*Exeunt*]

[Act 1 Scene 3]

Enter Capulet's Wife and Nurse

LADY CAPULET   Nurse, where's my daughter? Call her forth to
       me.

NURSE   Now by my maidenhead at twelve year old,
       I bade her come. What, lamb! What, ladybird!
       God forbid, where's this girl? What, Juliet!

Enter Juliet

---

85 **unattainted** unbiased/uninfected   89 **Maintains** upholds   **falsehood** untruth/
faithlessness/deception   90 **these** i.e. my eyes (which cannot drown however often they are
flooded with **tears**)   91 **Transparent** clear (like **eyes**)/obvious and easily detected (like **heretics**)
heretics holders of unorthodox religious beliefs; those suspected of heresy or witchcraft were
tested by being thrown into water, if they floated they were considered guilty and might be
burnt at the stake   95 **poised** balanced, weighed   97 **Your lady's love** the love you bear your
lady/the negligible amount of love your lady may bear you   99 **scant** scarcely   101 **splendour**
the brilliant light   **mine own** i.e. the sight of my own Rosaline   **1.3 Location: the Capulets'
house, Verona**   2 **by . . . old** the Nurse cannot swear to having been a virgin at thirteen
3 **What** an expression of impatience   4 **God forbid** either an apologetic exclamation for the fact
that **ladybird**, as well as being a term of endearment, could also mean "lewd woman," or an
expression of concern for Juliet's well-being

5	JULIET	How now? Who calls?
	NURSE	Your mother.
	JULIET	Madam, I am here. What is your will?
	LADY CAPULET	This is the matter.— Nurse, give leave awhile,

We must talk in secret.— Nurse, come back again,
10   I have remembered me, thou's hear our counsel.
Thou know'st my daughter's of a pretty age.

NURSE   Faith, I can tell her age unto an hour.

LADY CAPULET   She's not fourteen.

NURSE   I'll lay fourteen of my teeth — and yet, to my teen
15   be it spoken, I have but four — she's not fourteen. How long
is it now to Lammas-tide?

LADY CAPULET   A fortnight and odd days.

NURSE   Even or odd, of all days in the year, come Lammas
Eve at night shall she be fourteen. Susan and she — God rest
20   all Christian souls! — were of an age. Well, Susan is with
God: she was too good for me. But as I said, on Lammas Eve
at night shall she be fourteen, that shall she, marry, I
remember it well. 'Tis since the earthquake now eleven
years, and she was weaned — I never shall forget it — of all
25   the days of the year, upon that day, for I had then laid
wormwood to my dug, sitting in the sun under the
dovehouse wall. My lord and you were then at Mantua —
nay, I do bear a brain — but, as I said, when it did taste the
wormwood on the nipple of my dug and felt it bitter, pretty
30   fool, to see it tetchy and fall out with the dug! 'Shake', quoth
the dovehouse: 'twas no need, I trow, to bid me trudge. And

---

8 give leave give us leave (i.e. leave us alone)   **10 thou's** thou shalt   **11 pretty** fair/proper
14 teen sorrow (punning on the suffix of **fourteen**)   **16 Lammas-tide** 1 August, the harvest
festival   **18 Even . . . stinted and said "Ay"** all the early texts print this speech as prose,
though it has some verse rhythms within it, which have led many editors to set it as verse; the
same goes for the Nurse's remaining speeches in the scene   **Even or odd** the Nurse has
misunderstood Lady Capulet's sense of **odd** (i.e. a few)   **Lammas . . . night** the evening of
31 July   **19 Susan** the Nurse's dead daughter   **25 laid . . . dug** applied the bitter-tasting
plant wormwood to my breast (as a means of weaning the baby)   **27 Mantua** city in
northern Italy   **28 bear a brain** i.e. have a good memory   **30 fool** a term of endearment
"Shake" . . . dovehouse i.e. the dovehouse shook as a result of the **earthquake**/the shaking
of the dovehouse instructed the Nurse to stir herself   **quoth** said   **31 trow** am sure
trudge depart, walk off

since that time it is eleven years, for then she could stand
alone, nay, by th'rood, she could have run and waddled all
about, for even the day before, she broke her brow, and then
35   my husband — God be with his soul, a was a merry man —
took up the child, 'Yea,' quoth he, 'dost thou fall upon thy
face? Thou wilt fall backward when thou hast more wit, wilt
thou not, Jule?' And by my holidam, the pretty wretch left
crying and said 'Ay'. To see now how a jest shall come about!
40   I warrant, an I should live a thousand years, I never should
forget it: 'Wilt thou not, Jule?' quoth he, and, pretty fool, it
stinted and said 'Ay'.

LADY CAPULET   Enough of this, I pray thee, hold thy peace.

NURSE   Yes, madam, yet I cannot choose but laugh, to think
45   it should leave crying and say 'Ay'. And yet I warrant it had
upon it brow a bump as big as a young cock'rel's stone, a
perilous knock, and it cried bitterly. 'Yea,' quoth my
husband, 'fall'st upon thy face? Thou wilt fall backward
when thou comest to age, wilt thou not, Jule?' It stinted and
50   said 'Ay'.

JULIET   And stint thou too, I pray thee, Nurse, say I.

NURSE   Peace, I have done. God mark thee to his grace!
Thou wast the prettiest babe that e'er I nursed. An I might
live to see thee married once, I have my wish.

55   LADY CAPULET   Marry, that 'marry' is the very theme
I came to talk of. Tell me, daughter Juliet,
How stands your disposition to be married?

JULIET   It is an honour that I dream not of.

NURSE   An honour! Were not I thine only nurse, I would say
60   thou hadst sucked wisdom from thy teat.

LADY CAPULET   Well, think of marriage now: younger than you,
Here in Verona, ladies of esteem,

---

33 th'rood Christ's cross   34 broke banged, grazed   35 a was he was   37 fall backward i.e.
for sex   wit understanding   38 holidam holiness/what I consider holy   39 come about
come true   40 warrant assure you   42 stinted stopped (crying)   46 it its   stone testicle
51 say I puns on said "Ay"   52 mark . . . grace single you out for mercy   54 once one day
57 disposition inclination   60 thy teat the breast that fed you

Are made already mothers. By my count,
I was your mother much upon these years
65 That you are now a maid. Thus then in brief:
The valiant Paris seeks you for his love.

NURSE   A man, young lady! Lady, such a man as all the
world — why, he's a man of wax.

LADY CAPULET   Verona's summer hath not such a flower.

70 NURSE   Nay, he's a flower, in faith, a very flower.

LADY CAPULET   What say you? Can you love the gentleman?
This night you shall behold him at our feast:
Read o'er the volume of young Paris' face,
And find delight writ there with beauty's pen,
75 Examine every several lineament,
And see how one another lends content
And what obscured in this fair volume lies
Find written in the margent of his eyes.
This precious book of love, this unbound lover,
80 To beautify him, only lacks a cover.
The fish lives in the sea, and 'tis much pride
For fair without the fair within to hide.
That book in many's eyes doth share the glory,
That in gold clasps locks in the golden story:
85 So shall you share all that he doth possess,
By having him, making yourself no less.

NURSE   No less? Nay, bigger: women grow by men.

LADY CAPULET   Speak briefly, can you like of Paris' love?

JULIET   I'll look to like, if looking liking move:

---

64 much . . . years at much the same age   68 man of wax i.e. perfect, as if modeled from wax
75 several individual, separate (an apparently purposeful Folio emendation of Quarto's
"married lineament")   lineament facial feature (playing on the sense of "line or sketch")
76 content happiness, satisfaction (plays on the sense of "contents of a volume")   78 margent
margin (which might contain additional commentary)   79 unbound unmarried/without a
book's binding   80 cover plays on the notion of "embracing wife" and puns on the phrase
"feme covert" (a wife)   81 The . . . hide the fish is in his element within the confines of the
sea, and it is an excellent thing for a beautiful exterior to cover and compliment the beauty that
lies within   83 book binding   84 clasps fastenings on a book/embraces   87 women . . . men
i.e. in pregnancy   88 like of be pleased by   89 look expect/use my eyes   liking move may
generate liking

90 But no more deep will I endart mine eye
Than your consent gives strength to make it fly.

Enter a Servingman

SERVINGMAN   Madam, the guests are come, supper served up,
you called, my young lady asked for, the nurse cursed in the
pantry, and everything in extremity. I must hence to wait: I
95 beseech you, follow straight.   *Exit*

LADY CAPULET   We follow thee.— Juliet, the county stays.

NURSE   Go, girl, seek happy nights to happy days.   *Exeunt*

[Act 1 Scene 4]
running scene 4

Enter Romeo, Mercutio, Benvolio, with five or six other Masquers,
Torchbearers

ROMEO   What, shall this speech be spoke for our excuse?
Or shall we on without apology?

BENVOLIO   The date is out of such prolixity:
We'll have no Cupid hoodwinked with a scarf,
5 Bearing a Tartar's painted bow of lath,
Scaring the ladies like a crow-keeper.
But let them measure us by what they will,
We'll measure them a measure, and be gone.

ROMEO   Give me a torch, I am not for this ambling.
10 Being but heavy, I will bear the light.

MERCUTIO   Nay, gentle Romeo, we must have you dance.

---

90 **endart mine eye** gaze piercingly as if firing one of Cupid's arrows   95 **straight** straight away
96 **county** count (i.e. Paris)   **stays** awaits   **1.4** *Location: near the Capulets' house; the*
action then shifts indoors   **Masquers** masked performers   1 **speech . . . excuse**
traditionally one of the masquers would make a speech excusing the group's intrusion and
complimenting the company   3 **The . . . prolixity** such long-windedness is out of fashion
4 **Cupid** i.e. boy dressed as Cupid who would deliver the speech for the masquers   **hoodwinked**
blindfolded   5 **Tartar's . . . lath** imitation bow made out of a narrow strip of wood and painted
to look like the powerful lip-shaped bow of a Tartar (person from central Asia)   6 **crow-keeper**
scarecrow   7 **measure** judge   8 **measure . . . measure** mete out a dance to them/pace out a
dance   9 **ambling** affected way of walking or dancing   10 **heavy** melancholy (plays on the
sense of "weighty," enabling Romeo to pun on **light**)

ROMEO   Not I, believe me. You have dancing shoes
             With nimble soles, I have a soul of lead
             So stakes me to the ground I cannot move.

15 MERCUTIO   You are a lover, borrow Cupid's wings,
             And soar with them above a common bound.

ROMEO   I am too sore enpiercèd with his shaft
             To soar with his light feathers and so bound,
             I cannot bound a pitch above dull woe:

20   Under love's heavy burden do I sink.

MERCUTIO   And to sink in it should you burden love,
             Too great oppression for a tender thing.

ROMEO   Is love a tender thing? It is too rough,
             Too rude, too boist'rous, and it pricks like thorn.

25 MERCUTIO   If love be rough with you, be rough with love:
             Prick love for pricking, and you beat love down.
             Give me a case to put my visage in,
             A visor for a visor! What care I   *Puts on a mask*
             What curious eye doth quote deformities?

30   Here are the beetle brows shall blush for me.

BENVOLIO   Come, knock and enter, and no sooner in,
             But every man betake him to his legs.

ROMEO   A torch for me: let wantons light of heart
             Tickle the senseless rushes with their heels,

16 **common bound** ordinary limit (**bound** puns on the senses of "leap in a dance" and "state of
being shackled")   17 **enpiercèd** pierced through   **shaft** arrow   18 **bound** fastened
down/imprisoned   19 **pitch** degree/height (literally, highest point of a falcon's flight)
dull heavy/dim/gloomy   21 **And . . . love** plays on the senses of "and if you penetrated your
lover sexually you would weigh her down with your body/and if you lost your erection during
sex you would disappoint your lover"   22 **oppression** misfortune/physical pressure
thing plays on sense of "vagina" (Romeo then shifts the punning sense to "penis")   24 **rude**
harsh/turbulent/vulgar/large and coarse   **boist'rous** painful to the feelings/turbulent/stiff
(with sexual connotations)   **pricks** plays on sense of "penetrates, thrusts like a penis"
26 **Prick** wound, stab/penetrate sexually/stimulate sexually (i.e. masturbate)   **for** in return
for   **beat love down** get the better of love/get rid of your erection   27 **case** mask
28 **visor . . . visor** mask for a face/mask for a face so ugly it resembles a grotesque mask
29 **quote** take note of   30 **beetle brows** bushy or overhanging eyebrows (on the mask)
32 **betake . . . legs** i.e. dance   33 **wantons** lively/promiscuous people   **light of heart**
carefree/promiscuous   34 **Tickle** plays on sense of "stimulate sexually"   **senseless** lacking
feeling   **rushes** commonly used to cover floors   **heels** often associated with sexual licence

35   For I am proverbed with a grandsire phrase,
      I'll be a candle-holder, and look on.
      The game was ne'er so fair, and I am done.

MERCUTIO   Tut, dun's the mouse, the constable's own word:
      If thou art dun, we'll draw thee from the mire
40   Or — save your reverence — love, wherein thou stick'st
      Up to the ears. Come, we burn daylight, ho!

ROMEO   Nay, that's not so.

MERCUTIO   I mean, sir, in delay
      We waste our lights in vain, light lights by day.
45   Take our good meaning, for our judgement sits
      Five times in that ere once in our five wits.

ROMEO   And we mean well in going to this masque,
      But 'tis no wit to go.

MERCUTIO   Why, may one ask?

50   ROMEO   I dreamt a dream tonight.

MERCUTIO   And so did I.

ROMEO   Well, what was yours?

MERCUTIO   That dreamers often lie.

ROMEO   In bed asleep, while they do dream things true.

55   MERCUTIO   O, then I see Queen Mab hath been with you:
      She is the fairies' midwife, and she comes
      In shape no bigger than an agate-stone
      On the forefinger of an alderman,

---

35 proverbed . . . phrase furnished with an old proverb   **36 I'll . . . on** may refer to the
proverb "a good candle-holder proves a good gamester" (i.e. one is better off as a spectator)
37 The . . . done refers to the proverb "when play is at the best, it is time to leave"
38 dun's . . . word a reference to the quiet and hidden nature of a dun mouse, hence "be still,"
the sort of cautionary phrase a **constable** might utter   **dun** gray-brown; puns on **done**
39 draw . . . mire refers to the game "Dun is in the mire" in which players heave a horse called
Dun, represented by a heavy log, out of imaginary mud   **40 save your reverence** if you'll
excuse my language   **41 burn daylight** waste time (Romeo interprets this literally and
disagrees on the grounds that it is nighttime)   **45 Take . . . wits** understand my true meaning,
for good sense is five times more likely to be found there (through the use of reason) than in
the exercise of the senses   **47 mean** intend (playing on Mercutio's sense of "signify")
48 wit wisdom   **50 tonight** last night   **55 Queen Mab** possibly from the Celtic fairy queen
"Mabh," but **queen** puns on "quean" (i.e. prostitute) and **mab** could also mean "promiscuous
woman"   **57 agate-stone** precious stone often set in a ring and carved with tiny figures
58 alderman influential member of a local council

Drawn with a team of little atomies
60   Over men's noses as they lie asleep:
Her wagon-spokes made of long spinners' legs,
The cover of the wings of grasshoppers,
Her traces of the smallest spider's web,
Her collars of the moonshine's wat'ry beams,
65   Her whip of cricket's bone, the lash of film,
Her wagoner a small grey-coated gnat,
Not half so big as a round little worm
Pricked from the lazy finger of a maid,
Her chariot is an empty hazel-nut
70   Made by the joiner squirrel or old grub,
Time out o'mind the fairies' coachmakers.
And in this state she gallops night by night
Through lovers' brains, and then they dream of love,
On courtiers' knees, that dream on curtsies straight,
75   O'er lawyers' fingers, who straight dream on fees,
O'er ladies' lips, who straight on kisses dream,
Which oft the angry Mab with blisters plagues,
Because their breath with sweetmeats tainted are:
Sometime she gallops o'er a courtier's nose,
80   And then dreams he of smelling out a suit:
And sometime comes she with a tithe-pig's tail
Tickling a parson's nose as a lies asleep,
Then he dreams of another benefice.
Sometime she driveth o'er a soldier's neck,
85   And then dreams he of cutting foreign throats,

---

59 atomies creatures as tiny as atoms   **61 spinners** spiders   **63 traces** straps linking the collar round an animal's neck to the crossbar of the **chariot**   **65 lash** flexible cord of the whip **film** fine gossamer-like thread   **66 wagoner** driver   **67 worm . . . maid** worms were said to breed in the fingers of lazy maids   **70 joiner** skilled craftsman who works in wood **grub** insect larva or worm that bores holes   **74 curtsies** bows   **straight** straight away **78 sweetmeats** candied fruit/confectionary   **80 smelling . . . suit** finding someone with a petition to present at court from whom he may claim a fee for his assistance   **81 tithe-pig** pig given to the **parson** as part of the tithe (the tenth of one's goods due to the Church annually) **83 another benefice** additional Church position (with property and income)

Of breaches, ambuscadoes, Spanish blades,
Of healths five-fathom deep, and then anon
Drums in his ear, at which he starts and wakes,
And being thus frighted swears a prayer or two
90 And sleeps again. This is that very Mab
That plaits the manes of horses in the night,
And bakes the elflocks in foul sluttish hairs,
Which once untangled, much misfortune bodes.
This is the hag, when maids lie on their backs,
95 That presses them and learns them first to bear,
Making them women of good carriage:
This is she—

ROMEO   Peace, peace, Mercutio, peace!
Thou talk'st of nothing.

100 MERCUTIO   True, I talk of dreams,
Which are the children of an idle brain,
Begot of nothing but vain fantasy,
Which is as thin of substance as the air
And more inconstant than the wind, who woos
105 Even now the frozen bosom of the north,
And being angered puffs away from thence,
Turning his side to the dew-dropping south.

BENVOLIO   This wind you talk of blows us from ourselves
Supper is done, and we shall come too late.

110 ROMEO   I fear too early, for my mind misgives
Some consequence yet hanging in the stars
Shall bitterly begin his fearful date

---

86 **breaches** gaps in fortifications inflicted by artillery   **ambuscadoes** ambushes   **Spanish blades** Spanish swords, especially those made in Toledo, were famed for being of superior quality   87 **healths five-fathom deep** toasts drunk from extremely deep glasses   **anon** shortly   92 **bakes** stiffens/forms into a mass   **elflocks** tangles (which superstition held to be the work of elves)   94 **hag** evil spirit in female form (here the incubus that **presses** on sleepers and causes nightmares or erotic dreams)   95 **learns** teaches   **bear** bear the weight of a man/bear children   96 **carriage** deportment/ability to carry a burden (i.e. a man or a baby)   99 **nothing** plays on the sense of "vagina"   102 **Begot** conceived, created   **vain** worthless, empty, idle   107 **Turning his side** changing direction/changing allegiance   110 **misgives** fears/is full of foreboding about   112 **fearful** fear-inspiring   **date** appointed time

With this night's revels and expire the term
Of a despisèd life closed in my breast
115   By some vile forfeit of untimely death.
But he that hath the steerage of my course,
Direct my suit. On, lusty gentlemen!

BENVOLIO   Strike, drum.

They march about the stage and Servingmen come forth with their
napkins

Enter [Chief] Servant

CHIEF SERVINGMAN   Where's Potpan, that he helps not to take
120   away? He shift a trencher? He scrape a trencher?

FIRST SERVINGMAN   When good manners shall lie in one or two
men's hands and they unwashed too, 'tis a foul thing.

CHIEF SERVINGMAN   Away with the joint-stools, remove the
court-cupboard, look to the plate. Good thou, save me a piece
125   of marchpane, and as thou lovest me, let the porter let in
Susan Grindstone and Nell.— Antony, and Potpan!

SECOND SERVINGMAN   Ay, boy, ready.

CHIEF SERVINGMAN   You are looked for and called for, asked for
and sought for, in the great chamber.

130   FIRST SERVINGMAN   We cannot be here and there too. Cheerly,
boys, be brisk awhile, and the longer liver take all.

Exeunt [some Servingmen]

Enter all the Guests and Gentlewomen to the Masquers

CAPULET   Welcome, gentlemen! Ladies that have their toes
Unplagued with corns will walk a bout with you.
Ah, my mistresses, which of you all

---

113 expire cause to expire   **term** duration/agreed period for repayment (Romeo has
mortgaged his life)   **115 forfeit** penalty/loss   **118 drum** drummer   **119 take away** i.e. clear
the table   **120 trencher** wooden plate   **121 manners** may quibble on the Latin *manuarius* to
suggest "belonging to the hand"   **122 foul** bad/dirty   **123 joint-stools** stools made of parts
fitted together by a joiner   **124 court-cupboard** sideboard   **plate** silver or gold tableware
125 marchpane marzipan   **126 Grindstone** like **Potpan**, a name that suggests the character
has a domestic function, though Grindstone, used to sharpen knives, may additionally be
sexually suggestive ("to grind" had a slang sense of "to have sex," a "stone" could also mean a
"testicle")   **130 Cheerly** cheerily   **131 the . . . all** a proverb equivalent to "the winner takes
all"   **133 walk a bout** dance a round

135 Will now deny to dance? She that makes dainty,
 She I'll swear hath corns. Am I come near ye now?
 Welcome, gentlemen! I have seen the day
 That I have worn a visor and could tell
 A whispering tale in a fair lady's ear,
140 Such as would please: 'tis gone, 'tis gone, 'tis gone.
 You are welcome, gentlemen! Come, musicians, play.

Music plays, and they dance

 A hall, hall, give room! And foot it, girls.
 More light, you knaves, and turn the tables up,
 And quench the fire, the room is grown too hot.
145 Ah, sirrah, this unlooked-for sport comes well.
 Nay, sit, nay, sit, good cousin Capulet,
 For you and I are past our dancing days:
 How long is't now since last yourself and I
 Were in a mask?

150 SECOND CAPULET By'r lady, thirty years.

 CAPULET What, man? 'Tis not so much, 'tis not so much:
 'Tis since the nuptial of Lucentio,
 Come Pentecost as quickly as it will,
 Some five and twenty years, and then we masked.

155 SECOND CAPULET 'Tis more, 'tis more, his son is elder, sir:
 His son is thirty.

 CAPULET Will you tell me that?
 His son was but a ward two years ago.

 ROMEO What lady is that, which doth *To a Servingman*
 enrich the hand
160 Of yonder knight?

 SERVINGMAN I know not, sir.

---

135 deny refuse **makes dainty** is coyly reluctant **136 Am . . . now?** Have I touched a
sensitive spot/hit home with this? **142 A hall** i.e. clear the hall **143 turn . . . up** clear the
tables to one side, probably by removing the boards from trestle tables **145 sirrah** sir (used to
a social inferior, here either a servant, younger male guest, Capulet himself or, affectionately,
the **cousin**) **unlooked-for** unexpected **150 By'r lady** by Our Lady (the Virgin Mary)
153 Pentecost Whit Sunday (the seventh Sunday after Easter) **158 ward** minor under the
control of a guardian (i.e. under twenty-one)

ROMEO   O, she doth teach the torches to burn bright!
It seems she hangs upon the cheek of night
As a rich jewel in an Ethiope's ear:
165   Beauty too rich for use, for earth too dear!
So shows a snowy dove trooping with crows,
As yonder lady o'er her fellows shows.
The measure done, I'll watch her place of stand,
And touching hers, make blessèd my rude hand.
170   Did my heart love till now? Forswear it, sight,
For I ne'er saw true beauty till this night.

TYBALT   This, by his voice, should be a Montague.
Fetch me my rapier, boy.— What dares the slave

                                    [*Exit a Servingman*]

Come hither, covered with an antic face,
175   To fleer and scorn at our solemnity?
Now, by the stock and honour of my kin,
To strike him dead I hold it not a sin.

CAPULET   Why, how now, kinsman? Wherefore storm you so?

TYBALT   Uncle, this is a Montague, our foe,
180   A villain that is hither come in spite,
To scorn at our solemnity this night.

CAPULET   Young Romeo is it?

TYBALT   'Tis he, that villain Romeo.

CAPULET   Content thee, gentle coz, let him alone:
185   A bears him like a portly gentleman,
And to say truth, Verona brags of him
To be a virtuous and well-governed youth.
I would not for the wealth of all this town
Here in my house do him disparagement:
190   Therefore be patient, take no note of him.
It is my will, the which if thou respect,

---

164 Ethiope's Ethiopian's   **165 Beauty** possibly puns on "booty"   **use** plays on sense
of "financial interest"   **earth** life on earth/death and burial   **dear** beloved/costly
168 her . . . stand where she stands   **169 rude** rough/uncivilized   **170 Forswear** it deny
it/renounce my former vows of love (to Rosaline)   **173 rapier** lightweight sword   **174 antic**
grotesque (refers to Romeo's mask)   **175 fleer** mock, laugh scornfully   **solemnity** celebration
176 stock ancestry   **185 portly** of good bearing/dignified

Show a fair presence and put off these frowns,
An ill-beseeming semblance for a feast.

TYBALT   It fits when such a villain is a guest:
195   I'll not endure him.

CAPULET   He shall be endured.
What, goodman boy? I say, he shall: go to.
Am I the master here or you? Go to.
You'll not endure him? God shall mend my soul,
200   You'll make a mutiny among my guests?
You will set cock-a-hoop? You'll be the man?

TYBALT   Why, uncle, 'tis a shame.

CAPULET   Go to, go to.
You are a saucy boy. Is't so, indeed?
205   This trick may chance to scathe you, I know what.
You must contrary me? Marry, 'tis time.—
Well said, my hearts!— You are a   *To Dancers/To Tybalt*
    princox. Go,
Be quiet, or— More light, more light!—   *To Servants*
    for shame,   *To Tybalt*
I'll make you quiet.— What, cheerly, my hearts!   *To Dancers*
210 TYBALT   Patience perforce with wilful choler meeting
Makes my flesh tremble in their different greeting.
I will withdraw, but this intrusion shall
Now seeming sweet convert to bitter gall.   *Exit*

ROMEO   If I profane with my unworthiest hand   *To Juliet*
215   This holy shrine, the gentle sin is this:
My lips, two blushing pilgrims, ready stand

---

193 **semblance** appearance   197 **goodman boy** a contemptuous and belittling expression
goodman a man below the rank of gentleman   **go to** an expression of impatience and
reproof   199 **God . . . soul** an oath   201 **set cock-a-hoop** behave recklessly/provoke
disorder   **be the man** play the big man   204 **saucy** insolent   205 **scathe** injure
I know what I assure you/I know how much   206 **contrary** contradict, defy   **time** i.e. time
you complied/time you were taught a lesson/time I concerned myself with my guests
207 **said** done   **hearts** fine friends (i.e. the guests)   **princox** conceited, impertinent youth
210 **perforce** enforced   **choler** anger   211 **different** antagonistic, clashing   214 **profane**
desecrate, defile   215 **shrine** i.e. Juliet's hand

To smooth that rough touch with a tender kiss.

JULIET   Good pilgrim, you do wrong your hand too much,
Which mannerly devotion shows in this,

220   For saints have hands that pilgrims' hands do touch,
And palm to palm is holy palmers' kiss.

ROMEO   Have not saints lips, and holy palmers too?

JULIET   Ay, pilgrim, lips that they must use in prayer.

ROMEO   O, then, dear saint, let lips do what hands do:

225   They pray, grant thou, lest faith turn to despair.

JULIET   Saints do not move, though grant for prayers' sake.

ROMEO   Then move not, while my prayer's effect I take.
Thus from my lips, by thine, my sin is purged.   *Kisses her*

JULIET   Then have my lips the sin that they have took.

230 ROMEO   Sin from my lips? O, trespass sweetly urged!
Give me my sin again.   *Kisses her again*

JULIET   You kiss by th'book.

NURSE   Madam, your mother craves a word   *Juliet stands aside*
with you.

ROMEO   What is her mother?

235 NURSE   Marry, bachelor,
Her mother is the lady of the house,
And a good lady, and a wise and virtuous.
I nursed her daughter, that you talked withal.
I tell you, he that can lay hold of her

240   Shall have the chinks.

ROMEO   Is she a Capulet?   *Aside?*
O, dear account! My life is my foe's debt.

---

219 mannerly . . . this shows proper devotion in this action   **220 saints** i.e. images of saints
221 palmers pilgrims who have traveled to the Holy Land and returned with a palm leaf as a
symbol of their visit (playing on **palm** of the hand)   **225 grant thou** you must concede/grant
their prayers   **226 move** entreat, pray (Romeo shifts the sense to "change position")
230 urged argued/provoked   **232 by th'book** expertly, by the rules/religiously, in accordance
with the Bible   **234 What** who   **235 bachelor** young man   **238 withal** with   **239 lay hold**
of with sexual connotations   **240 the chinks** lots of money (plays on sense of "vagina")
242 dear account costly debt, heavy reckoning (**dear** puns on sense of "beloved")   **my foe's**
debt a debt I owe to my foe

BENVOLIO	Away, begone, the sport is at the best.	*Comes forward*
ROMEO	Ay, so I fear, the more is my unrest.	

245 CAPULET Nay, gentlemen, prepare not to be gone,   *The guests*
We have a trifling foolish banquet towards.   *indicate that they*
Is it e'en so? Why then I thank you all.   *have to leave*
I thank you, honest gentlemen, goodnight.—
More torches here!— Come on, then let's to bed.   *To Servingmen*
250 Ah, sirrah, by my fay, it waxes late:
I'll to my rest.   *[Exeunt all but Juliet and Nurse]*

JULIET Come hither, nurse. What is yond gentleman?

NURSE The son and heir of old Tiberio.

JULIET What's he that now is going out of door?

255 NURSE Marry, that I think be young Petruchio.

JULIET What's he that follows here, that would not dance?

NURSE I know not.

JULIET Go ask his name.— If he be marrièd,   *The Nurse goes*
My grave is like to be my wedding bed.

260 NURSE His name is Romeo, and a Montague,   *Returning*
The only son of your great enemy.

JULIET My only love sprung from my only hate!
Too early seen unknown, and known too late!
Prodigious birth of love it is to me,
265 That I must love a loathèd enemy.

NURSE What's this? What's this?

JULIET A rhyme I learned even now
Of one I danced withal.

One calls within 'Juliet!'

NURSE Anon, anon!
270 Come, let's away: the strangers all are gone.   *Exeunt*

---

243 **the . . . best** another allusion to the proverb "when play is at the best, it is time to
leave"   246 **banquet** light meal/course of sweetmeats, fruit and wine   **towards** ready,
imminent   248 **honest** honorable   250 **fay** faith   252 **yond** yonder, that   259 **like** likely
264 **Prodigious** abnormal (used to describe a deformed baby)/ill-omened   269 **Anon** coming,
just a minute

[Act 2]

[Enter] Chorus

CHORUS   Now old desire doth in his death-bed lie,
And young affection gapes to be his heir:
That fair for which love groaned for and would die,
With tender Juliet matched, is now not fair.
5   Now Romeo is beloved and loves again,
Alike bewitchèd by the charm of looks,
But to his foe supposed he must complain,
And she steal love's sweet bait from fearful hooks.
Being held a foe, he may not have access
10   To breathe such vows as lovers use to swear,
And she as much in love, her means much less
To meet her new-belovèd anywhere:
But passion lends them power, time means, to meet,
Temp'ring extremities with extreme sweet.   *[Exit]*

[Act 2 Scene 1]   *running scene 5*

Enter Romeo alone

ROMEO   Can I go forward when my heart is here?
Turn back, dull earth, and find thy centre out.   *Stands aside*

Enter Benvolio with Mercutio

BENVOLIO   Romeo! My cousin Romeo, Romeo!

MERCUTIO   He is wise,
5   And on my life hath stol'n him home to bed.

BENVOLIO   He ran this way and leapt this orchard wall.
Call, good Mercutio.

2.0 2 gapes waits eagerly   **3 fair** beauty (i.e. Rosaline)   **groaned ... die** perhaps with sexual connotations ("to die" can mean "to orgasm")   **4 matched** compared   **5 again** in return
6 Alike both equally   **looks** physical appearance/gazes   **7 foe supposed** i.e. Juliet
complain make a lover's laments   **8 fearful** frightening   **10 use** are accustomed
14 Temp'ring extremities modifying severe hardships   **2.1 Location:** *outside the Capulets' walled orchard; the action then shifts to the orchard itself*   **1 go forward** move on, leave
2 earth i.e. his body   **centre** i.e. heart/Juliet   **6 orchard** garden/land devoted to herbs and fruit trees

MERCUTIO   Nay, I'll conjure too.
Romeo! Humours! Madman! Passion! Lover!
10   Appear thou in the likeness of a sigh,
Speak but one rhyme, and I am satisfied:
Cry but 'Ay me', pronounce but 'love' and 'dove',
Speak to my gossip Venus one fair word,
One nickname for her purblind son and heir,
15   Young Abraham Cupid, he that shot so true,
When King Cophetua loved the beggar-maid!—
He heareth not, he stirreth not, he moveth not,   *Aside*
The ape is dead, and I must conjure him.—
I conjure thee by Rosaline's bright eyes,
20   By her high forehead and her scarlet lip,
By her fine foot, straight leg and quiv'ring thigh,
And the demesnes that there adjacent lie,
That in thy likeness thou appear to us.
BENVOLIO   An if he hear thee, thou wilt anger him.
25   MERCUTIO   This cannot anger him: 'twould anger him
To raise a spirit in his mistress' circle
Of some strange nature, letting it there stand
Till she had laid it and conjured it down:
That were some spite. My invocation
30   Is fair and honest, and in his mistress' name
I conjure only but to raise up him.

---

8 conjure summon him with an incantation as one would a spirit   9 Humours! (creature of)
moods   11 rhyme i.e. verse of love poetry   13 gossip old friend   Venus Roman goddess of
love   14 purblind blind   15 Abraham Cupid i.e. one who is both young and old, and a
patriarch like the biblical Abraham   16 King . . . beggar-maid the tale of the African King
Cophetua, who fell in love with a beggar, was popularized in a ballad   18 The . . . dead
probably refers to performing apes who played dead as part of an act (ape is also an
affectionate term)   22 demesnes lands (i.e. the vaginal area)   26 raise a spirit summon a
supernatural spirit/get an erect penis   circle magic circle/vagina   27 strange supernatural/
belonging to someone other than Romeo   stand continues to play on the idea of having an
erection   28 laid . . . down subdued the spirit/provided sex and caused the erection to subside
29 spite vexation   30 honest honorable (plays on the sense of "chaste")

BENVOLIO   Come, he hath hid himself among these trees,
To be consorted with the humorous night:
Blind is his love and best befits the dark.

35 MERCUTIO   If love be blind, love cannot hit the mark.
Now will he sit under a medlar tree,
And wish his mistress were that kind of fruit
As maids call medlars, when they laugh alone.—
O Romeo, that she were, O, that she were

40 An open arse and thou a pop'rin pear!
Romeo, goodnight: I'll to my truckle-bed,
This field-bed is too cold for me to sleep.—
Come, shall we go?

BENVOLIO   Go, then, for 'tis in vain

45 To seek him here that means not to be found.

Exeunt [Benvolio and Mercutio]

ROMEO   He jests at scars that never felt   *Comes forward*
a wound.

[Enter Juliet above]

But, soft, what light through yonder window breaks?
It is the east, and Juliet is the sun.
Arise, fair sun, and kill the envious moon,

50 Who is already sick and pale with grief,
That thou her maid art far more fair than she:
Be not her maid, since she is envious:
Her vestal livery is but sick and green
And none but fools do wear it, cast it off.

55 It is my lady, O, it is my love!
O, that she knew she were!

---

33 **consorted with** associated with/part of (plays on the sense of "sexually intimate with")
humorous damp/subject to varying moods   35 **hit the mark** strike the target/penetrate the
vagina   36 **medlar** fruit with a deep hollow at the top, hence a slang term for the vagina (also
puns on "meddler"—i.e. "fornicator")   39 **O** another vaginal pun   40 **open arse** medlar
fruit, with obvious sexual sense   **pop'rin pear** pear from Poperinghe in Flanders and a slang
term for the penis; puns on "pop her in" (where "her" signifies "it")   41 **truckle-bed** small
wheeled bed stored under a larger bed   42 **field-bed** bed on the ground   *above* i.e. on the
upper staging level or gallery; the entry, or the sight of Juliet, might be delayed until "It is my
lady"   51 **maid** votary (of Diana, Roman goddess of the moon and chastity)   53 **vestal livery**
virginal clothing

She speaks yet she says nothing: what of that?
Her eye discourses: I will answer it.
I am too bold, 'tis not to me she speaks:
60   Two of the fairest stars in all the heaven,
Having some business, do entreat her eyes
To twinkle in their spheres till they return.
What if her eyes were there, they in her head?
The brightness of her cheek would shame those stars,
65   As daylight doth a lamp, her eye in heaven
Would through the airy region stream so bright
That birds would sing and think it were not night.
See how she leans her cheek upon her hand!
O, that I were a glove upon that hand,
70   That I might touch that cheek!

JULIET   Ay me!

ROMEO   She speaks: *Aside*
O, speak again, bright angel, for thou art
As glorious to this night, being o'er my head
75   As is a wingèd messenger of heaven
Unto the white upturnèd wond'ring eyes
Of mortals that fall back to gaze on him
When he bestrides the lazy puffing clouds,
And sails upon the bosom of the air.

80   JULIET   O Romeo, Romeo, wherefore art thou Romeo?
Deny thy father and refuse thy name,
Or if thou wilt not, be but sworn my love,
And I'll no longer be a Capulet.

ROMEO   Shall I hear more, or shall I speak at this?   *Aside*
85   JULIET   'Tis but thy name that is my enemy,
Thou art thyself, though not a Montague.
What's Montague? It is nor hand, nor foot,

---

62 spheres orbits; stars and planets were thought to be contained within transparent concentric spheres that rotated around the earth   **74 glorious** magnificent/ illustrious/shining   **76 white upturnèd** looking upward, so that the whites of the eyes are visible   **80 wherefore** why   **86 though** even if you were

Nor arm, nor face, nor any other part
Belonging to a man. O, be some other name.
90 What's in a name? That which we call a rose
By any other word would smell as sweet,
So Romeo would, were he not Romeo called,
Retain that dear perfection which he owes
Without that title. Romeo, doff thy name,
95 And for thy name, which is no part of thee,
Take all myself.

ROMEO   I take thee at thy word: *To her*
Call me but love, and I'll be new baptized,
Henceforth I never will be Romeo.

100 JULIET   What man art thou that thus bescreened in night
So stumblest on my counsel?

ROMEO   By a name
I know not how to tell thee who I am:
My name, dear saint, is hateful to myself,
105 Because it is an enemy to thee.
Had I it written, I would tear the word.

JULIET   My ears have yet not drunk a hundred words
Of thy tongue's uttering, yet I know the sound:
Art thou not Romeo and a Montague?

110 ROMEO   Neither, fair maid, if either thee dislike.

JULIET   How cam'st thou hither, tell me, and wherefore?
The orchard walls are high and hard to climb,
And the place death, considering who thou art,
If any of my kinsmen find thee here.

115 ROMEO   With love's light wings did I o'er-perch these walls,
For stony limits cannot hold love out,
And what love can do that dares love attempt:
Therefore thy kinsmen are no stop to me.

JULIET   If they do see thee, they will murder thee.

---

93 owes owns   **94 doff** cast off   **95 for** in exchange for   **100 bescreened** concealed
101 counsel private thoughts   **115 o'er-perch** fly over

120 ROMEO   Alack, there lies more peril in thine eye
             Than twenty of their swords: look thou but sweet,
             And I am proof against their enmity.

     JULIET   I would not for the world they saw thee here.

     ROMEO   I have night's cloak to hide me from their eyes,
125   And but thou love me, let them find me here:
             My life were better ended by their hate,
             Than death prorogued, wanting of thy love.

     JULIET   By whose direction found'st thou out this place?

     ROMEO   By love, that first did prompt me to inquire:
130   He lent me counsel and I lent him eyes.
             I am no pilot, yet wert thou as far
             As that vast shore washed with the farthest sea,
             I should adventure for such merchandise.

     JULIET   Thou know'st the mask of night is on my face,
135   Else would a maiden blush bepaint my cheek
             For that which thou hast heard me speak tonight
             Fain would I dwell on form, fain, fain deny
             What I have spoke: but farewell compliment!
             Dost thou love me? I know thou wilt say 'Ay',
140   And I will take thy word. Yet if thou swear'st,
             Thou mayst prove false: at lovers' perjuries
             They say Jove laughs. O gentle Romeo,
             If thou dost love, pronounce it faithfully:
             Or if thou think'st I am too quickly won,
145   I'll frown and be perverse and say thee nay,
             So thou wilt woo, but else not for the world.
             In truth, fair Montague, I am too fond,
             And therefore thou mayst think my behaviour light:
             But trust me, gentleman, I'll prove more true

---

122 **proof** impervious/armored   125 **but** unless   127 **prorogued** postponed   **wanting of** lacking   130 **counsel** advice, guidance   131 **pilot** navigator, one who directs the course of a ship   137 **Fain** willingly   **form** formality, decorum   138 **compliment** etiquette   142 **Jove** Jupiter, Roman king of the gods   143 **pronounce** declare   146 **So** so long as   **else** otherwise   147 **fond** loving/infatuated/foolish   148 **light** frivolous/forward/unchaste

150 Than those that have more coying to be strange.
I should have been more strange, I must confess,
But that thou overheard'st, ere I was ware,
My true love's passion: therefore pardon me,
And not impute this yielding to light love,
155 Which the dark night hath so discoverèd.

ROMEO   Lady, by yonder blessèd moon I vow
That tips with silver all these fruit-tree tops—

JULIET   O, swear not by the moon, th'inconstant moon,
That monthly changes in her circlèd orb,
160 Lest that thy love prove likewise variable.

ROMEO   What shall I swear by?

JULIET   Do not swear at all:
Or if thou wilt, swear by thy gracious self,
Which is the god of my idolatry,
165 And I'll believe thee.

ROMEO   If my heart's dear love—

JULIET   Well, do not swear. Although I joy in thee,
I have no joy of this contract tonight:
It is too rash, too unadvised, too sudden,
170 Too like the lightning, which doth cease to be
Ere one can say 'It lightens'. Sweet, goodnight!
This bud of love, by summer's ripening breath,
May prove a beauteous flower when next we meet.
Goodnight, goodnight, as sweet repose and rest
175 Come to thy heart as that within my breast!

ROMEO   O, wilt thou leave me so unsatisfied?

JULIET   What satisfaction canst thou have tonight?

ROMEO   Th'exchange of thy love's faithful vow for mine.

JULIET   I gave thee mine before thou didst request it:
180 And yet I would it were to give again.

ROMEO   Wouldst thou withdraw it? For what purpose, love?

---

150 coying coyness, affected reluctance   strange aloof, reserved   152 ware aware (of you)
155 Which which yielding   discoverèd revealed   159 circlèd orb i.e. celestial sphere
163 gracious full of divine grace   168 contract i.e. mutual declarations of love
177 satisfaction may pick up on the sense of "sexual satisfaction"   180 were were mine

JULIET   But to be frank and give it thee again.
And yet I wish but for the thing I have.
My bounty is as boundless as the sea,
185   My love as deep: the more I give to thee,
The more I have, for both are infinite.
I hear some noise within. Dear love, adieu!—
[*Nurse*] *calls within*
Anon, good nurse!— Sweet Montague, be true.
Stay but a little, I will come again.   [*Exit, above*]
190   ROMEO   O blessèd, blessèd night! I am afeard,
Being in night, all this is but a dream,
Too flattering-sweet to be substantial.
[*Enter Juliet, above*]
JULIET   Three words, dear Romeo, and goodnight indeed.
If that thy bent of love be honourable,
195   Thy purpose marriage, send me word tomorrow,
By one that I'll procure to come to thee,
Where and what time thou wilt perform the rite,
And all my fortunes at thy foot I'll lay,
And follow thee my lord throughout the world.
[*Nurse calls*] *within 'Madam!'*
200   I come, anon.— But if thou mean'st not well,
I do beseech thee—
[*Nurse calls*] *within 'Madam!'*
By and by, I come.—
To cease thy strife, and leave me to my grief.
Tomorrow will I send.
205   ROMEO   So thrive my soul—
JULIET   A thousand times goodnight!   *Exit, [above]*
ROMEO   A thousand times the worse, to want thy light.
Love goes toward love as schoolboys from their books,
But love from love, toward school with   *Romeo starts*
heavy looks.   *to go*
Enter Juliet again, [above]

---

182 frank generous/candid   **184 bounty** generosity   **194 bent** intention, inclination
203 strife antagonism/strivings, efforts   **207 want** lack

210 JULIET   Hist, Romeo, hist! O, for a falc'ner's voice,
                  To lure this tassel-gentle back again!
                  Bondage is hoarse, and may not speak aloud,
                  Else would I tear the cave where Echo lies,
                  And make her airy tongue more hoarse than mine,
215   With repetition of my 'Romeo'.

ROMEO   It is my soul that calls upon my name.
                  How silver-sweet sound lovers' tongues by night,
                  Like softest music to attending ears!

JULIET   Romeo!

220 ROMEO   My nyas?

JULIET   What o'clock tomorrow shall I send to thee?

ROMEO   By the hour of nine.

JULIET   I will not fail: 'tis twenty years till then.
                  I have forgot why I did call thee back.

225 ROMEO   Let me stand here till thou remember it.

JULIET   I shall forget, to have thee still stand there,
                  Rememb'ring how I love thy company.

ROMEO   And I'll still stay, to have thee still forget,
                  Forgetting any other home but this.

230 JULIET   'Tis almost morning, I would have thee gone:
                  And yet no further than a wanton's bird,
                  That lets it hop a little from his hand,
                  Like a poor prisoner in his twisted gyves,
                  And with a silken thread plucks it back again,
235   So loving-jealous of his liberty.

ROMEO   I would I were thy bird.

JULIET   Sweet, so would I:
                  Yet I should kill thee with much cherishing.
                  Goodnight, goodnight! Parting is such sweet sorrow,
240   That I shall say goodnight till it be morrow.   *Exit, [above]*

---

210 **Hist** a whispered call for attention   211 **tassel-gentle** tercel gentle, a male falcon
212 **Bondage is hoarse** i.e. one who is confined can only whisper   213 **Echo** in Greek
mythology, Echo, rejected by Narcissus, pined away in caves until only her voice was left
220 **nyas** young hawk (which has yet to fly)   226 **to** in order to   **still** yet/always (Romeo
plays with these meanings and with the sense of "motionless")   231 **wanton's** spoiled child's
233 **gyves** fetters

ROMEO   Sleep dwell upon thine eyes, peace in thy breast!
Would I were sleep and peace, so sweet to rest!
// The grey-eyed morn smiles on the frowning night, //
// Check'ring the eastern clouds with streaks of light, //
245   // And darkness fleckled like a drunkard reels //
// From forth day's pathway, made by Titan's wheels. //
Hence will I to my ghostly friar's close cell,
His help to crave, and my dear hap to tell.   *Exit*

[Act 2 Scene 2]   *running scene 6*

Enter Friar Laurence alone with a basket

FRIAR LAURENCE   The grey-eyed morn smiles on the frowning
night,
Check'ring the eastern clouds with streaks of light,
And fleckled darkness like a drunkard reels
From forth day's path and Titan's burning wheels:
5   Now, ere the sun advance his burning eye,
The day to cheer and night's dank dew to dry,
I must upfill this osier cage of ours
With baleful weeds and precious-juicèd flowers.
The earth that's nature's mother is her tomb:
10   What is her burying grave, that is her womb,
And from her womb children of divers kind
We sucking on her natural bosom find:
Many for many virtues excellent,
None but for some and yet all different.
15   O, mickle is the powerful grace that lies
In plants, herbs, stones, and their true qualities:

---

245 fleckled dappled   **246 From forth** away from, out of   **Titan** Roman sun god, who drove
the sun across the heavens in a chariot   **247 ghostly** holy, spiritual   **close cell** humble
dwelling, especially that of a monk   **248 dear hap** good fortune (though **dear** may quibble
ominously on "dire, grievous")   **2.2 Location:** *near Friar Laurence's cell, Verona*
5 advance raise   **7 osier cage** willow basket   **8 baleful** deadly   **11 divers** various
14 None . . . some there are none that do not have some useful properties   **15 mickle** great
grace beneficent virtue

For nought so vile that on the earth doth live
But to the earth some special good doth give,
Nor aught so good but strained from that fair use
20 Revolts from true birth, stumbling on abuse.
Virtue itself turns vice, being misapplied,
And vice sometime by action dignified.

Enter Romeo

Within the infant rind of this weak flower
Poison hath residence and medicine power:
25 For this, being smelt, with that part cheers each part,
Being tasted, slays all senses with the heart.
Two such opposèd kings encamp them still
In man as well as herbs, grace and rude will:
And where the worser is predominant,
30 Full soon the canker death eats up that plant.

ROMEO Good morrow, father.

FRIAR LAURENCE *Benedicite!*
What early tongue so sweet saluteth me?
Young son, it argues a distempered head
35 So soon to bid good morrow to thy bed:
Care keeps his watch in every old man's eye,
And where care lodges, sleep will never lie,
But where unbruisèd youth with unstuffed brain
Doth couch his limbs, there golden sleep doth reign:
40 Therefore thy earliness doth me assure
Thou art uproused with some distemp'rature,
Or if not so, then here I hit it right,
Our Romeo hath not been in bed tonight.

ROMEO That last is true, the sweeter rest was mine.

45 FRIAR LAURENCE God pardon sin! Wast thou with Rosaline?

ROMEO With Rosaline, my ghostly father? No,
I have forgot that name, and that name's woe.

---

19 aught anything   **strained** forced   **25 that part** i.e. its smell   **26 slays** some editors prefer the Second Quarto's "stays"   **with** along with   **27 them still** themselves always   **30 canker** worm that destroys plants   **32 *Benedicite!*** Bless you!   **34 argues** suggests   **distempered** disordered, unhappy   **36 Care** worry   **39 couch** lay, rest

FRIAR LAURENCE   That's my good son: but where hast thou been,
then?

ROMEO   I'll tell thee ere thou ask it me again:
50   I have been feasting with mine enemy,
Where on a sudden one hath wounded me,
That's by me wounded: both our remedies
Within thy help and holy physic lies.
I bear no hatred, blessèd man, for lo,
55   My intercession likewise steads my foe.

FRIAR LAURENCE   Be plain, good son, rest homely in thy drift,
Riddling confession finds but riddling shrift.

ROMEO   Then plainly know my heart's dear love is set
On the fair daughter of rich Capulet:
60   As mine on hers, so hers is set on mine;
And all combined, save what thou must combine
By holy marriage. When and where and how
We met, we wooed and made exchange of vow,
I'll tell thee as we pass, but this I pray,
65   That thou consent to marry us today.

FRIAR LAURENCE   Holy Saint Francis, what a change is here!
Is Rosaline, that thou didst love so dear,
So soon forsaken? Young men's love then lies
Not truly in their hearts, but in their eyes.
70   Jesu Maria, what a deal of brine
Hath washed thy sallow cheeks for Rosaline!
How much salt water thrown away in waste,
To season love, that of it doth not taste!
The sun not yet thy sighs from heaven clears,
75   Thy old groans yet ringing in my ancient ears:
Lo, here upon thy cheek the stain doth sit
Of an old tear that is not washed off yet.
If e'er thou wast thyself and these woes thine,
Thou and these woes were all for Rosaline.

---

53 physic medicine, healing   **54 lo** look (a common speech marker)   **55 intercession**
petition, entreaty   **steads** helps   **56 rest homely** remain simple   **drift** meaning/aim
57 shrift absolution   **75 old** former/abundant

80   And art thou changed? Pronounce this sentence then:
        Women may fall, when there's no strength in men.

ROMEO   Thou chid'st me oft for loving Rosaline.

FRIAR LAURENCE   For doting, not for loving, pupil mine.

ROMEO   And bad'st me bury love.

85 FRIAR LAURENCE   Not in a grave,
        To lay one in, another out to have.

ROMEO   I pray thee, chide me not. Her I love now
        Doth grace for grace and love for love allow:
        The other did not so.

90 FRIAR LAURENCE   O, she knew well
        Thy love did read by rote that could not spell.
        But come, young waverer, come, go with me,
        In one respect I'll thy assistant be:
        For this alliance may so happy prove,

95   To turn your households' rancour to pure love.

ROMEO   O, let us hence! I stand on sudden haste.

FRIAR LAURENCE   Wisely and slow: they stumble that run fast.

                                        Exeunt

[Act 2 Scene 3]   *running scene 7*

Enter Benvolio and Mercutio

MERCUTIO   Where the devil should this Romeo be?
        Came he not home tonight?

BENVOLIO   Not to his father's: I spoke with his man.

MERCUTIO   Why, that same pale hard-hearted wench, that
        Rosaline,

5   Torments him so, that he will sure run mad.

BENVOLIO   Tybalt, the kinsman to old Capulet,
        Hath sent a letter to his father's house.

MERCUTIO   A challenge, on my life.

---

80 **sentence** maxim, saying   82 **chid'st** rebuked   84 **bad'st** bade, instructed   88 **grace**
favor   91 **read by rote** recite by memory, without understanding   93 **In one respect** for one
reason   96 **stand** insist/depend   **2.3** *Location: a public place in Verona*   2 **tonight** last
night   3 **man** servant

BENVOLIO	Romeo will answer it.
10 MERCUTIO	Any man that can write may answer a letter.
BENVOLIO	Nay, he will answer the letter's master, how he dares, being dared.
MERCUTIO	Alas, poor Romeo, he is already dead, stabbed with a white wench's black eye, run through the ear with a love-song, the very pin of his heart cleft with the blind bow-boy's butt-shaft: and is he a man to encounter Tybalt?
BENVOLIO	Why, what is Tybalt?
MERCUTIO	More than prince of cats, O, he's the courageous captain of compliments: he fights as you sing prick-song, keeps time, distance and proportion: he rests his minim rests, one, two, and the third in your bosom — the very butcher of a silk button — a duellist, a duellist, a gentleman of the very first house, of the first and second cause. Ah, the immortal *passado*, the *punto reverso*, the *hay*!
25 BENVOLIO	The what?
MERCUTIO	The pox of such antic, lisping, affecting phantasimes, these new tuners of accent! 'Jesu, a very good blade, a very tall man, a very good whore!' Why, is not this a lamentable thing, grandsire, that we should be thus afflicted with these strange flies, these fashion-mongers, these 'pardon-me's',

---

9 **answer it** accept the challenge (in the following line Mercutio plays on the literal meaning)
12 **dared** challenged   14 **eye** plays on sense of "vagina"   15 **pin** wooden peg at the center of
a target (plays on sense of "penis")   **blind bow-boy's** i.e. Cupid's   16 **butt-shaft** strong
unbarbed arrow (in archery used for shooting at the butt, a mound on which the target stood)
18 **prince of cats** an allusion to Tybert, the cat in the moral tale *Reynard the Fox*   19 **captain
of compliments** master of the fastidious etiquette of duelling   **prick-song** written music
20 **rests . . . rests** pauses very briefly (between feinting thrusts), like a musician pausing
momentarily between very short notes   21 **third** i.e. third thrust (the genuine one)
butcher . . . button i.e. so precise he can pierce his opponent's button   23 **first house** best
fencing school   **first . . . cause** in the rules of fencing, the two valid reasons for undertaking a
duel   24 *passado* forward thrust with one foot advanced   *punto reverso* backhanded thrust
hay penetrating thrust   26 **The pox of** a plague upon   **affecting** affected, pretentious
phantasimes fanciful, extravagant men   27 **these . . . accent** those whose speech is peppered
with fashionable foreign phrases/those who pronounce words in an affected manner or with a
foreign inflection   **blade** sword/fine fellow   28 **tall** brave/fine   29 **grandsire** Mercutio
addresses an imaginary old man or grandfather   30 **strange flies** bizarre or foreign parasites

who stand so much on the new form, that they cannot sit at ease on the old bench? O, their bones, their bones!

Enter Romeo

BENVOLIO   Here comes Romeo, here comes Romeo.

MERCUTIO   Without his roe, like a dried herring: O flesh, flesh,
35   how art thou fishified! Now is he for the numbers that Petrarch flowed in: Laura to his lady was a kitchen-wench — marry, she had a better love to berhyme her — Dido a dowdy, Cleopatra a gypsy, Helen and Hero hildings and harlots, Thisbe a grey eye or so, but not to the purpose.— Signior
40   Romeo, *bon jour:* there's a French salutation to your French slop. You gave us the counterfeit fairly last night.

ROMEO   Good morrow to you both. What counterfeit did I give you?

MERCUTIO   The slip, sir, the slip — can you not conceive?

45   **ROMEO**   Pardon, good Mercutio, my business was great, and in such a case as mine a man may strain courtesy.

MERCUTIO   That's as much as to say, such a case as yours constrains a man to bow in the hams.

---

31 stand insist (plays on the literal sense)   **form** code of behavior, etiquette (plays on sense of **bench**)   **32 old bench** i.e. traditional behavior and customs   **their bones** i.e. their bones are so tender they cannot sit on a hard bench/their bones are corrupted from venereal disease (plays on the way such men fill their speech with foreign words, here the French *bon*, i.e. "good")   **34 roe** female deer/semen   i.e. he is sexually exhausted (plays on the first syllable of Romeo's name, leaving "me, o," the lament of a lover)   **dried herring** withered penis (**roe** was removed from the herring during the curing process)   **flesh** plays on sense of "penis/erection"   **35 fishified** made fish-like, i.e. coldblooded/dried out (impotent)/obsessed with your mistress's vagina   **numbers . . . in** the Italian poet **Petrarch** wrote passionate verse (**numbers**) to his love **Laura**   **36 flowed in** wrote fluently/overflowed in/swam in **to** compared to   **37 better love** i.e. Petrarch   **Dido** the legendary Queen of Carthage who committed suicide after her lover Aeneas deserted her   **dowdy** shabbily dressed woman **38 Cleopatra** Egyptian queen of the first century BC who committed suicide after the loss of her kingdom and the death of her lover Antony   **Helen and Hero** the famously beautiful Helen of Troy, and Hero, lover of Leander, who committed suicide when he drowned swimming the Hellespont to see her   **hildings** good-for-nothings/whores   **39 Thisbe** the lover of Pyramus committed suicide after his death   **grey** considered a particularly beautiful eye color   **not** nothing   **40 *bon jour*** "good day" (French)   **to . . . slop** to match your French-style loose breeches   **41 the counterfeit** i.e. the slip (a counterfeit coin was known as a **slip**)   **44 conceive** understand, work it out   **46 case** situation (Mercutio then shifts the sense to "vagina")   **48 bow . . . hams** bow from the waist (playing on **courtesy**, a form of **curtsy**)/hunch over after a heavy bout of sexual activity or with the pain of venereal disease **hams** thighs and buttocks

ROMEO	Meaning, to curtsy.
50 MERCUTIO	Thou hast most kindly hit it.
ROMEO	A most courteous exposition.
MERCUTIO	Nay, I am the very pink of courtesy.
ROMEO	Pink for flower.
MERCUTIO	Right.
55 ROMEO	Why, then is my pump well flowered.
MERCUTIO	Sure wit, follow me this jest now till thou hast worn out thy pump, that when the single sole of it is worn, the jest may remain after the wearing sole singular.
ROMEO	O single-soled jest, solely singular for the singleness.
60 MERCUTIO	Come between us, good Benvolio, my wits faints.
ROMEO	Switch and spurs, switch and spurs, or I'll cry a match.
MERCUTIO	Nay, if our wits run the wild-goose chase, I am done, for thou hast more of the wild-goose in one of thy wits
65	than I am sure I have in my whole five. Was I with you there for the goose?
ROMEO	Thou wast never with me for anything when thou wast not there for the goose.
MERCUTIO	I will bite thee by the ear for that jest.
70 ROMEO	Nay, good goose, bite not.
MERCUTIO	Thy wit is a very bitter sweeting: it is a most sharp sauce.

---

49 curtsy bow   **50 kindly hit it** readily got it/naturally had sex   **52 very pink** most excellent example (Romeo plays on the fact that a pink is a type of **flower** and on the verb "to pink" (i.e. to ornament a **pump** or garment by punching small holes or designs into it)   **55 pump** light shoe   **flowered** decorated with flowers/pinked   **56 Sure** sure-footed, secure   **follow me** follow me (**me** is emphatic)   **57 single** only/thin   **58 sole singular** uniquely individual/alone   **59 single-soled . . . singleness** slight, poor jest, only noteworthy for the fact that there is only one of it/that it is simple   **61 Switch and spurs** i.e. urge your wits on   **Switch** whip   **cry a match** declare the contest is over/declare my victory   **63 wild-goose chase** horse race in which the leading rider chose the course and the others were obliged to follow him anywhere/a pointless pursuit   **64 of the wild-goose** i.e. foolishness (geese were proverbially stupid)   **65 Was . . . goose?** Have I evened the score with my jest about the goose?   **68 for the goose** as a stupid person/in search of a prostitute   **71 sweeting** sweet apple   **sharp sauce** biting riposte/stinging impudence/bitter sauce for food

ROMEO   And is it not then well served into a sweet goose?

MERCUTIO   O, here's a wit of cheverel, that stretches from an
75   inch narrow to an ell broad!

ROMEO   I stretch it out for that word 'broad', which added to
the goose, proves thee far and wide a broad goose.

MERCUTIO   Why, is not this better now than groaning for love?
Now art thou sociable, now art thou Romeo, now art thou
80   what thou art, by art as well as by nature: for this drivelling
love is like a great natural, that runs lolling up and down to
hide his bauble in a hole.

BENVOLIO   Stop there, stop there.

MERCUTIO   Thou desirest me to stop in my tale against the hair.

85   BENVOLIO   Thou wouldst else have made thy tale large.

MERCUTIO   O, thou art deceived: I would have made it short, for
I was come to the whole depth of my tale, and meant indeed
to occupy the argument no longer.

Enter Nurse and her man [Peter]

ROMEO   Here's goodly gear. A sail, a sail!

90   MERCUTIO   Two, two: a shirt and a smock.

NURSE   Peter?

PETER   Anon.

NURSE   My fan, Peter.

---

73 And . . . goose? Romeo may allude to the proverb "sweet meat must have sour sauce"; he
may also shift the sense of **sauce** to "semen," so that **served** plays on the sense of sexual
service, and **goose** continues to play on the sense of "prostitute"   **74 wit** plays on sense of
"penis"   **cheverel** easily stretched kid leather   **75 ell** forty-five inches/penis   **77 broad**
large/obvious/outspoken/indecent (may pun on "brood-goose" and on "abroad," i.e. out and
about)   **80 drivelling** tedious/dribbling   **81 natural** idiot, fool   **lolling** with tongue (or
bauble) hanging out   **82 bauble** baton with a carved head on one end traditionally carried by
a fool/penis (fools were supposed to be particularly well-endowed)   **hole** plays on the sense of
"vagina"   **83 there** i.e. now, at this point in your jesting (but Mercutio plays on the sense of
"in the **hole**")   **84 stop in** cease telling/stuff in   **tale** puns on "tail," i.e. penis   **84 against
the hair** against my wish/up against the pubic hair   **85 large** long/vulgar/erect
86 short plays on the sense of "flaccid, no longer erect"   **87 was . . . depth** had reached
the conclusion/had achieved orgasm (**whole** puns on hole)   **88 occupy** continue/have sex
with   **argument** topic (almost certainly plays on a sense of "vagina")   **89 goodly gear**
applies either to the joke ("good stuff" quibbling on the sense of "fine genitals") or to the nurse
("fine clothing/good new matter for a joke")   **A sail** the cry given when a ship is sighted (here
a reference to the Nurse's appearance or manner of approach)   **90 shirt . . . smock** i.e. man
and a woman

MERCUTIO	Good Peter, to hide her face, for her fan's the fairer
95	face.
NURSE	God ye good morrow, gentlemen.
MERCUTIO	God ye good e'en, fair gentlewoman.
NURSE	Is it good e'en?
MERCUTIO	'Tis no less, I tell you, for the bawdy hand of the dial
100	is now upon the prick of noon.
NURSE	Out upon you! What a man are you?
ROMEO	One, gentlewoman, that God hath made himself to
	mar.
NURSE	By my troth, it is well said: 'for himself to mar',
105	quoth a? Gentlemen, can any of you tell me where I may find
	the young Romeo?
ROMEO	I can tell you, but young Romeo will be older when
	you have found him than he was when you sought him: I am
	the youngest of that name, for fault of a worse.
110 NURSE	You say well.
MERCUTIO	Yea, is the worst well? Very well took, i'faith, wisely,
	wisely.
NURSE	If you be he, sir, I desire some confidence with you.
BENVOLIO	She will indite him to some supper.
115 MERCUTIO	A bawd, a bawd, a bawd! So ho!
ROMEO	What hast thou found?
MERCUTIO	No hare, sir, unless a hare, sir, in a Lenten pie, that is
	something stale and hoar ere it be spent.
	An old hare hoar, *Sings*
120 | And an old hare hoar, |

99 hand of the clock (plays on the sense of "human hand")   **100 prick** mark on the clock face indicating the hour/penis   **101 Out upon you!** expression of indignant reproach **What** what kind of   **102 that . . . mar** i.e. though made in God's image, such a man will ruin it through sin   **104 troth** faith   **105 quoth a** said he   **109 fault** lack   **111 took** taken, interpreted   **113 confidence** malapropism for "conference"/private conversation **114 indite** intentional malapropism for "invite"   **supper** also euphemistic for sex **115 bawd** hare/procurer, pimp   **So ho!** a hunting cry given when game is sighted   **117 hare** plays on the sense of "prostitute"   **Lenten pie** pie consumed during Lent when meat eating was prohibited (in theory such a pie should be meatless so this hare pie may be a leftover or one made of old meat that has been obtained illicitly; **pie** was also a slang term for the vagina) **118 stale** plays on the sense of "prostitute"   **hoar** mouldy, old (puns on "whore")   **be spent** used up, eaten/employed sexually

Is very good meat in Lent.
But a hare that is hoar
Is too much for a score,
When it hoars ere it be spent.

125 Romeo, will you come to your father's? We'll to dinner,
thither.

ROMEO   I will follow you.

MERCUTIO   Farewell, ancient lady, farewell, 'lady,   *Sings*
lady, lady'.   *Exeunt Mercutio, Benvolio*

130 NURSE   I pray you, sir, what saucy merchant was this that
was so full of his ropery?

ROMEO   A gentleman, nurse, that loves to hear himself talk,
and will speak more in a minute than he will stand to in a
month.

135 NURSE   An a speak anything against me, I'll take him down,
an a were lustier than he is, and twenty such Jacks, and if I
cannot, I'll find those that shall. Scurvy knave, I am none of
his flirt-gills, I am none of his skains-mates.—   *To Peter*
And thou must stand by too, and suffer every knave to use

140 me at his pleasure?

PETER   I saw no man use you at his pleasure: if I had, my
weapon should quickly have been out, I warrant you. I dare
draw as soon as another man, if I see occasion in a good
quarrel, and the law on my side.

145 NURSE   Now, afore God, I am so vexed that every part about
me quivers. Scurvy knave!— Pray you, sir, a word: *To Romeo*
and as I told you, my young lady bid me inquire you out:

---

121 meat plays on sense of "sexual goods/vagina"   **122 hoar** the word now takes on sense of
"syphilitic"   **123 too . . . score** not worth paying for/not worth having sex with   **124 hoars**
becomes mouldy/is diseased/infects with venereal disease   **130 merchant** fellow   **131 ropery**
roguery/trickery/lewdness   **133 stand to** uphold, abide by (plays on the idea of sustaining an
erection)   **135 An a** if he   **take him down** humble him, take him down a peg or two (plays
on sense of "quell his erection")   **136 lustier** livelier/more lustful   **Jacks** knaves (and
possibly "penises")   **138 flirt-gills** loose women, whores   **skains-mates** a "skene" is a dagger,
hence "knife-wielding companions/whores" (literally, the sheath for his phallic dagger)
139 use . . . pleasure treat me as he wishes (Peter plays on the sense of "have sex with me")
142 weapon sword/penis   **145 part** with vaginal connotations

what she bid me say, I will keep to myself. But first let me tell
ye, if ye should lead her in a fool's paradise, as they say, it
150   were a very gross kind of behaviour, as they say, for the
gentlewoman is young, and therefore, if you should deal
double with her, truly it were an ill thing to be offered to any
gentlewoman, and very weak dealing.

ROMEO   Nurse, commend me to thy lady and mistress. I
155   protest unto thee—

NURSE   Good heart, and i'faith I will tell her as much. Lord,
Lord, she will be a joyful woman.

ROMEO   What wilt thou tell her, nurse? Thou dost not mark
me.

160 **NURSE**   I will tell her, sir, that you do protest, which, as I take
it, is a gentlemanlike offer.

ROMEO   Bid her devise
Some means to come to shrift this afternoon,
And there she shall at Friar Laurence' cell
165   Be shrived and married. Here is for thy pains.   *Attempts to*

NURSE   No truly, sir, not a penny.   *give money*

ROMEO   Go to, I say you shall.

NURSE   This afternoon, sir? Well, she shall be there.

ROMEO   And stay, good nurse, behind the abbey wall:
170   Within this hour my man shall be with thee
And bring thee cords made like a tackled stair,
Which to the high top-gallant of my joy
Must be my convoy in the secret night.
Farewell, be trusty and I'll quit thy pains.
175   Farewell, commend me to thy mistress.

NURSE   Now God in heaven bless thee! Hark you, sir.

ROMEO   What say'st thou, my dear nurse?

---

151 deal double with deceive/betray sexually ("to deal" was to have sex)   **153 weak** poor,
contemptible   **155 protest** declare/vow   **158 mark** listen to   **163 shrift** confession
165 shrived absolved   **171 cords . . . stair** a rope ladder   **172 top-gallant** highest point
(literally the platform at the top of the tallest mast on a ship)   **174 quit** requite, reward

NURSE   Is your man secret? Did you ne'er hear say,
      'Two may keep counsel, putting one away'?

180 ROMEO   Warrant thee, my man's as true as steel.

NURSE   Well, sir, my mistress is the sweetest lady — Lord,
      Lord! When 'twas a little prating thing — O, there is a
      nobleman in town, one Paris, that would fain lay knife
      aboard, but she, good soul, had as lief see a toad, a very toad,
185   as see him. I anger her sometimes and tell her that Paris is
      the properer man, but, I'll warrant you, when I say so, she
      looks as pale as any clout in the versal world. Doth not
      rosemary and Romeo begin both with a letter?

ROMEO   Ay, nurse, what of that? Both with an R.

190 NURSE   A mocker! That's the dog's name: R is for the— no, I
      know it begins with some other letter — and she hath the
      prettiest sententious of it, of you and rosemary, that it would
      do you good to hear it.

ROMEO   Commend me to thy lady.   [*Exit Romeo*]

195 NURSE   Ay, a thousand times.— Peter?

PETER   Anon.

NURSE   Before and apace.   *Exeunt Nurse and Peter*

[Act 2 Scene 4]   *running scene 8*

Enter Juliet

JULIET   The clock struck nine when I did send the nurse:
      In half an hour she promised to return.
      Perchance she cannot meet him: that's not so.

---

178 secret trustworthy   **179 "Two . . . away"** proverbial saying meaning that two may keep a
secret in the absence of a third party   **180 Warrant thee** be assured   **182 prating** chattering,
babbling   **183 fain . . . aboard** willingly lay a claim to her (from the practice of bringing one's
own knife to the dinner table, or "board," and using it to mark one's place); to "lay aboard"
could also refer to boarding a vessel, and plays on the sense of sexual boarding (**knife** has
phallic connotations)   **184 as lief** rather, as soon   **186 properer** finer/better-looking
187 clout piece of cloth/sail   **versal** whole (from "universal")   **188 rosemary** the herb
symbolized fidelity and remembrance, and was used at weddings and funerals   **190 dog's
name** because "r" sounds like a dog's growl   **R is for the—** the Nurse may be about to say
"arse"   **192 sententious** malapropism for "sentences," i.e. maxims   **197 apace** quickly
2.4 Location: *either the Capulets' house or their garden*

O, she is lame! Love's herald should be thoughts,
5 Which ten times faster glides than the sun's beams,
Driving back shadows over louring hills:
Therefore do nimble-pinioned doves draw love,
And therefore hath the wind-swift Cupid wings.
Now is the sun upon the highmost hill
10 Of this day's journey, and from nine till twelve
Is three long hours, yet she is not come.
Had she affections and warm youthful blood,
She would be as swift in motion as a ball:
My words would bandy her to my sweet love,
15 And his to me.
But old folks, many feign as they were dead,
Unwieldy, slow, heavy and pale as lead.

Enter Nurse [and Peter]

O God, she comes! O honey nurse, what news?
Hast thou met with him? Send thy man away.

20 **NURSE**   Peter, stay at the gate.   [*Exit Peter*]

JULIET   Now, good sweet nurse — O Lord, why look'st thou
sad?
Though news be sad, yet tell them merrily:
If good, thou sham'st the music of sweet news
By playing it to me with so sour a face.

25 **NURSE**   I am aweary, give me leave awhile.
Fie, how my bones ache! What a jaunt have I had!

JULIET   I would thou hadst my bones, and I thy news:
Nay, come, I pray thee speak, good, good nurse, speak.

NURSE   Jesu, what haste? Can you not stay awhile?
30 Do you not see that I am out of breath?

JULIET   How art thou out of breath, when thou hast breath
To say to me that thou art out of breath?
The excuse that thou dost make in this delay
Is longer than the tale thou dost excuse.

---

4 lame slow/unsatisfactory   **herald** messenger   **6 louring** frowning, darkened   **7 nimble-pinioned . . . love** Venus, the Roman goddess of love, had a chariot drawn by swift-winged doves   **14 bandy** toss (to and fro, like a **ball** in tennis)   **26 jaunt** tiring, troublesome journey

35   Is thy news good or bad? Answer to that.
        Say either, and I'll stay the circumstance:
        Let me be satisfied, is't good or bad?

NURSE   Well, you have made a simple choice, you know not
        how to choose a man: Romeo? No, not he, though his face be
40   better than any man's, yet his leg excels all men's, and for a
        hand and a foot and a body, though they be not to be talked
        on, yet they are past compare: he is not the flower of
        courtesy, but, I'll warrant him, as gentle as a lamb. Go thy
        ways, wench, serve God. What, have you dined at home?

45 JULIET   No, no. But all this did I know before.
        What says he of our marriage? What of that?

NURSE   Lord, how my head aches! What a head have I!
        It beats as it would fall in twenty pieces.
        My back o't'other side — O, my back, my back!
50   Beshrew your heart for sending me about,
        To catch my death with jaunting up and down!

JULIET   I'faith, I am sorry that thou art not well.
        Sweet, sweet, sweet nurse, tell me, what says my love?

NURSE   Your love says, like an honest gentleman, and a
55   courteous, and a kind, and a handsome, and, I warrant, a
        virtuous— Where is your mother?

JULIET   Where is my mother? Why, she is within,
        Where should she be? How oddly thou repliest:
        'Your love says, like an honest gentleman,
60   Where is your mother?'

NURSE   O God's lady dear!
        Are you so hot? Marry, come up, I trow.
        Is this the poultice for my aching bones?
        Henceforward do your messages yourself.

65 JULIET   Here's such a coil! Come, what says Romeo?

NURSE   Have you got leave to go to shrift today?

JULIET   I have.

---

36 stay the circumstance wait for the details   **38 simple** foolish   **50 Beshrew** curse
54 honest honorable   **61 God's lady** the Virgin Mary   **62 hot** eager/fervent/impatient
(with a play on the sense of "lustful")   **come up** expression of indignant surprise and reproof
63 poultice hot preparation applied to the skin to soothe aches   **65 coil** fuss

NURSE   Then hie you hence to Friar Laurence' cell,
             There stays a husband to make you a wife:
70   Now comes the wanton blood up in your cheeks,
             They'll be in scarlet straight at any news.
             Hie you to church, I must another way,
             To fetch a ladder, by the which your love
             Must climb a bird's nest soon when it is dark:
75   I am the drudge and toil in your delight,
             But you shall bear the burden soon at night.
             Go, I'll to dinner: hie you to the cell.
JULIET   Hie to high fortune! Honest nurse, farewell.   *Exeunt*

[Act 2 Scene 5]   *running scene 9*

Enter Friar and Romeo

FRIAR LAURENCE   So smile the heavens upon this holy act,
             That after-hours with sorrow chide us not.
ROMEO   Amen, amen. But come what sorrow can,
             It cannot countervail the exchange of joy
5   That one short minute gives me in her sight:
             Do thou but close our hands with holy words,
             Then love-devouring death do what he dare,
             It is enough I may but call her mine.
FRIAR LAURENCE   These violent delights have violent ends,
10   And in their triumph die, like fire and powder,
             Which as they kiss consume. The sweetest honey
             Is loathsome in his own deliciousness,
             And in the taste confounds the appetite:
             Therefore love moderately, long love doth so:
15   Too swift arrives as tardy as too slow.
Enter Juliet   *Running*
             Here comes the lady. O, so light a foot

---

68 hie hurry   **70 wanton** unrestrained/lively/sexually passionate   **74 bird's nest** i.e. Juliet's
room (**bird** plays on the sense of "young woman" and **nest** on the sense of "vagina")   **76 bear
the burden** do the work/bear the weight of Romeo's body   **2.5 *Location: Friar Laurence's
cell*   4 countervail** counterbalance   **6 close** join   **10 powder** gunpowder   **11 consume**
are destroyed (with a play on sexual consummation)   **13 confounds** ruins

Will ne'er wear out the everlasting flint:
A lover may bestride the gossamers
That idles in the wanton summer air,
20 And yet not fall, so light is vanity.

JULIET Good even to my ghostly confessor.

FRIAR LAURENCE Romeo shall thank thee, daughter, for us both.

JULIET As much to him, else is his thanks too much.

ROMEO Ah, Juliet, if the measure of thy joy
25 Be heaped like mine, and that thy skill be more
To blazon it, then sweeten with thy breath
This neighbour air, and let rich music's tongue
Unfold the imagined happiness that both
Receive in either by this dear encounter.

30 JULIET Conceit, more rich in matter than in words,
Brags of his substance, not of ornament:
They are but beggars that can count their worth,
But my true love is grown to such excess
I cannot sum up sum of half my wealth.

35 FRIAR LAURENCE Come, come with me, and we will make short
work,
For, by your leaves, you shall not stay alone
Till holy church incorporate two in one.   [*Exeunt*]

[Act 3 Scene 1]   *running scene 10*

Enter Mercutio, Benvolio and Men

BENVOLIO I pray thee, good Mercutio, let's retire:
The day is hot, the Capulets abroad,
And if we meet, we shall not scape a brawl,
For now, these hot days, is the mad blood stirring.

---

17 **flint** i.e. stone floor 18 **gossamers** fine cobwebs 19 **wanton** playful 20 **light** not
heavy/worthless **vanity** transitory worldly joy 22 **thank thee** i.e. with a kiss
23 **As . . . much** i.e. I must kiss him in return or I shall have been overpaid 25 **that** if
26 **blazon** describe/proclaim 27 **music's tongue** i.e. Juliet's voice and words 28 **imagined**
i.e. not yet expressed 29 **in either** from one another 30 **Conceit** imagination/idea/
understanding **matter** genuine substance 31 **ornament** i.e. descriptive words 34 **sum up**
sum calculate the total **3.1 *Location: a public place in Verona*** 3 **scape** escape

5   MERCUTIO   Thou art like one of these fellows that when he
enters the confines of a tavern, claps me his sword upon the
table and says 'God send me no need of thee!' and by the
operation of the second cup draws him on the drawer, when
indeed there is no need.

10   BENVOLIO   Am I like such a fellow?

MERCUTIO   Come, come, thou art as hot a Jack in thy mood as
any in Italy, and as soon moved to be moody, and as soon
moody to be moved.

BENVOLIO   And what to?

15   MERCUTIO   Nay, an there were two such, we should have none
shortly, for one would kill the other. Thou? Why, thou wilt
quarrel with a man that hath a hair more or a hair less in his
beard than thou hast. Thou wilt quarrel with a man for
cracking nuts, having no other reason but because thou

20   hast hazel eyes: what eye but such an eye would spy out such
a quarrel? Thy head is as full of quarrels as an egg is full of
meat, and yet thy head hath been beaten as addle as an egg
for quarrelling: thou hast quarrelled with a man for
coughing in the street, because he hath wakened thy dog

25   that hath lain asleep in the sun: didst thou not fall out with a
tailor for wearing his new doublet before Easter? With
another for tying his new shoes with old ribbon. And yet
thou wilt tutor me from quarrelling?

BENVOLIO   An I were so apt to quarrel as thou art, any man

30   should buy the fee-simple of my life for an hour and a
quarter.

MERCUTIO   The fee-simple? O, simple!

Enter Tybalt, Petruchio and others

BENVOLIO   By my head, here comes the Capulets.

MERCUTIO   By my heel, I care not.

6 claps me claps (me is emphatic)   7 by . . . cup by the time his second drink has taken effect
8 draws . . . drawer draws his sword on the innkeeper   11 Jack knave   mood anger
12 moved provoked   13 to be at being   15 two puns on to   22 meat edible matter
addle rotten/muddled, confused   26 doublet close-fitting jacket with a flared base
Easter i.e. the time after Lent when new clothes were worn   28 from to avoid   30 fee-simple
absolute possession (term relating to property)   for . . . quarter i.e. were he so quarrelsome,
his life would be over very soon   32 simple foolish

35 TYBALT   Follow me close, for I will speak to them.—   *To his*
              Gentlemen, good e'en, a word with one of you.   *companions*

   MERCUTIO   And but one word with one of us? Couple it with
              something, make it a word and a blow.

   TYBALT   You shall find me apt enough to that, sir, an you will
40   give me occasion.

   MERCUTIO   Could you not take some occasion without giving?

   TYBALT   Mercutio, thou consort'st with Romeo—

   MERCUTIO   Consort? What, dost thou make us minstrels? An
              thou make minstrels of us, look to hear nothing but
45   discords. Here's my fiddlestick, here's that shall   *Points to*
              make you dance. Come, consort!   *his sword*

   BENVOLIO   We talk here in the public haunt of men:
              Either withdraw unto some private place,
              Or reason coldly of your grievances,
50   Or else depart: here all eyes gaze on us.

   MERCUTIO   Men's eyes were made to look, and let them gaze:
              I will not budge for no man's pleasure, I.

   Enter Romeo

   TYBALT   Well, peace be with you, sir, here comes my man.

   MERCUTIO   But I'll be hanged, sir, if he wear your livery.
55   Marry, go before to field, he'll be your follower:
              Your worship in that sense may call him 'man'.

   TYBALT   Romeo, the love I bear thee can afford
              No better term than this: thou art a villain.

   ROMEO   Tybalt, the reason that I have to love thee
60   Doth much excuse the appertaining rage
              To such a greeting: villain am I none;
              Therefore farewell, I see thou know'st me not.

---

42 consort'st associate with (Mercutio deliberately interprets this as "play in a musical group,
or consort")   **43 minstrels** musicians   **44 look** expect   **49 coldly** calmly   **54 your livery**
the uniform of your servant (Mercutio has deliberately interpreted **man** as "manservant")
55 go . . . field should you go to the duelling field   **follower** manservant/pursuer
60 excuse . . . greeting excuse me from displaying the rage that is the appropriate response to
such a greeting

TYBALT	Boy, this shall not excuse the injuries
	That thou hast done me: therefore turn and draw.
65 ROMEO	I do protest I never injured thee,
	But love thee better than thou canst devise,
	Till thou shalt know the reason of my love:
	And so, good Capulet — which name I tender
	As dearly as my own — be satisfied.
70 MERCUTIO	O calm, dishonourable, vile submission!
	Alla stoccado carries it away.
	Tybalt, you rat-catcher, will you walk? *Draws his sword*
TYBALT	What wouldst thou have with me?
MERCUTIO	Good king of cats, nothing but one of your nine
75	lives that I mean to make bold withal, and as you shall use
	me hereafter, dry-beat the rest of the eight. Will you pluck
	your sword out of his pilcher by the ears? Make haste, lest
	mine be about your ears ere it be out.
TYBALT	I am for you. *Draws*
80 ROMEO	Gentle Mercutio, put thy rapier up.
MERCUTIO	Come, sir, your *passado*. *They fight*
ROMEO	Draw, Benvolio, beat down their weapons.—
	Gentlemen, for shame, forbear this outrage!
	Tybalt, Mercutio, the prince expressly hath *Tries to part them*
85	Forbidden bandying in Verona streets:
	Hold, Tybalt! Good Mercutio! *Tybalt stabs Mercutio*
	Exit Tybalt
MERCUTIO	I am hurt.
	A plague o'both the houses! I am sped.
	Is he gone and hath nothing?
90 BENVOLIO	What, art thou hurt?

---

66 devise conceive   **68 tender** value/cherish   **71 *Alla stoccado*** Italian fencing term
meaning "at the thrust" (here a reference to Tybalt)   **carries it away** wins the day   **72 will
you walk** are you leaving/will you walk aside with me (for a duel)   **75 make bold withal** take
liberties with   **as . . . hereafter** depending on how you treat me subsequently   **76 dry-beat**
beat severely (without using a sword)   **77 pilcher** scabbard   **81 *passado*** forward thrust with
one foot advanced   **83 forbear** stop   **85 bandying** exchanging blows   **86 Hold** desist
88 sped gone, dispatched

MERCUTIO   Ay, ay, a scratch, a scratch, marry, 'tis enough.
Where is my page? Go, villain, fetch a surgeon.   [*Exit Page*]

ROMEO   Courage, man, the hurt cannot be much.

MERCUTIO   No, 'tis not so deep as a well, nor so wide as a church
95   door, but 'tis enough, 'twill serve: ask for me tomorrow, and
you shall find me a grave man. I am peppered, I warrant,
for this world. A plague o'both your houses! What? A dog, a
rat, a mouse, a cat, to scratch a man to death! A braggart,
a rogue, a villain, that fights by the book of arithmetic!—
100   Why the devil came you between us? I was hurt   *To Romeo*
under your arm.

ROMEO   I thought all for the best.

MERCUTIO   Help me into some house, Benvolio,
Or I shall faint. A plague o'both your houses!
105   They have made worms' meat of me. I have it,
And soundly too. Your houses!   *Exeunt*   *Benvolio helping*
                                                      Mercutio

ROMEO   This gentleman, the prince's near ally,
My very friend, hath got his mortal hurt
In my behalf: my reputation stained
110   With Tybalt's slander — Tybalt, that an hour
Hath been my cousin. O sweet Juliet,
Thy beauty hath made me effeminate,
And in my temper softened valour's steel!

Enter Benvolio

BENVOLIO   O Romeo, Romeo, brave Mercutio is dead!
115   That gallant spirit hath aspired the clouds,
Which too untimely here did scorn the earth.

ROMEO   This day's black fate on more days doth depend,
This but begins the woe others must end.

Enter Tybalt

BENVOLIO   Here comes the furious Tybalt back again.

---

92 **villain** rogue/servant   96 **grave** serious, dignified/dead and buried   **peppered** done for,
ruined   99 **by . . . arithmetic** by the fencing manual/precisely   107 **ally** relative   108 **very**
true   113 **temper** disposition (plays on the sense of "hardness of a sword after it has been
tempered, i.e. heated and immersed in water")   115 **aspired** ascended to   117 **more** i.e.
future   **depend** hang over   118 **others** i.e. other days

120	ROMEO	He gone in triumph and Mercutio slain?

Away to heaven, respective lenity,
And fire and fury be my conduct now!
Now, Tybalt, take the 'villain' back again,
That late thou gav'st me, for Mercutio's soul
125 Is but a little way above our heads,
Staying for thine to keep him company:
Either thou or I, or both, must go with him.

TYBALT   Thou, wretched boy, that didst consort him here,
Shalt with him hence.

130 ROMEO   This shall determine that.

They fight. Tybalt falls

BENVOLIO   Romeo, away, begone!
The citizens are up, and Tybalt slain.
Stand not amazed: the prince will doom thee death,
If thou art taken. Hence, begone, away!

135 ROMEO   O, I am fortune's fool!

BENVOLIO   Why dost thou stay?   *Exit Romeo*

Enter Citizens

CITIZEN   Which way ran he that killed Mercutio?
Tybalt, that murderer, which way ran he?

BENVOLIO   There lies that Tybalt.

140 CITIZEN   Up, sir, go with me:
I charge thee in the prince's name, obey.

Enter Prince, Old Montague, Capulet, their Wives and all

PRINCE   Where are the vile beginners of this fray?

BENVOLIO   O, noble prince, I can discover all
The unlucky manage of this fatal brawl:
145 There lies the man, slain by young Romeo,
That slew thy kinsman, brave Mercutio.

LADY CAPULET   Tybalt, my cousin? O my brother's child!

---

121 respective lenity considerate mercy, discriminating mildness   **122 conduct** guide
128 consort associate with   **130 This** i.e. his sword   **133 amazed** overwhelmed/stunned/
bewildered   **doom** sentence   **135 fool** dupe/plaything/jester   **141 charge** order
143 discover reveal   **144 unlucky** unfortunate/ill-omened   **manage** conduct   **fatal** deadly/
fateful   **147 cousin** a general term for a relative

O prince! O cousin! Husband! O, the blood is spilled
Of my dear kinsman! Prince, as thou art true,
150   For blood of ours, shed blood of Montague.
O cousin, cousin!

PRINCE   Benvolio, who began this bloody fray?

BENVOLIO   Tybalt, here slain, whom Romeo's hand did slay.
Romeo that spoke him fair, bid him bethink
155   How nice the quarrel was, and urged withal
Your high displeasure: all this utterèd
With gentle breath, calm look, knees humbly bowed,
Could not take truce with the unruly spleen
Of Tybalt, deaf to peace, but that he tilts
160   With piercing steel at bold Mercutio's breast,
Who, all as hot, turns deadly point to point,
And with a martial scorn, with one hand beats
Cold death aside, and with the other sends
It back to Tybalt, whose dexterity
165   Retorts it. Romeo he cries aloud,
'Hold, friends! Friends, part!' and swifter than his tongue,
His agile arm beats down their fatal points,
And 'twixt them rushes, underneath whose arm
An envious thrust from Tybalt hit the life
170   Of stout Mercutio, and then Tybalt fled.
But by and by comes back to Romeo,
Who had but newly entertained revenge,
And to't they go like lightning, for, ere I
Could draw to part them, was stout Tybalt slain.
175   And as he fell, did Romeo turn and fly.
This is the truth, or let Benvolio die.

LADY CAPULET   He is a kinsman to the Montague,
Affection makes him false, he speaks not true:
Some twenty of them fought in this black strife,

---

155 nice trivial   withal moreover   158 take truce make peace   spleen fiery temper
159 tilts thrusts   162 with one . . . back Mercutio is fighting with a dagger in one hand, with
which he deflects blows, and a sword in the other, with which he attacks   165 Retorts returns
169 envious malicious   170 stout brave   171 by and by immediately   178 Affection
partiality/love

180   And all those twenty could but kill one life.
        I beg for justice, which thou, prince, must give:
        Romeo slew Tybalt, Romeo must not live.
      PRINCE   Romeo slew him, he slew Mercutio:
        Who now the price of his dear blood doth owe?
185   MONTAGUE   Not Romeo, prince, he was Mercutio's friend:
        His fault concludes but what the law should end,
        The life of Tybalt.
      PRINCE   And for that offence
        Immediately we do exile him hence.
190   I have an interest in your hearts' proceeding,
        My blood for your rude brawls doth lie a-bleeding:
        But I'll amerce you with so strong a fine
        That you shall all repent the loss of mine.
        It will be deaf to pleading and excuses,
195   Nor tears nor prayers shall purchase out abuses:
        Therefore use none. Let Romeo hence in haste,
        Else, when he is found, that hour is his last.
        Bear hence this body and attend our will:
        Mercy but murders, pardoning those that kill.   *Exeunt*

[Act 3 Scene 2]

running scene 11

Enter Juliet alone
      JULIET   Gallop apace, you fiery-footed steeds,
        Towards Phoebus' lodging: such a wagoner
        As Phaethon would whip you to the west,
        And bring in cloudy night immediately.
5   Spread thy close curtain, love-performing night,

---

190 **interest** plays on the sense of "legal claim"   **proceeding** plays on the sense of "legal action"   **191 My blood** Mercutio was the prince's relative   **192 amerce** punish   **195 purchase out abuses** redeem these wrongs   **199 Mercy . . . kill** i.e. leniency merely encourages murder   **3.2 Location: the Capulets' house**   **1 apace** swiftly   **2 Phoebus** Greek god of the sun, whose chariot was drawn by fiery horses   **lodging** i.e. the west, where the sun sets   **3 Phaethon** Phoebus' son, who, unable to control his father's chariot, was felled by one of Zeus' thunderbolts when he burned part of the earth   **5 close** private/ secretive/enclosing

That runaway's eyes may wink and Romeo
Leap to these arms, untalked of and unseen.
Lovers can see to do their amorous rites
By their own beauties, or if love be blind,
10 It best agrees with night. Come, civil night,
Thou sober-suited matron all in black,
And learn me how to lose a winning match,
Played for a pair of stainless maidenhoods:
Hood my unmanned blood, bating in my cheeks,
15 With thy black mantle, till strange love grow bold,
Think true love acted simple modesty.
Come night, come Romeo, come thou day in night,
For thou wilt lie upon the wings of night
Whiter than new snow upon a raven's back.
20 Come, gentle night, come, loving, black-browed night,
Give me my Romeo, and when I shall die,
Take him and cut him out in little stars,
And he will make the face of heaven so fine
That all the world will be in love with night
25 And pay no worship to the garish sun.
O, I have bought the mansion of a love,
But not possessed it, and though I am sold,
Not yet enjoyed. So tedious is this day
As is the night before some festival
30 To an impatient child that hath new robes
And may not wear them. O, here comes my nurse,

Enter Nurse, with cords

And she brings news, and every tongue that speaks
But Romeo's name speaks heavenly eloquence.—

---

6 **runaway's** i.e. Phaethon's/any roaming fugitive's/a night wanderer's   **wink** close
10 **civil** soberly dressed/grave/seemly   **12 learn** teach   **lose . . . match** Juliet will win Romeo
by surrendering to him   **13 maidenhoods** virginities (those of Juliet and Romeo)   **14 Hood**
cover up, blindfold (as a hawk was when it was not pursuing game)   **unmanned** untrained
(another term from falconry; plays on the sense of "without a husband")   **bating** fluttering
impatiently (used of a hawk; puns on "beating")   **15 strange** new, unfamiliar/reserved, shy
21 die may play on the sense of "orgasm"   **27 possessed** with sexual connotations (like
enjoyed)   *cords* i.e. the rope ladder

Now, nurse, what news? What hast thou there? The cords
35 That Romeo bid thee fetch?

NURSE   Ay, ay, the cords.   *Drops the cords*

JULIET   Ay me, what news? Why dost thou wring thy hands?

NURSE   Ah, welladay! He's dead, he's dead, he's dead!
We are undone, lady, we are undone.
40 Alack the day, he's gone, he's killed, he's dead!

JULIET   Can heaven be so envious?

NURSE   Romeo can,
Though heaven cannot: O Romeo, Romeo!
Whoever would have thought it? Romeo!

45 JULIET   What devil art thou that dost torment me thus?
This torture should be roared in dismal hell.
Hath Romeo slain himself? Say thou but 'Ay',
And that bare vowel 'I' shall poison more
Than the death-darting eye of cockatrice:
50 I am not I, if there be such an ay,
Or those eyes shut, that makes thee answer 'Ay'.
If he be slain, say 'Ay', or if not, 'No':
Brief sounds determine of my weal or woe.

NURSE   I saw the wound, I saw it with mine eyes —
55 God save the mark! — here on his manly breast: *Points*
A piteous corpse, a bloody piteous corpse;
Pale, pale as ashes, all bedaubed in blood,
All in gore-blood: I swoonèd at the sight.

JULIET   O, break, my heart, poor bankrupt, break at once!
60 To prison, eyes, ne'er look on liberty!
Vile earth, to earth resign, end motion here,
And thou and Romeo press one heavy bier!

---

38 welladay expression of sorrow   39 undone ruined   41 envious malicious/full of ill-will at
Juliet's happiness   49 cockatrice basilisk, a mythical reptile with a gaze that could kill
51 those eyes shut i.e. Romeo's eyes, shut in death   53 weal well-being   55 God . . . mark
an apologetic exclamation excusing the mention of unpleasant matters   58 gore-blood
congealing blood   59 break plays on the sense of "become financially ruined"   61 Vile earth
i.e. her body   resign surrender (yourself)   motion movement, i.e. life (plays on sense of
"strong emotion")   62 bier stretcher-like structure on which a corpse is carried to the grave

NURSE   O Tybalt, Tybalt, the best friend I had!
O courteous Tybalt, honest gentleman,
65 That ever I should live to see thee dead!

JULIET   What storm is this that blows so contrary?
Is Romeo slaughtered, and is Tybalt dead,
My dearest cousin, and my dearer lord?
Then, dreadful trumpet, sound the general doom,
70 For who is living, if those two are gone?

NURSE   Tybalt is gone, and Romeo banishèd,
Romeo that killed him, he is banishèd.

JULIET   O, God! Did Romeo's hand shed Tybalt's blood?

NURSE   It did, it did, alas the day, it did!

75 JULIET   O serpent heart, hid with a flow'ring face!
Did ever dragon keep so fair a cave?
Beautiful tyrant, fiend angelical,
Dove-feathered raven, wolvish-ravening lamb,
Despisèd substance of divinest show!
80 Just opposite to what thou justly seem'st,
A damnèd saint, an honourable villain!
O nature, what hadst thou to do in hell,
When thou didst bower the spirit of a fiend
In mortal paradise of such sweet flesh?
85 Was ever book containing such vile matter
So fairly bound? O, that deceit should dwell
In such a gorgeous palace!

NURSE   There's no trust,
No faith, no honesty in men: all perjured,
90 All forsworn, all naught, all dissemblers.
Ah, where's my man? Give me some aqua vitae:
These griefs, these woes, these sorrows make me old.
Shame come to Romeo!

---

68 lord husband   **69 trumpet** i.e. the last trumpet, the sound of which, according to the Bible, would announce the end of the world   **76 keep** live in   **80 Just** exact (**justly** shifts the sense to "truly, rightfully")   **83 bower** shelter/lodge   **90 dissemblers** deceivers   **91 aqua vitae** strong alcoholic drink (literally "water of life")

JULIET   Blistered be thy tongue
95   For such a wish! He was not born to shame:
        Upon his brow shame is ashamed to sit;
        For 'tis a throne where honour may be crowned
        Sole monarch of the universal earth.
        O, what a beast was I to chide at him!
100 NURSE   Will you speak well of him that killed your cousin?
    JULIET   Shall I speak ill of him that is my husband?
        Ah, poor my lord, what tongue shall smooth thy name,
        When I, thy three-hours' wife, have mangled it?
        But wherefore, villain, didst thou kill my cousin?—
105   That villain cousin would have killed my husband.
        Back, foolish tears, back to your native spring,
        Your tributary drops belong to woe,
        Which you mistaking offer up to joy.
        My husband lives that Tybalt would have slain,
110   And Tybalt dead that would have slain my husband:
        All this is comfort, wherefore weep I then?
        Some word there was, worser than Tybalt's death,
        That murdered me. I would forget it fain,
        But, O, it presses to my memory,
115   Like damnèd guilty deeds to sinners' minds:
        'Tybalt is dead, and Romeo banishèd.'
        That 'banishèd', that one word 'banishèd',
        Hath slain ten thousand Tybalts. Tybalt's death
        Was woe enough if it had ended there:
120   Or if sour woe delights in fellowship
        And needly will be ranked with other griefs,
        Why followed not, when she said 'Tybalt's dead',
        Thy father, or thy mother, nay, or both,
        Which modern lamentation might have moved?
125   But with a rearward following Tybalt's death,

---

102 poor my lord my poor lord   **107 tributary** serving as an offering or tribute (playing on the sense of "stream-like")   **121 needly** of necessity   **ranked** accompanied/drawn up in rows (like soldiers)   **123 Thy . . . mother** i.e. news of one of their deaths   **124 modern . . . moved** might have provoked ordinary sorrow   **125 rearward** rearguard action ("ward" puns on "word")

'Romeo is banishèd': to speak that word,
Is father, mother, Tybalt, Romeo, Juliet,
All slain, all dead. 'Romeo is banishèd'!
There is no end, no limit, measure, bound,
130   In that word's death: no words can that woe sound.
Where is my father and my mother, nurse?

NURSE   Weeping and wailing over Tybalt's corpse.
Will you go to them? I will bring you thither.

JULIET   Wash they his wounds with tears: mine shall be
spent,
135   When theirs are dry, for Romeo's banishment.
Take up those cords.— Poor ropes, you are beguiled,
Both you and I, for Romeo is exiled:
He made you for a highway to my bed,
But I, a maid, die maiden-widowèd.
140   Come cord, come nurse, I'll to my wedding-bed,
And death, not Romeo, take my maidenhead!

NURSE   Hie to your chamber, I'll find Romeo
To comfort you: I wot well where he is.
Hark ye, your Romeo will be here at night.
145   I'll to him, he is hid at Laurence' cell.

JULIET   O, find him! Give this ring to my true knight,
And bid him come to take his last farewell.   *Exeunt*

[Act 3 Scene 3]   *running scene 12*

Enter Friar and Romeo   *Romeo hesitating*

FRIAR LAURENCE   Romeo, come forth, come forth, thou fearful
man:
Affliction is enamoured of thy parts,
And thou art wedded to calamity.

---

130 **word's death** word's fatal nature (or possibly "word is death")   **sound** give voice
to/measure the depth of   136 **beguiled** deceived, foiled   143 **wot** know   **3.3 Location:**
Friar Laurence's cell   1 **fearful** full of fear   2 **parts** personal or physical qualities

ROMEO   Father, what news? What is the prince's doom?
5   What sorrow craves acquaintance at my hand,
          That I yet know not?
FRIAR LAURENCE   Too familiar
          Is my dear son with such sour company:
          I bring thee tidings of the prince's doom.
10   ROMEO   What less than doomsday is the prince's doom?
FRIAR LAURENCE   A gentler judgement vanished from his lips:
          Not body's death, but body's banishment.
ROMEO   Ha, banishment? Be merciful, say 'death',
          For exile hath more terror in his look,
15   Much more than death. Do not say 'banishment'.
FRIAR LAURENCE   Here from Verona art thou banishèd.
          Be patient, for the world is broad and wide.
ROMEO   There is no world without Verona walls,
          But purgatory, torture, hell itself.
20   Hence banishèd is banished from the world,
          And world's exile is death: then banishèd,
          Is death mistermed. Calling death banishèd,
          Thou cutt'st my head off with a golden axe,
          And smil'st upon the stroke that murders me.
25   FRIAR LAURENCE   O deadly sin! O rude unthankfulness!
          Thy fault our law calls death, but the kind prince,
          Taking thy part, hath rushed aside the law,
          And turned that black word 'death' to 'banishment'.
          This is dear mercy, and thou see'st it not.
30   ROMEO   'Tis torture and not mercy. Heaven is here,
          Where Juliet lives, and every cat and dog
          And little mouse, every unworthy thing,
          Live here in heaven and may look on her,
          But Romeo may not. More validity,

---

4 doom judgement   10 doomsday Judgement Day, the end of the world (i.e. death)
11 vanished was expelled, issued into thin air   18 without outside of   20 Hence banishèd
banished from here   21 world's exile exile from the world   26 Thy . . . death legally, the
crime that you have committed requires the death penalty   27 rushed forced   34 validity
worth

35   More honourable state, more courtship lives
      In carrion-flies than Romeo: they may seize
      On the white wonder of dear Juliet's hand
      And steal immortal blessing from her lips,
      Who even in pure and vestal modesty,
40   Still blush, as thinking their own kisses sin.
      This may flies do, when I from this must fly —
      And say'st thou yet that exile is not death? —
      But Romeo may not: he is banishèd.
      Hadst thou no poison mixed, no sharp-ground knife,
45   No sudden mean of death, though ne'er so mean,
      But 'banishèd' to kill me? 'Banishèd'?
      O friar, the damnèd use that word in hell,
      Howling attends it: how hast thou the heart,
      Being a divine, a ghostly confessor,
50   A sin-absolver, and my friend professed,
      To mangle me with that word 'banishèd'?

FRIAR LAURENCE   Then, fond mad man, hear me a little speak.

ROMEO   O, thou wilt speak again of banishment.

FRIAR LAURENCE   I'll give thee armour to keep off that word:
55   Adversity's sweet milk, philosophy,
      To comfort thee, though thou art banishèd.

ROMEO   Yet 'banishèd'? Hang up philosophy!
      Unless philosophy can make a Juliet,
      Displant a town, reverse a prince's doom,
60   It helps not, it prevails not: talk no more.

FRIAR LAURENCE   O, then I see that madmen have no ears.

ROMEO   How should they, when wise men have no eyes?

FRIAR LAURENCE   Let me dispute with thee of thy estate.

---

35 courtship courtliness/wooing   36 carrion-flies flies that feed on rotting flesh   39 vestal
virginal   40 their own kisses the fact that they naturally touch one another   45 mean
method   mean lowly, base   46 But . . . Banishèd the sequence of clauses is confusing here,
suggesting some textual error, perhaps due to undeleted authorial first thoughts; Folio omits a
Second Quarto line, "They are freemen, but I am banishèd" , whereas it should perhaps have
deleted this line instead   49 divine clergyman   52 fond foolish (plays on sense of "loving")
57 Yet still   Hang up hang   59 Displant uproot   63 dispute reason, talk   estate situation

ROMEO   Thou canst not speak of that thou dost not feel:
65   Wert thou as young as I, Juliet thy love,
An hour but married, Tybalt murderèd,
Doting like me and like me banishèd,
Then mightst thou speak, then mightst thou tear thy hair,
And fall upon the ground as I do now,
70   Taking the measure of an unmade grave.

Enter Nurse and knocks   *From the other*
side of a door

FRIAR LAURENCE   Arise, one knocks. Good Romeo,
hide thyself.

ROMEO   Not I, unless the breath of heartsick groans,
Mist-like, enfold me from the search of eyes.

Knock   *Romeo remains*

FRIAR LAURENCE   Hark, how they knock!— Who's   *on the floor*
there?— Romeo, arise,
75   Thou wilt be taken.— Stay awhile!— Stand up,

Knock

Run to my study.— By and by!— God's will,   *Romeo does*
What simpleness is this?— I come, I come!   *not move*

Knock

Who knocks so hard? Whence come you? What's your will?

NURSE   Let me come in, and you shall know   *From the other*
my errand: *side of the door*
80   I come from Lady Juliet.

FRIAR LAURENCE   Welcome, then.

NURSE   O holy friar, O, tell me, holy friar,
Where's my lady's lord? Where's Romeo?

FRIAR LAURENCE   There on the ground, with his own tears made
drunk.

85   NURSE   O, he is even in my mistress' case,
Just in her case. O, woeful sympathy!
Piteous predicament! Even so lies she,
Blubb'ring and weeping, weeping and blubb'ring.

---

64 **that** that which   67 **Doting** loving madly   75 **taken** arrested   77 **simpleness** foolishness
85 **even** exactly   **case** state (the nurse unintentionally plays on the sense of "vagina")
86 **sympathy** unity, affinity

Stand up, stand up, stand, an you be a man:

90   For Juliet's sake, for her sake, rise and stand.

Why should you fall into so deep an O?

ROMEO   Nurse!

NURSE   Ah sir, ah sir! Death's the end of all.

ROMEO   Speak'st thou of Juliet? How is it with her?

95   Doth not she think me an old murderer,

Now I have stained the childhood of our joy

With blood removed but little from her own?

Where is she? And how doth she? And what says

My concealed lady to our cancelled love?

100   **NURSE**   O, she says nothing, sir, but weeps and weeps,

And now falls on her bed, and then starts up,

And Tybalt calls, and then on Romeo cries,

And then down falls again.

ROMEO   As if that name,

105   Shot from the deadly level of a gun,

Did murder her, as that name's cursèd hand

Murdered her kinsman. O, tell me, friar, tell me,

In what vile part of this anatomy

Doth my name lodge? Tell me, that I may sack

110   The hateful mansion.   *Draws his sword*

FRIAR LAURENCE   Hold thy desperate hand.

Art thou a man? Thy form cries out thou art:

Thy tears are womanish, thy wild acts denote

The unreasonable fury of a beast.

115   Unseemly woman in a seeming man,

And ill-beseeming beast in seeming both,

Thou hast amazed me. By my holy order,

I thought thy disposition better tempered.

Hast thou slain Tybalt? Wilt thou slay thyself?

---

89 **stand** unconscious play on "get an erection" (**rise** has the same connotations)   **an** if
91 **O** groan (plays on sense of "vagina")   93 **Death** plays on sense of "orgasm"
95 **old** practiced, experienced   99 **cancelled** invalidated, nullified (puns on **concealed**)
102 **on Romeo cries** calls upon Romeo/cries out against Romeo   105 **level** aim   109 **sack**
plunder, destroy   118 **tempered** balanced (plays on "temper," i.e. **disposition**)

120 And slay thy lady that in thy life lives,
By doing damnèd hate upon thyself?
Why rail'st thou on thy birth, the heaven and earth?
Since birth, and heaven, and earth, all three do meet
In thee at once, which thou at once wouldst lose.

125 Fie, fie, thou sham'st thy shape, thy love, thy wit,
Which like a usurer abound'st in all,
And usest none in that true use indeed
Which should bedeck thy shape, thy love, thy wit.
Thy noble shape is but a form of wax,

130 Digressing from the valour of a man:
Thy dear love sworn but hollow perjury,
Killing that love which thou hast vowed to cherish:
Thy wit, that ornament to shape and love,
Misshapen in the conduct of them both,

135 Like powder in a skilless soldier's flask,
Is set afire by thine own ignorance,
And thou dismembered with thine own defence.
What, rouse thee, man! Thy Juliet is alive,
For whose dear sake thou wast but lately dead:

140 There art thou happy. Tybalt would kill thee,
But thou slew'st Tybalt: there art thou happy.
The law that threatened death became thy friend
And turned it to exile: there art thou happy.
A pack of blessings light upon thy back,

145 Happiness courts thee in her best array,
But like a mishavèd and sullen wench,
Thou pouts upon thy fortune and thy love:
Take heed, take heed, for such die miserable.

---

123 heaven, and earth i.e. soul and body   **125 Fie** expression of reproach or disgust
wit intelligence, reason   **126 Which** (you) who   **usurer** moneylender (notorious for
charging high interest)   **127 in . . . use** for its proper purpose (**use** plays on the sense of
"financial interest")   **128 bedeck** adorn   **shape** physical appearance   **130 Digressing**
deviating   **valour** honor/courage   **134 Misshapen** deformed/ill-directed   **conduct**
guidance/management   **135 powder** gunpowder   **flask** container for gunpowder
137 dismembered . . . defence blown to bits by the weapon that should have been used to
protect you (i.e. **wit/powder**)   **139 dead** i.e. suicidal   **140 happy** fortunate   **145 array**
clothing   **146 mishavèd** misbehaved

Go, get thee to thy love as was decreed,
150 Ascend her chamber, hence and comfort her:
But look thou stay not till the watch be set,
For then thou canst not pass to Mantua,
Where thou shalt live till we can find a time
To blaze your marriage, reconcile your friends,
155 Beg pardon of thy prince, and call thee back
With twenty hundred thousand times more joy
Than thou went'st forth in lamentation.—
Go before, nurse, commend me to thy lady,
And bid her hasten all the house to bed,
160 Which heavy sorrow makes them apt unto:
Romeo is coming.

NURSE   O Lord, I could have stayed here all night
To hear good counsel. O, what learning is!—
My lord, I'll tell my lady you will come.

165 ROMEO   Do so, and bid my sweet prepare to chide.

NURSE   Here, sir, a ring she bid me give you, sir:
Hie you, make haste, for it grows very late.   [*Exit*]

ROMEO   How well my comfort is revived by this!

FRIAR LAURENCE   Go hence, goodnight, and here stands all your
state:
170 Either be gone before the watch be set,
Or by the break of day disguised from hence.
Sojourn in Mantua: I'll find out your man,
And he shall signify from time to time
Every good hap to you that chances here.
175 Give me thy hand, 'tis late. Farewell, goodnight.

ROMEO   But that a joy past joy calls out on me,
It were a grief, so brief to part with thee. Farewell.

Exeunt

---

149 **decreed** decided (earlier)   151 **watch be set** night watchmen take up their posts at the
city gates   154 **blaze** proclaim, make public   **friends** relatives   160 **apt unto** ready for
169 **here . . . state** your fortunes depend on what happens now   173 **signify** inform you
174 **good hap** favorable event   177 **brief** hurriedly

[Act 3 Scene 4]   *running scene 13*

Enter Old Capulet, his Wife and Paris

CAPULET   Things have fall'n out, sir, so unluckily
That we have had no time to move our daughter:
Look you, she loved her kinsman Tybalt dearly,
And so did I.— Well, we were born to die.

5   'Tis very late, she'll not come down tonight.
I promise you, but for your company,
I would have been abed an hour ago.

PARIS   These times of woe afford no times to woo.
Madam, goodnight, commend me to your daughter.

10   LADY CAPULET   I will, and know her mind early tomorrow:
Tonight she is mewed up to her heaviness.

CAPULET   Sir Paris, I will make a desperate tender
Of my child's love: I think she will be ruled
In all respects by me, nay, more, I doubt it not.—

15   Wife, go you to her ere you go to bed,
Acquaint her here of my son Paris' love,
And bid her, mark you me, on Wednesday next —
But, soft, what day is this?

PARIS   Monday, my lord,

20   CAPULET   Monday? Ha, ha! Well, Wednesday is too soon,
O'Thursday let it be: o'Thursday, tell her,
She shall be married to this noble earl.
Will you be ready? Do you like this haste?
We'll keep no great ado — a friend or two,

25   For hark you, Tybalt being slain so late,
It may be thought we held him carelessly,
Being our kinsman, if we revel much:
Therefore we'll have some half a dozen friends,
And there an end. But what say you to Thursday?

3.4 Location: the Capulets' house   **2 move** persuade/encourage   **11 mewed . . . heaviness**
confined with her sorrow (a "mew" was a cage for a moulting hawk)   **12 desperate**
reckless/bold   **tender** offer   **16 son** (future) son-in-law   **17 mark you me** listen to me, pay
attention   **24 ado** fuss   **25 late** recently   **26 held him carelessly** did not regard him highly

30	PARIS	My lord, I would that Thursday were tomorrow.
	CAPULET	Well get you gone: o'Thursday be it, then.—

Go you to Juliet ere you go to bed,   *To Lady Capulet*
Prepare her, wife, against this wedding day.—
Farewell, my lord. Light to my chamber, ho!
35   Afore me! It is so very late,
That we may call it early by and by.
Goodnight.   *Exeunt*

[Act 3 Scene 5]   *running scene 14*

Enter Romeo and Juliet aloft

JULIET   Wilt thou be gone? It is not yet near day.
It was the nightingale, and not the lark,
That pierced the fearful hollow of thine ear;
Nightly she sings on yon pom'granate tree.
5   Believe me, love, it was the nightingale.
ROMEO   It was the lark, the herald of the morn,
No nightingale: look, love, what envious streaks
Do lace the severing clouds in yonder east:
Night's candles are burnt out, and jocund day
10   Stands tiptoe on the misty mountains tops.
I must be gone and live or stay and die.
JULIET   Yon light is not daylight, I know it, I:
It is some meteor that the sun exhales,
To be to thee this night a torchbearer,
15   And light thee on thy way to Mantua.
Therefore stay yet: thou need'st not to be gone.
ROMEO   Let me be ta'en, let me be put to death,
I am content, so thou wilt have it so.
I'll say yon grey is not the morning's eye,

---

33 against in anticipation of   **35 Afore me!** either an instruction to a servant bearing a light
or a mild oath   **3.5   7 envious** malicious/jealous   **8 severing** separating (the **clouds** drift
apart, and in doing so will separate Romeo and Juliet)   **9 jocund** merry, sprightly
13 meteor . . . exhales ill-omened meteors were believed to be formed of vapors drawn up
("exhaled") from the earth by the sun   **17 ta'en** arrested   **18 so thou** provided

20   'Tis but the pale reflex of Cynthia's brow,
        Nor that is not the lark, whose notes do beat
        The vaulty heaven so high above our heads.
        I have more care to stay than will to go:
        Come, death, and welcome! Juliet wills it so.
25   How is't, my soul? Let's talk, it is not day.

JULIET   It is, it is: hie hence, begone, away!
        It is the lark that sings so out of tune,
        Straining harsh discords and unpleasing sharps.
        Some say the lark makes sweet division;
30   This doth not so, for she divideth us:
        Some say the lark and loathèd toad change eyes,
        O, now I would they had changed voices too,
        Since arm from arm that voice doth us affray,
        Hunting thee hence with hunt's-up to the day.
35   O, now begone, more light and light it grows.

ROMEO   More light and light, more dark and dark our woes!

Enter Nurse

NURSE   Madam!

JULIET   Nurse?

NURSE   Your lady mother is coming to your chamber:
40   The day is broke, be wary, look about.   [*Exit*]

JULIET   Then, window, let day in, and let life out.

ROMEO   Farewell, farewell! One kiss, and I'll descend.

JULIET   Art thou gone so? Love, lord, ay, husband, friend,
        I must hear from thee every day in the hour,
45   For in a minute there are many days.
        O, by this count I shall be much in years
        Ere I again behold my Romeo!

20 reflex reflection   Cynthia another name for the goddess of the moon   22 vaulty vaulted,
arched   23 care concern/inclination   26 hie hurry   28 Straining singing (plays on the
sense of "forcing, making an unnatural effort")   29 division rapid melodic music
31 change exchange   33 arm from arm from one another's arms   affray frighten
34 hunt's-up song used to rouse hunters in the morning and sometimes played to the bride the
morning after her wedding   43 friend lover   46 much in years very old

ROMEO   Farewell!
I will omit no opportunity
50   That may convey my greetings, love, to thee.
JULIET   O, think'st thou we shall ever meet again?
ROMEO   I doubt it not, and all these woes shall serve
For sweet discourses in our time to come.
JULIET   O God, I have an ill-divining soul!
55   Methinks I see thee, now thou art so low,
As one dead in the bottom of a tomb:
Either my eyesight fails or thou look'st pale.
ROMEO   And trust me, love, in my eye so do you:
Dry sorrow drinks our blood. Adieu, adieu!   *Exit*
60   JULIET   O fortune, fortune, all men call thee fickle:
If thou art fickle, what dost thou with him.
That is renowned for faith? Be fickle, fortune,
For then I hope thou wilt not keep him long,
But send him back.

Enter Mother   *Below*

65   LADY CAPULET   Ho, daughter, are you up?
JULIET   Who is't that calls? It is my lady mother.
Is she not down so late, or up so early?
What unaccustomed cause procures her hither?

Juliet could exit aloft and enter below

LADY CAPULET   Why, how now, Juliet!
70   JULIET   Madam, I am not well.
LADY CAPULET   Evermore weeping for your cousin's death?
What, wilt thou wash him from his grave with tears?
An if thou couldst, thou couldst not make him live:
Therefore, have done. Some grief shows much of love,
75   But much of grief shows still some want of wit.
JULIET   Yet let me weep for such a feeling loss.
LADY CAPULET   So shall you feel the loss, but not the friend
Which you weep for.

---

54 ill-divining foreseeing evil   **59 Dry** thirsty (each sigh was thought to drain the heart of
a drop of blood)   **67 not . . . late** not yet in bed   **68 procures** brings   **73 An if** even if
76 feeling powerfully felt   **77 feel** experience (the **loss**)/touch (the living **friend**)
friend relative (in her response Juliet privately intends "lover")

JULIET   Feeling so the loss,
80   I cannot choose but ever weep the friend.
LADY CAPULET   Well, girl, thou weep'st not so much for his death,
As that the villain lives which slaughtered him.
JULIET   What villain, madam?
LADY CAPULET   That same villain, Romeo.
85   JULIET   Villain and he be many miles asunder.—   *Aside?*
God pardon him! I do with all my heart:
And yet no man like he doth grieve my heart.
LADY CAPULET   That is because the traitor lives.
JULIET   Ay, madam, from the reach of these my hands:
90   Would none but I might venge my cousin's death!
LADY CAPULET   We will have vengeance for it, fear thou not:
Then weep no more. I'll send to one in Mantua,
Where that same banished runagate doth live,
Shall give him such an unaccustomed dram,
95   That he shall soon keep Tybalt company,
And then I hope, thou wilt be satisfied.
JULIET   Indeed, I never shall be satisfied
With Romeo, till I behold him — dead —
Is my poor heart so for a kinsman vexed.
100   Madam, if you could find out but a man
To bear a poison, I would temper it,
That Romeo should upon receipt thereof,
Soon sleep in quiet. O, how my heart abhors
To hear him named and cannot come to him,
105   To wreak the love I bore my cousin
Upon his body that hath slaughtered him!
LADY CAPULET   Find thou the means, and I'll find such a man.
But now I'll tell thee joyful tidings, girl.
JULIET   And joy comes well in such a needy time:
110   What are they, beseech your ladyship?

---

87 like so much as   **grieve** make sorrowful/anger, vex   **93 runagate** fugitive   **94 dram**
measure (of poisoned drink)   **97 be satisfied** be content/be revenged (on)/have enough
(of)/be sexually satisfied   **98 dead** can apply to either **him** or to **heart**   **99 kinsman** cousin
(Tybalt)/husband (Romeo)   **101 temper** mix/modify and make safe   **103 sleep in quiet**
die/fall into a harmless sleep   **105 wreak** avenge/bestow   **109 needy** destitute

LADY CAPULET   Well, well, thou hast a careful father, child,
One who, to put thee from thy heaviness,
Hath sorted out a sudden day of joy,
That thou expects not, nor I looked not for.

115 JULIET   Madam, in happy time, what day is that?

LADY CAPULET   Marry, my child, early next Thursday morn,
The gallant, young and noble gentleman,
The County Paris, at St Peter's Church,
Shall happily make thee there a joyful bride.

120 JULIET   Now, by St Peter's Church and Peter too,
He shall not make me there a joyful bride.
I wonder at this haste, that I must wed
Ere he that should be husband comes to woo.
I pray you tell my lord and father, madam,

125 I will not marry yet, and, when I do, I swear
It shall be Romeo, whom you know I hate,
Rather than Paris. These are news indeed!

LADY CAPULET   Here comes your father: tell him so yourself,
And see how he will take it at your hands.

Enter Capulet and Nurse

130 CAPULET   When the sun sets, the earth doth drizzle dew,
But for the sunset of my brother's son
It rains downright.
How now? A conduit, girl? What, still in tears?
Evermore show'ring? In one little body

135 Thou counterfeits a bark, a sea, a wind,
For still thy eyes, which I may call the sea,
Do ebb and flow with tears: the bark thy body is,
Sailing in this salt flood: the winds, thy sighs,
Who, raging with thy tears and they with them,

140 Without a sudden calm, will overset

---

111 careful caring, solicitous   113 sorted out chosen   114 looked not for did not expect
115 in happy time this is opportune   116 Marry plays on the marital sense of the word
133 conduit fountain   135 counterfeits imitates   bark small ship   138 flood sea/torrent
140 overset overwhelm/capsize

Thy tempest-tossèd body. How now, wife?
Have you delivered to her our decree?

LADY CAPULET   Ay, sir, but she will none, she gives you thanks.
I would the fool were married to her grave.

145   CAPULET   Soft, take me with you, take me with you, wife.
How, will she none? Doth she not give us thanks?
Is she not proud? Doth she not count her blest,
Unworthy as she is, that we have wrought
So worthy a gentleman to be her bridegroom?

150   JULIET   Not proud you have, but thankful that you have:
Proud can I never be of what I hate,
But thankful even for hate, that is meant love.

CAPULET   How now? How now? Chopped-logic? What is this?
'Proud' and 'I thank you' and 'I thank you not',
155   And yet 'not proud', mistress minion you?
Thank me no thankings nor proud me no prouds,
But fettle your fine joints gainst Thursday next,
To go with Paris to St Peter's Church,
Or I will drag thee on a hurdle thither.
160   Out, you green-sickness carrion, out, you baggage,
You tallow-face!

LADY CAPULET   Fie, fie, what, are you mad?

JULIET   Good father, I beseech you on my knees,   *Kneels*
Hear me with patience but to speak a word.

165   CAPULET   Hang thee, young baggage, disobedient wretch!
I tell thee what: get thee to church o'Thursday,
Or never after look me in the face.
Speak not, reply not, do not answer me:
My fingers itch. Wife, we scarce thought us blest

---

144 **would** wish   145 **take . . . you** let me understand you properly   146 **How** what
147 **her** herself   148 **wrought** arranged (for)/persuaded   152 **hate . . . love** something
hateful that was nevertheless arranged for me out of love   153 **Chopped-logic** specious, false
logic or one who argues in such a manner   157 **fettle** prepare; literally, "groom (a horse)"
159 **hurdle** frame on which traitors were dragged to execution   160 **Out** expression of
indignation and scorn   **green-sickness** anaemic illness affecting pubescent girls, hence
"pale"   **carrion** corpse/worthless wretch   161 **tallow-face** person with a pale, waxen face
tallow animal fat used for making candles and soap   169 **itch** i.e. to beat you

170   That God had lent us but this only child,
        But now I see this one is one too much,
        And that we have a curse in having her.
        Out on her, hilding!

NURSE   God in heaven bless her!

175   You are to blame, my lord, to rate her so.

CAPULET   And why, my lady wisdom? Hold your   *To Nurse*
        tongue,
        Good prudence, smatter with your gossips, go.

NURSE   I speak no treason.

CAPULET   O, God gi' good e'en.

180 **NURSE**   May not one speak?

CAPULET   Peace, you mumbling fool!
        Utter your gravity o'er a gossip's bowl,
        For here we need it not.

LADY CAPULET   You are too hot.

185 **CAPULET**   God's bread, it makes me mad!
        Day, night, hour, tide, time, work, play,
        Alone, in company, still my care hath been
        To have her matched: and having now provided
        A gentleman of noble parentage,

190   Of fair demesnes, youthful, and nobly allied,
        Stuffed, as they say, with honourable parts,
        Proportioned as one's thought would wish a man,
        And then to have a wretched puling fool,
        A whining mammet, in her fortune's tender,

195   To answer 'I'll not wed, I cannot love,
        I am too young, I pray you pardon me.'
        But, an you will not wed, I'll pardon you:
        Graze where you will you shall not house with me.

---

173 hilding hussy, good-for-nothing   **175 rate** berate, scold   **177 smatter** chatter, talk
ignorantly   **gossips** women friends   **179 God . . . e'en** i.e. for God's sake/go away (literally,
good evening)   **182 gravity** words of wisdom   **bowl** drinking vessel   **185 God's bread** an
oath referring to the bread used in the Christian sacrament of Communion   **187 still** always
190 demesnes lands   **191 parts** qualities   **193 puling** whining   **194 mammet**
doll/contemptible weakling   **in . . . tender** when fortune makes her an offer   **197 pardon** the
sense now shifts from "excuse, forgive" to "give permission to leave"

Look to't, think on't, I do not use to jest.

200 Thursday is near, lay hand on heart, advise:

An you be mine, I'll give you to my friend,

An you be not, hang, beg, starve, die in the streets,

For, by my soul, I'll ne'er acknowledge thee,

Nor what is mine shall never do thee good.

205 Trust to't, bethink you, I'll not be forsworn.   *Exit*

JULIET   Is there no pity sitting in the clouds,

That sees into the bottom of my grief?

O, sweet my mother, cast me not away!

Delay this marriage for a month, a week,

210 Or if you do not, make the bridal bed

In that dim monument where Tybalt lies.

LADY CAPULET   Talk not to me, for I'll not speak a word:

Do as thou wilt, for I have done with thee.   *Exit*

JULIET   O God!— O nurse, how shall this be prevented?

215 My husband is on earth, my faith in heaven:

How shall that faith return again to earth,

Unless that husband send it me from heaven

By leaving earth? Comfort me, counsel me.

Alack, alack, that heaven should practise stratagems

220 Upon so soft a subject as myself!

What say'st thou? Hast thou not a word of joy?

Some comfort, nurse.

NURSE   Faith, here it is:

Romeo is banished, and all the world to nothing,

225 That he dares ne'er come back to challenge you,

Or if he do, it needs must be by stealth.

Then, since the case so stands as now it doth,

I think it best you married with the county.

O, he's a lovely gentleman!

230 Romeo's a dishclout to him. An eagle, madam,

---

199 do . . . jest am not in the habit of joking   200 advise consider   205 be forsworn break
my word   211 monument tomb   215 faith i.e. marriage vows   219 practise plot
224 all . . . nothing the odds are overwhelming   225 challenge lay claim to   230 dishclout
dishcloth

Hath not so green, so quick, so fair an eye
As Paris hath. Beshrew my very heart,
I think you are happy in this second match,
For it excels your first: or if it did not,
235   Your first is dead, or 'twere as good he were,
As living here and you no use of him.

JULIET   Speakest thou from thy heart?

NURSE   And from my soul too,
Or else beshrew them both.

240   JULIET   Amen.

NURSE   What?

JULIET   Well, thou hast comforted me marv'llous much.
Go in and tell my lady I am gone,
Having displeased my father, to Laurence' cell,
245   To make confession and to be absolved.

NURSE   Marry, I will, and this is wisely done.   [*Exit*]

JULIET   Ancient damnation! O most wicked fiend!
Is it more sin to wish me thus forsworn,
Or to dispraise my lord with that same tongue
250   Which she hath praised him with above compare
So many thousand times? Go, counsellor,
Thou and my bosom henceforth shall be twain.
I'll to the friar, to know his remedy:
If all else fail, myself have power to die.   *Exit*

[Act 4 Scene 1]   *running scene 15*

Enter Friar and County Paris

FRIAR LAURENCE   On Thursday, sir? The time is very short.

PARIS   My father Capulet will have it so,
And I am nothing slow to slack his haste.

231 **quick** lively/keen   232 **Beshrew** curse   236 **use** plays on the sense of "sexual employment"   240 **Amen** expression of agreement (to the Nurse's advice/to **beshrew them both**)   247 **Ancient damnation!** Damned old woman!   248 **forsworn** perjured (by breaking marriage vows)   252 **bosom** i.e. private thoughts   **twain** separated   **4.1** *Location: Friar Laurence's cell*   3 **nothing slow** in no way reluctant

	FRIAR LAURENCE	You say you do not know the lady's mind?

FRIAR LAURENCE   You say you do not know the lady's mind?

5   Uneven is the course, I like it not.

PARIS   Immoderately she weeps for Tybalt's death,
And therefore have I little talk of love,
For Venus smiles not in a house of tears.
Now, sir, her father counts it dangerous

10   That she doth give her sorrow so much sway,
And in his wisdom hastes our marriage,
To stop the inundation of her tears,
Which too much minded by herself alone
May be put from her by society:

15   Now do you know the reason of this haste.

FRIAR LAURENCE   I would I knew not why it should be   *Aside*
slowed.—
Look, sir, here comes the lady towards my cell.

Enter Juliet

PARIS   Happily met, my lady and my wife!

JULIET   That may be, sir, when I may be a wife.

20   PARIS   That 'may be' must be, love, on Thursday next.

JULIET   What must be shall be.

FRIAR LAURENCE   That's a certain text.

PARIS   Come you to make confession to this father?

JULIET   To answer that, I should confess to you.

25   PARIS   Do not deny to him that you love me.

JULIET   I will confess to you that I love him.

PARIS   So will ye, I am sure, that you love me.

JULIET   If I do so, it will be of more price,
Being spoke behind your back, than to your face.

30   PARIS   Poor soul, thy face is much abused with tears.

JULIET   The tears have got small victory by that,
For it was bad enough before their spite.

---

4 mind opinion   8 Venus the goddess/the planet   house plays on the astrological senses of "one of the twelve parts of the heavens" and "sign of the zodiac in which a particular planet has influence"   10 sway rule, influence   13 minded dwelt on, attended to   14 society companionship   18 Happily gladly/fortunately   22 text saying, proverb   28 price value

| PARIS | Thou wrong'st it more than tears with that report. |

PARIS   Thou wrong'st it more than tears with that report.

JULIET   That is no slander, sir, which is a truth,

35   And what I spake, I spake it to my face.

PARIS   Thy face is mine, and thou hast slandered it.

JULIET   It may be so, for it is not mine own.—
Are you at leisure, holy father, now,
Or shall I come to you at evening mass?

40 FRIAR LAURENCE   My leisure serves me, pensive daughter, now.—
My lord, we must entreat the time alone.

PARIS   God shield I should disturb devotion!
Juliet, on Thursday early will I rouse ye:
Till then, adieu, and keep this holy kiss.   *Kisses Juliet on forehead*

                                    Exit Paris   *or hand or cheek*

45 JULIET   O, shut the door, and when thou hast done so,
Come weep with me, past hope, past care, past help!

FRIAR LAURENCE   O, Juliet, I already know thy grief,
It strains me past the compass of my wits:
I hear thou must, and nothing may prorogue it,

50   On Thursday next be married to this county.

JULIET   Tell me not, friar, that thou hearest of this,
Unless thou tell me how I may prevent it:
If in thy wisdom thou canst give no help,
Do thou but call my resolution wise,

55   And with this knife I'll help it presently.   *Shows a dagger*
God joined my heart and Romeo's, thou our hands,
And ere this hand, by thee to Romeo sealed,
Shall be the label to another deed,
Or my true heart with treacherous revolt

60   Turn to another, this shall slay them both:
Therefore, out of thy long-experienced time,
Give me some present counsel, or, behold,
'Twixt my extremes and me this bloody knife

---

35 my face openly/about my face   37 not mine own Juliet privately means "as my face
belongs to Romeo"   40 pensive sorrowful, full of melancholy musing   42 shield forbid
48 compass bounds   49 prorogue defer   55 presently immediately   58 label seal
(technically the strip of paper to which the seal was affixed)   deed action/legal document
60 both i.e. hand and heart   61 time age   63 extremes desperate hardships

Shall play the umpire, arbitrating that
65 Which the commission of thy years and art
Could to no issue of true honour bring.
Be not so long to speak, I long to die,
If what thou speak'st speak not of remedy.

FRIAR LAURENCE   Hold, daughter: I do spy a kind of hope,
70 Which craves as desp'rate an execution
As that is desperate which we would prevent.
If, rather than to marry County Paris,
Thou hast the strength of will to slay thyself,
Then is it likely thou wilt undertake
75 A thing like death to chide away this shame,
That cop'st with death himself to scape from it:
And if thou dar'st, I'll give thee remedy.

JULIET   O, bid me leap, rather than marry Paris,
From off the battlements of any tower,
80 Or walk in thievish ways, or bid me lurk
Where serpents are, chain me with roaring bears,
Or hide me nightly in a charnel-house,
O'er-covered quite with dead men's rattling bones,
With reeky shanks and yellow chapless skulls,
85 Or bid me go into a new-made grave
And hide me with a dead man in his tomb —
Things that to hear them told have made me tremble —
And I will do it without fear or doubt,
To live an unstained wife to my sweet love.

90 FRIAR LAURENCE   Hold, then. Go home, be merry, give consent
To marry Paris. Wednesday is tomorrow:
Tomorrow night look that thou lie alone,
Let not thy nurse lie with thee in thy chamber:
Take thou this vial, being then in bed,   *Shows a vial*

---

64 **umpire** technically, one brought in to decide a legal matter when arbitrators cannot agree
65 **commission** authority/authority to perform judicial functions   **art** skill, knowledge
66 **issue** outcome   76 **That cop'st** you who would embrace   80 **thievish ways** streets
frequented by thieves   82 **charnel-house** vault containing dead bodies   84 **reeky shanks**
stinking shinbones   **chapless** jawless

95 And this distilling liquor drink thou off,
    When presently through all thy veins shall run
    A cold and drowsy humour, for no pulse
    Shall keep his native progress, but surcease.
    No warmth, no breath shall testify thou liv'st:
100 The roses in thy lips and cheeks shall fade
    To wanny ashes, thy eyes' windows fall,
    Like death when he shuts up the day of life.
    Each part, deprived of supple government,
    Shall stiff and stark and cold appear like death:
105 And in this borrowed likeness of shrunk death
    Thou shalt continue two-and-forty hours,
    And then awake as from a pleasant sleep.
    Now when the bridegroom in the morning comes
    To rouse thee from thy bed, there art thou dead:
110 Then as the manner of our country is,
    In thy best robes uncovered on the bier,
    // Be borne to burial in thy kindred's grave //
    Thou shalt be borne to that same ancient vault
    Where all the kindred of the Capulets lie.
115 In the mean time, against thou shalt awake,
    Shall Romeo by my letters know our drift,
    And hither shall he come, and he and I
    Will watch thy waking, and that very night
    Shall Romeo bear thee hence to Mantua.
120 And this shall free thee from this present shame,
    If no inconstant toy, nor womanish fear,
    Abate thy valour in the acting it.

JULIET   Give me, give me! O, tell not me of fear!   *Takes the vial*

FRIAR LAURENCE   Hold, get you gone, be strong and prosperous
125 In this resolve: I'll send a friar with speed
    To Mantua, with my letters to thy lord.

---

95 **distilling** distilled/infusing   **liquor** liquid   **off** i.e. entirely   97 **humour** fluid
98 **native** natural   **surcease** cease   101 **wanny** wan, pale   **eyes' windows** i.e. eyelids
103 **supple government** power of movement   115 **against** in anticipation of the time when
116 **drift** scheme/intention   121 **toy** aversion/whim   124 **prosperous** successful/fortunate

JULIET   Love give me strength, and strength shall help afford.
Farewell, dear father!   *Exeunt*

[Act 4 Scene 2]   *running scene 16*

Enter Father Capulet, Mother, Nurse and Servingmen, two or three
CAPULET   So many guests invite as here are writ.—

                                          [*Exit a Servingman*]

Sirrah, go hire me twenty cunning cooks.
SERVINGMAN   You shall have none ill, sir, for I'll try if they can
lick their fingers.

5   CAPULET   How canst thou try them so?
SERVINGMAN   Marry, sir, 'tis an ill cook that cannot lick his own
fingers: therefore he that cannot lick his fingers goes not
with me.
CAPULET   Go, begone.   [*Exit the Servingman*]

10   We shall be much unfurnished for this time.
What, is my daughter gone to Friar Laurence?
NURSE   Ay, forsooth.
CAPULET   Well, he may chance to do some good on her.
A peevish self-willed harlotry it is.

Enter Juliet

15   NURSE   See where she comes from shrift with merry look.
CAPULET   How now, my headstrong? Where have you been
gadding?
JULIET   Where I have learned me to repent the sin
Of disobedient opposition
To you and your behests, and am   ↓*Falls prostrate or kneels*↓
enjoined

20   By holy Laurence to fall prostrate here,

---

127 help afford supply help   **4.2 *Location: the Capulets' house***   2 cunning skillful
3 none ill no bad ones   try test   6 'tis . . . fingers proverbial phrase for one who has no faith
in his abilities   10 unfurnished unprovided, unprepared   12 forsooth indeed, in truth
14 peevish foolish/obstinate/headstrong   harlotry harlot/wretch   16 gadding wandering,
roving idly   19 behests commands

To beg your pardon. Pardon, I beseech you!
Henceforward I am ever ruled by you.

CAPULET   Send for the county, go tell him of this:
I'll have this knot knit up tomorrow morning.

25 **JULIET**   I met the youthful lord at Laurence' cell,
And gave him what becomèd love I might,
Not stepping o'er the bounds of modesty.

CAPULET   Why, I am glad on't, this is well — stand
up —   *She rises*
This is as't should be. Let me see the county.

30 Ay, marry, go, I say, and fetch him hither.
Now, afore God, this reverend holy friar,
All our whole city is much bound to him.

JULIET   Nurse, will you go with me into my closet,
To help me sort such needful ornaments

35 As you think fit to furnish me tomorrow?

LADY CAPULET   No, not till Thursday: there's time enough.

CAPULET   Go, nurse, go with her: we'll to church tomorrow.
                                    Exeunt Juliet and Nurse

LADY CAPULET   We shall be short in our provision,
'Tis now near night.

40 **CAPULET**   Tush, I will stir about,
And all things shall be well, I warrant thee, wife:
Go thou to Juliet, help to deck up her:
I'll not to bed tonight, let me alone.
I'll play the housewife for this once. What, ho!

45 They are all forth. Well, I will walk myself
To County Paris, to prepare him up
Against tomorrow. My heart is wondrous light,
Since this same wayward girl is so reclaimed.
                                    Exeunt Father and Mother

---

26 becomèd befitting, seemly   **33 closet** private room   **34 ornaments** clothing/accessories
38 short lacking   **42 deck up her** adorn her, prepare her   **45 They** i.e. the servants   **forth**
out of the house (on errands)

[Act 4 Scene 3]   *running scene 17*

Enter Juliet and Nurse   *A curtained bed is provided onstage*

JULIET   Ay, those attires are best, but, gentle nurse,
I pray thee leave me to myself tonight,
For I have need of many orisons
To move the heavens to smile upon my state,
5   Which, well thou know'st, is cross and full of sin.

Enter Mother

LADY CAPULET   What, are you busy, ho? Need you my help?

JULIET   No, madam, we have culled such necessaries
As are behoveful for our state tomorrow.
So please you, let me now be left alone,
10   And let the nurse this night sit up with you,
For I am sure you have your hands full all,
In this so sudden business.

LADY CAPULET   Goodnight.
Get thee to bed, and rest, for thou hast need.

Exeunt [Lady Capulet and Nurse]

15   JULIET   Farewell! God knows when we shall meet again.
I have a faint cold fear thrills through my veins,
That almost freezes up the heat of life.
I'll call them back again to comfort me.—
Nurse!— What should she do here?
20   My dismal scene I needs must act alone.
Come, vial.
What if this mixture do not work at all?
Shall I be married then tomorrow morning?
No, no, this shall forbid it.— Lie thou   *Lays down a dagger*
there.—
25   What if it be a poison, which the friar
Subtly hath ministered to have me dead,

4.3 *Location: Juliet's bedroom in the Capulets' house*   **3 orisons** prayers   **5 cross**
perverse/unfavorable   **7 culled** selected   **8 behoveful** useful, necessary   **state** ceremony
16 thrills pierces/passes with a shudder of emotion   **20 dismal** ominous/disastrous
26 Subtly craftily

Lest in this marriage he should be dishonoured,
Because he married me before to Romeo?
I fear it is, and yet methinks it should not,
30   For he hath still been tried a holy man.
How if, when I am laid into the tomb,
I wake before the time that Romeo
Come to redeem me? There's a fearful point!
Shall I not then be stifled in the vault,
35   To whose foul mouth no healthsome air breathes in,
And there die strangled ere my Romeo comes?
Or if I live, is it not very like,
The horrible conceit of death and night,
Together with the terror of the place —
40   As in a vault, an ancient receptacle,
Where for these many hundred years the bones
Of all my buried ancestors are packed:
Where bloody Tybalt, yet but green in earth,
Lies fest'ring in his shroud, where, as they say,
45   At some hours in the night spirits resort —
Alack, alack, is it not like that I,
So early waking what with loathsome smells,
And shrieks like mandrakes torn out of the earth,
That living mortals, hearing them, run mad —
50   O, if I wake, shall I not be distraught,
Environèd with all these hideous fears?
And madly play with my forefather's joints?
And pluck the mangled Tybalt from his shroud?
And in this rage, with some great kinsman's bone,
55   As with a club, dash out my desp'rate brains?
O, look! Methinks I see my cousin's ghost
Seeking out Romeo that did spit his body

---

30 still always   **tried** proved   **36 strangled ere** suffocated before   **37 like** likely   **38 conceit**
conception, idea   **43 green in earth** newly buried (**green** also suggests putrefying flesh)
48 mandrakes plants with forked roots that resembled the human form and were said to shriek
when pulled from the ground, causing madness or death in any who heard them   **50 distraught**
driven to madness   **51 Environèd** surrounded   **54 rage** madness   **57 spit** impale

Upon a rapier's point. Stay, Tybalt, stay!
Romeo, Romeo, Romeo! Here's drink: I drink to thee.

She drinks and falls onto the bed within the curtains

[Act 4 Scene 4]   *running scene 17 continues*

Enter Lady of the house and Nurse

LADY CAPULET   Hold, take these keys, and fetch more spices,
    nurse.

NURSE   They call for dates and quinces in the pastry.

Enter Old Capulet

CAPULET   Come, stir, stir, stir! The second cock hath crowed,
The curfew-bell hath rung, 'tis three o'clock.

5   Look to the baked meats, good Angelica:
Spare not for cost.

NURSE   Go, you cotquean, go,   *To Capulet*
Get you to bed. Faith, you'll be sick tomorrow
For this night's watching.

10   CAPULET   No, not a whit. What, I have watched ere now
All night for less cause, and ne'er been sick.

LADY CAPULET   Ay, you have been a mouse-hunt in your time,
But I will watch you from such watching now.

Exeunt Lady and Nurse

CAPULET   A jealous hood, a jealous hood!—

15   Now fellow, what is there?   *Calls*

Enter three or four with spits, and logs and baskets

SERVINGMAN   Things for the cook, sir, but I know not what.

CAPULET   Make haste, make haste.—   *[Exit Servingman]*
Sirrah, fetch drier logs:
Call Peter, he will show thee where they are.

---

58 Stay stop   **4.4   2 quinces** pear-shaped fruits   **pastry** room in which pastry dishes were
made   **4 curfew-bell** bell that rang at a fixed hour in the morning   **5 baked meats** meat pies
Angelica either the Nurse or Lady Capulet (plays on the herb of the same name)   **7 cotquean**
man who interferes with the housework   **9 watching** wakefulness   **12 mouse-hunt** hunter
of mice (i.e. women, hence "fornicator")   **13 watch . . . watching** keep an eye on you to
prevent such wakeful (sexual) behavior   **14 A jealous hood** jealousy/a jealous woman/a
jealous spy (wearing a hood as a disguise)

ᴀɴᴏᴛʜᴇʀ sᴇʀᴠɪɴɢᴍᴀɴ   I have a head, sir, that will find out logs,
And never trouble Peter for the matter.   [*Exit*]
ᴄᴀᴘᴜʟᴇᴛ   Mass, and well said, a merry whoreson, ha!
Thou shalt be logger-head. Good Father, 'tis day:
Play music
The county will be here with music straight,
For so he said he would. I hear him near.—
Nurse! Wife! What, ho! What, Nurse, I say!
Enter Nurse
Go waken Juliet, go and trim her up,
I'll go and chat with Paris. Hie, make haste,
Make haste: the bridegroom he is come already.
Make haste, I say.   [*Exit*]
ɴᴜʀsᴇ   Mistress, what, mistress? Juliet?—
Fast, I warrant her, she.—   *Approaches the bed*
Why, lamb, why, lady! Fie, you slug-a-bed!
Why, love, I say, madam, sweetheart, why, bride!
What, not a word? You take your pennyworths now,
Sleep for a week, for the next night, I warrant,
The County Paris hath set up his rest,
That you shall rest but little. God forgive me,
Marry and amen.— How sound is she asleep!
I must needs wake her. Madam, madam, madam!
Ay, let the county take you in your bed,
He'll fright you up, i'faith. Will it not be?   *Draws the curtains*
What, dressed, and in your clothes, and down again?
I must needs wake you: lady, lady, lady!—
Alas, alas! Help, help! My lady's dead!
O, welladay, that ever I was born!
Some aqua vitae, ho! My lord! My lady!

25

30

35

40

45

---

20 l . . . logs I have a good head for finding things/having a wooden (i.e. stupid) head I can
easily find logs   **22 Mass** by the Mass (a common oath)   **whoreson** bastard, whore's son
(spoken jovially)   **23 logger-head** in charge of fetching logs/a blockhead   **24 straight**
straight away   **27 trim her up** adorn her, deck her out   **32 Fast** fast asleep   **35 take your
pennyworths** take what little sleep you can/sleep soundly   **37 set . . . rest** determined
(literally a card-playing term meaning "to stake all" and playing on the sense of "got an
erection in preparation for the assault")   **41 take** find/have sex with   **42 fright** puns on
"freight" (i.e. to load, burden)   **43 down** in bed

Enter Mother

LADY CAPULET   What noise is here?

NURSE   O lamentable day!

50   LADY CAPULET   What is the matter?

NURSE   Look, look! O heavy day!

LADY CAPULET   O me, O me! My child, my only life,
Revive, look up, or I will die with thee!
Help, help! Call help.

Enter Father

55   CAPULET   For shame, bring Juliet forth, her lord is come.

NURSE   She's dead, deceased, she's dead, alack the day!

LADY CAPULET   Alack the day, she's dead, she's dead, she's dead!

CAPULET   Ha? Let me see her. Out, alas, she's cold:
Her blood is settled, and her joints are stiff.

60   Life and these lips have long been separated:
Death lies on her like an untimely frost
Upon the sweetest flower of all the field.

NURSE   O lamentable day!

LADY CAPULET   O woeful time!

65   CAPULET   Death, that hath ta'en her hence to make me wail,
Ties up my tongue, and will not let me speak.

Enter Friar and the County   Musicians may enter here

FRIAR LAURENCE   Come, is the bride ready to go to church?

CAPULET   Ready to go, but never to return.—
O son, the night before thy wedding-day   To Paris

70   Hath Death lain with thy wife. There she lies,
Flower as she was, deflowered by him.
Death is my son-in-law, Death is my heir:
My daughter he hath wedded. I will die,
And leave him all: life, living, all is Death's.

75   PARIS   Have I thought long to see this morning's face,
And doth it give me such a sight as this?

LADY CAPULET   Accursed, unhappy, wretched, hateful day!
Most miserable hour that e'er time saw

---

58 Out, alas expression of sorrow   74 living being alive/possessions and property
75 thought long longed/been impatient

In lasting labour of his pilgrimage!
But one, poor one, one poor and loving child,
But one thing to rejoice and solace in,
And cruel death hath catched it from my sight!

NURSE   O woe! O woeful, woeful, woeful day!
Most lamentable day, most woeful day,
85 That ever, ever, I did yet behold!
O day, O day, O day, O hateful day!
Never was seen so black a day as this:
O woeful day, O woeful day!

PARIS   Beguiled, divorcèd, wrongèd, spited, slain!
90 Most detestable death, by thee beguiled,
By cruel cruel thee quite overthrown!
O love, O life! Not life, but love in death!

CAPULET   Despised, distressèd, hated, martyred, killed!
Uncomfortable time, why cam'st thou now
95 To murder, murder our solemnity?
O child, O child! My soul, and not my child!
Dead art thou! Alack, my child is dead,
And with my child my joys are burièd.

FRIAR LAURENCE   Peace, ho, for shame! Confusion's care lives not
100 In these confusions. Heaven and yourself
Had part in this fair maid, now heaven hath all,
And all the better is it for the maid:
Your part in her you could not keep from death,
But heaven keeps his part in eternal life.
105 The most you sought was her promotion,
For 'twas your heaven she should be advanced:
And weep ye now, seeing she is advanced
Above the clouds, as high as heaven itself?
O, in this love, you love your child so ill

79 lasting endless/unceasing   82 catched seized   89 Beguiled deceived, cheated
94 Uncomfortable comfortless/disquieting   95 solemnity celebration, marriage ceremony
99 Confusion disorder/destruction/disaster   care management, control   105 promotion
social advancement (through marriage to Paris)   106 heaven idea of bliss, of the utmost good

110 That you run mad, seeing that she is well.
    She's not well married that lives married long,
    But she's best married that dies married young.
    Dry up your tears, and stick your rosemary
    On this fair corpse, and as the custom is,
115 And in her best array bear her to church:
    For though some nature bids us all lament,
    Yet nature's tears are reason's merriment.
    CAPULET   All things that we ordainèd festival,
    Turn from their office to black funeral:
120 Our instruments to melancholy bells,
    Our wedding cheer to a sad burial feast,
    Our solemn hymns to sullen dirges change,
    Our bridal flowers serve for a buried corpse,
    And all things change them to the contrary.
125 FRIAR LAURENCE   Sir, go you in, and madam, go with him,
    And go, Sir Paris: everyone prepare
    To follow this fair corpse unto her grave.
    The heavens do lour upon you for some ill,
    Move them no more by crossing their high will.

                                    Exeunt [all but Nurse]

                              Musicians may enter here

130 FIRST MUSICIAN   Faith, we may put up our pipes, and be gone.
    NURSE   Honest goodfellows, ah, put up, put up,
    For well you know this is a pitiful case.   [*Exit*]
    FIRST MUSICIAN   Ay, by my troth, the case may be amended.
    Enter Peter
    PETER   Musicians, O, musicians, 'Heart's ease', 'Heart's
135 ease'. O, an you will have me live, play 'Heart's ease'.
    FIRST MUSICIAN   Why 'Heart's ease'?

---

113 **stick** fasten/place/attach as an adornment   **rosemary** the herb symbolized fidelity and
remembrance, and was used at weddings and funerals   117 **reason's merriment** i.e.
laughably irrational/a cause of joy to reason   118 **ordainèd festival** intended to be festive
119 **office** function, appointed role   121 **cheer** food and drink, provisions   122 **solemn**
ceremonious   **sullen** sombre, melancholy   128 **lour** frown, look threateningly
ill wrongdoing   129 **Move** provoke   130 **put up** put away, pack up   132 **case** situation (the
First Musician then plays on the sense of "case for a musical instrument")   133 **amended**
repaired   134 **"Heart's ease"** a popular song

PETER   O, musicians, because my heart itself plays 'My heart is full of woe'. O, play me some merry dump to comfort me.

FIRST MUSICIAN   Not a dump we, 'tis no time to play now.

140 PETER   You will not, then?

FIRST MUSICIAN   No.

PETER   I will then give it you soundly.

FIRST MUSICIAN   What will you give us?

PETER   No money, on my faith, but the gleek: I will give you

145 the minstrel.

FIRST MUSICIAN   Then will I give you the serving-creature.

PETER   Then will I lay the serving-creature's dagger on your pate. I will carry no crotchets: I'll re you, I'll fa you. Do you note me?

150 FIRST MUSICIAN   An you re us and fa us, you note us.

SECOND MUSICIAN   Pray you put up your dagger, and put out your wit. Then have at you with my wit!

PETER   I will dry-beat you with an iron wit, and put up my iron dagger. Answer me like men:

155   When griping griefs the heart doth wound,
           Then music with her silver sound—
        Why 'silver sound'? Why 'music with her silver sound'?
        What say you, Simon Catling?

FIRST MUSICIAN   Marry, sir, because silver hath a sweet sound.

160 PETER   Prates. What say you, Hugh Rebeck?

SECOND MUSICIAN   I say 'silver sound', because musicians sound for silver.

---

137 "My . . . woe" another popular song, possibly the "Ballad of Two Lovers"   138 dump melody/mournful tune   142 soundly thoroughly/with force (plays in the sense of "audibly, with sound")   144 gleek gibe, jest (to "give the gleek" meant to mock someone) give . . . minstrel call you a minstrel (i.e. a vagrant or worthless wanderer)   146 serving-creature derogatory term for a servingman   148 pate head   carry no crotchets put up with no whims/sing none of these notes   re . . . you re and fa are musical notes, used here as if they were verbs meaning "to beat"   149 note pay attention to (plays on the sense of "record in musical notation"; in his response the First Musician widens the pun to include "beat us so that we are marked like a musical score")   151 put out extinguish/display   153 dry-beat beat severely (without using a dagger)   155 When . . . sound the opening lines of Richard Edwards' song "In Commendation of Music," published in *The Paradise of Dainty Devices* (1576) griping painful/grasping   158 Catling a small lute-string made from catgut   160 Prates mere chatter   Rebeck a rebec was a medieval three-stringed fiddle   161 sound for silver play for money

PETER   Prates too. What say you, James Soundpost?

THIRD MUSICIAN   Faith, I know not what to say.

165   PETER   O, I cry you mercy, you are the singer: I will say for
you. It is 'music with her silver sound' because musicians
have no gold for sounding:
Then music with her silver sound
With speedy help doth lend redress.   *Exit*

170   FIRST MUSICIAN   What a pestilent knave is this same!

SECOND MUSICIAN   Hang him, Jack! Come, we'll in here, tarry for
the mourners, and stay dinner.   *Exeunt*

[Act 5 Scene 1]   *running scene 18*

Enter Romeo

ROMEO   If I may trust the flattering truth of sleep,
My dreams presage some joyful news at hand:
My bosom's lord sits lightly in his throne,
And all this day an unaccustomed spirit
5   Lifts me above the ground with cheerful thoughts.
I dreamt my lady came and found me dead —
Strange dream, that gives a dead man leave to think! —
And breathed such life with kisses in my lips,
That I revived, and was an emperor.
10   Ah me, how sweet is love itself possessed,
When but love's shadows are so rich in joy!

Enter Romeo's Man   *Wearing riding boots*

News from Verona!— How now, Balthasar!
Dost thou not bring me letters from the friar?
How doth my lady? Is my father well?
15   How doth my lady Juliet? That I ask again,
For nothing can be ill, if she be well.

163 **Soundpost** a supporting wooden peg on a violin or similar instrument   165 **cry you mercy** beg your pardon   167 **for sounding** as payment for playing/with which to make a jingling sound   171 **Jack** the rogue   172 **stay** await   5.1 *Location: Mantua*   1 **flattering** pleasing/deceptive   2 **presage** foretell   3 **bosom's lord** i.e. heart   10 **possessed** actually experienced, enjoyed   11 **shadows** images, dreams

BALTHASAR　Then she is well, and nothing can be ill:
　　　　Her body sleeps in Capel's monument,
　　　　And her immortal part with angels lives.
20　　　I saw her laid low in her kindred's vault,
　　　　And presently took post to tell it you.
　　　　O, pardon me for bringing these ill news,
　　　　Since you did leave it for my office, sir.

ROMEO　　Is it even so? Then I deny you, stars!—
25　　　Thou know'st my lodging, get me ink and paper,
　　　　And hire post-horses: I will hence tonight.

BALTHASAR　I do beseech you, sir, have patience:
　　　　Your looks are pale and wild, and do import
　　　　Some misadventure.

30　ROMEO　　Tush, thou art deceived:
　　　　Leave me, and do the thing I bid thee do.
　　　　Hast thou no letters to me from the friar?

BALTHASAR　No, my good lord.

ROMEO　　No matter: get thee gone,
35　　　And hire those horses, I'll be with thee straight.—　　*Exit Man*
　　　　Well, Juliet, I will lie with thee tonight.
　　　　Let's see for means. O mischief, thou art swift
　　　　To enter in the thoughts of desperate men!
　　　　I do remember an apothecary,
40　　　And hereabouts a dwells, which late I noted
　　　　In tattered weeds, with overwhelming brows,
　　　　Culling of simples: meagre were his looks,
　　　　Sharp misery had worn him to the bones,
　　　　And in his needy shop a tortoise hung,
45　　　An alligator stuffed, and other skins

---

21 **presently took post** immediately set off with a post-horse (i.e. horse kept standing by for the speedy delivery of messages)　　23 **for my office** as my responsibility　　24 **deny** repudiate, renounce (some editors emend to the First Quarto's "defy")　　26 **post-horses** horses kept at inns for the use of messengers or for hire by travelers　　28 **import** suggest, portend　　29 **misadventure** fatal misfortune　　37 **see for** seek out, think about　　**mischief** calamity, harm, wicked deeds　　39 **apothecary** person who prepared and sold drugs　　40 **a** he **which** whom　　41 **weeds** clothing　　**overwhelming brows** overhanging or bushy eyebrows　　42 **Culling of simples** gathering medicinal herbs　　44 **needy** impoverished

Of ill-shaped fishes, and about his shelves
A beggarly account of empty boxes,
Green earthen pots, bladders and musty seeds,
Remnants of packthread and old cakes of roses,
50 Were thinly scattered, to make up a show.
Noting this penury, to myself I said
'An if a man did need a poison now,
Whose sale is present death in Mantua,
Here lives a caitiff wretch would sell it him.'
55 O, this same thought did but forerun my need,
And this same needy man must sell it me.
As I remember, this should be the house.
Being holy-day, the beggar's shop is shut.
What, ho, apothecary!

Enter Apothecary

60 APOTHECARY   Who calls so loud?

ROMEO   Come hither, man. I see that thou art poor.
Hold, there is forty ducats: let me have   *Shows gold*
A dram of poison, such soon-speeding gear
As will disperse itself through all the veins
65 That the life-weary taker may fall dead
And that the trunk may be discharged of breath
As violently as hasty powder fired
Doth hurry from the fatal cannon's womb.

APOTHECARY   Such mortal drugs I have, but Mantua's law
70 Is death to any he that utters them.

ROMEO   Art thou so bare and full of wretchedness,
And fear'st to die? Famine is in thy cheeks,
Need and oppression starveth in thy eyes,
Contempt and beggary hangs upon thy back:

---

47 account number   **48 earthen** earthenware   **bladders** animal bladders were used for storing liquid   **49 packthread** twine used for tying up packages   **cakes of roses** preparation of rose petals compressed into a cake for use as perfume   **53 Whose . . . death** the sale of which is punishable by instant death   **54 caitiff** miserable/base   **62 ducats** gold coins used in most European countries   **63 soon-speeding gear** rapidly working stuff/stuff that kills quickly   **65 That** so that   **66 trunk** body/cylindrical case that discharges explosives in a weapon   **69 mortal** fatal   **70 he** man   **utters** sells

75 The world is not thy friend nor the world's law:
The world affords no law to make thee rich,
Then be not poor, but break it and take this.

APOTHECARY   My poverty, but not my will, consents.

ROMEO   I pray thy poverty, and not thy will.

80 APOTHECARY   Put this in any liquid thing you will
And drink it off, and if you had the strength
Of twenty men, it would dispatch you straight.

ROMEO   There's thy gold, worse poison to   *Gives gold*
men's souls,
Doing more murder in this loathsome world,
85 Than these poor compounds that thou mayst not sell.
I sell thee poison, thou hast sold me none.
Farewell, buy food, and get thyself in flesh.—
Come, cordial and not poison, go with me
To Juliet's grave, for there must I use thee.

Exeunt [separately]

[Act 5 Scene 2]   *running scene 19*

Enter Friar John to Friar Laurence

FRIAR JOHN   Holy Franciscan friar, brother, ho!

Enter Friar Laurence

FRIAR LAURENCE   This same should be the voice of Friar John.—
Welcome from Mantua: what says Romeo?
Or if his mind be writ, give me his letter.

5 FRIAR JOHN   Going to find a barefoot brother out,
One of our order, to associate me,
Here in this city visiting the sick,
And finding him, the searchers of the town,
Suspecting that we both were in a house

---

77 **it** i.e. the law   79 **pray** entreat (some editors emend to the First Quarto's "pay")
85 **compounds** mixtures   87 **get . . . flesh** fatten yourself up   88 **cordial** medicine that
invigorates the heart   **5.2 Location:** *Friar Laurence's cell*   5 **barefoot brother** i.e. a fellow
Franciscan friar   6 **associate** accompany   8 **searchers** officials whose job was to view dead
bodies and ascertain the cause of death

10   Where the infectious pestilence did reign,

    Sealed up the doors, and would not let us forth,

    So that my speed to Mantua there was stayed.

FRIAR LAURENCE   Who bare my letter then to Romeo?

FRIAR JOHN   I could not send it — here it is again —   *Shows the letter*

15   Nor get a messenger to bring it thee,

    So fearful were they of infection.

FRIAR LAURENCE   Unhappy fortune! By my brotherhood,

    The letter was not nice but full of charge,

    Of dear import, and the neglecting it

20   May do much danger. Friar John, go hence,

    Get me an iron crow, and bring it straight

    Unto my cell.

FRIAR JOHN   Brother, I'll go and bring it thee.   *Exit*

FRIAR LAURENCE   Now must I to the monument alone,

25   Within this three hours will fair Juliet wake:

    She will beshrew me much that Romeo

    Hath had no notice of these accidents,

    But I will write again to Mantua,

    And keep her at my cell till Romeo come.

30   Poor living corpse, closed in a dead man's tomb!   *Exit*

[Act 5 Scene 3]

                                               running scene 20

Enter Paris and his Page   *Carrying flowers and a torch*

PARIS   Give me thy torch, boy. Hence, and stand aloof.

    Yet put it out, for I would not be seen.

    Under yon yew trees lay thee all along,

    Holding thy ear close to the hollow ground,

5   So shall no foot upon the churchyard tread,

---

10 pestilence plague   **12 speed** successful journey, rapid progress   **stayed** prevented
18 nice trivial   **charge** importance   **19 dear import** major significance/costly consequence
20 danger harm   **21 crow** crowbar   **27 accidents** events   **5.3** *Location: the churchyard containing the Capulet family tomb, Verona; the action moves into the tomb itself*
1 aloof at a distance   **3 lay . . . along** lie stretched out

Being loose, unfirm with digging up of graves,
But thou shalt hear it: whistle then to me
As signal that thou hear'st something approach.
Give me those flowers. Do as I bid thee, go.

10 PAGE   I am almost afraid to stand alone   *Aside*
Here in the churchyard, yet I will adventure.   *Stands back*

PARIS   Sweet flower, with flowers thy bridal
bed I strew —   *Strews flowers*
O woe, thy canopy is dust and stones —   *and sprinkles*
Which with sweet water nightly I will dew,   *perfumed water*

15 Or wanting that, with tears distilled by moans;
The obsequies that I for thee will keep
Nightly shall be to strew thy grave and weep.

Whistle Boy
The boy gives warning something doth approach.
What cursèd foot wanders this way tonight,

20 To cross my obsequies and true love's rite?
What, with a torch? Muffle me, night, awhile.   *Stands back*

Enter Romeo and Balthasar   *Carrying a mattock and*
ROMEO   Give me that mattock and the   *wrenching iron*
wrenching iron.
Hold, take this letter: early in the morning   *Gives a letter*
See thou deliver it to my lord and father.

25 Give me the light. Upon thy life, I charge thee,   *Takes a torch*
Whate'er thou hear'st or see'st, stand all aloof,
And do not interrupt me in my course.
Why I descend into this bed of death
Is partly to behold my lady's face,

30 But chiefly to take thence from her dead finger
A precious ring, a ring that I must use
In dear employment: therefore hence, begone.
But if thou, jealous, dost return to pry

---

6 **Being** i.e. the soil being   **10 stand** remain   **11 adventure** risk it, take my chances
13 canopy covering or hangings of a bed   **16 obsequies** rites of remembrance   **20 cross**
thwart   ***mattock*** pickaxe   ***wrenching iron*** crowbar   **32 dear employment** important
business/costly purpose   **33 jealous** suspicious

In what I further shall intend to do,
35 By heaven, I will tear thee joint by joint
And strew this hungry churchyard with thy limbs:
The time and my intents are savage-wild,
More fierce and more inexorable far
Than empty tigers or the roaring sea.

40 **BALTHASAR** I will be gone, sir, and not trouble you.

ROMEO   So shalt thou show me friendship. Take   *Gives money*
thou that.
Live and be prosperous, and farewell, good fellow.

BALTHASAR For all this same, I'll hide me hereabout: *Aside*
His looks I fear, and his intents I doubt.   *Stands aside*

45 **ROMEO**   Thou detestable maw, thou womb of   *Romeo*
death,   *begins to*
Gorged with the dearest morsel of the earth: *open the tomb*
Thus I enforce thy rotten jaws to open,
And in despite I'll cram thee with more food.

PARIS   This is that banished haughty Montague,   *Aside*
50 That murdered my love's cousin, with which grief
It is supposèd the fair creature died,
And here is come to do some villainous shame
To the dead bodies. I will apprehend him.—
Stop thy unhallowed toil, vile Montague!   *Comes forward*
55 Can vengeance be pursued further than death?
Condemnèd villain, I do apprehend thee:
Obey and go with me, for thou must die.

ROMEO   I must indeed, and therefore came I hither.
Good gentle youth, tempt not a desp'rate man,
60 Fly hence, and leave me: think upon these gone,
Let them affright thee. I beseech thee, youth,
Put not another sin upon my head,
By urging me to fury: O, begone!
By heaven, I love thee better than myself,

---

43 For . . . same all the same, nonetheless   **44 doubt** suspect/fear   **45 maw** throat/stomach
womb belly   **48 in despite** in angry defiance/to spite you   **54 unhallowed** unholy, wicked
60 gone dead

65   For I come hither armed against myself.
     Stay not, begone, live, and hereafter say,
     A madman's mercy bid thee run away.

    PARIS   I do defy thy commiseration,
     And apprehend thee for a felon here.

70   **ROMEO**   Wilt thou provoke me? Then have at   *They fight*
     thee, boy!

    PAGE   O Lord, they fight! I will go call the watch.   *[Exit]*

    PARIS   O, I am slain! If thou be merciful,
     Open the tomb, lay me with Juliet.   *Dies*

    ROMEO   In faith, I will. Let me peruse this face.

75   Mercutio's kinsman, noble County Paris!
     What said my man, when my betossèd soul
     Did not attend him as we rode? I think
     He told me Paris should have married Juliet:
     Said he not so? Or did I dream it so?

80   Or am I mad, hearing him talk of Juliet,
     To think it was so? O, give me thy hand,
     One writ with me in sour misfortune's book!
     I'll bury thee in a triumphant grave.   *Opens the tomb,*
     A grave? O no, a lantern, slaughtered youth,   *revealing Juliet*

85   For here lies Juliet, and her beauty makes
     This vault a feasting presence full of light.
     Death, lie thou there, by a dead man interred.
     How oft when men are at the point of death
     Have they been merry, which their keepers call

90   A light'ning before death. O, how may I
     Call this a light'ning? O my love, my wife!
     Death that hath sucked the honey of thy breath,
     Hath had no power yet upon thy beauty:
     Thou art not conquered, beauty's ensign yet

95   Is crimson in thy lips and in thy cheeks,

---

68 commiseration compassion   **78 should have** was to have   **80 him** i.e. Paris
83 triumphant splendid   **84 lantern** many-windowed turret-like structure often found
at the top of a church   **86 presence** reception room in a palace or great house   **89 keepers**
nurses/jailers   **94 ensign** military banner

And death's pale flag is not advancèd there.—
Tybalt, liest thou there in thy bloody sheet?
O, what more favour can I do to thee
Than with that hand that cut thy youth in twain
100   To sunder his that was thy enemy?
Forgive me, cousin.— Ah, dear Juliet,
Why art thou yet so fair? Shall I believe
That unsubstantial death is amorous,
And that the lean abhorrèd monster keeps
105   Thee here in dark to be his paramour?
For fear of that, I still will stay with thee,
And never from this palace of dim night
//Depart again. Come lie thou in my arms.//
//Here's to thy health, where'er thou tumblest in.//
110   //O true apothecary,//
//Thy drugs are quick. Thus with a kiss I die.//
Depart again. Here, here will I remain
With worms that are thy chambermaids: O, here
Will I set up my everlasting rest,
115   And shake the yoke of inauspicious stars
From this world-wearied flesh. Eyes, look your last!
Arms, take your last embrace! And, lips, O you
The doors of breath, seal with a righteous kiss
A dateless bargain to engrossing death!   *Kisses Juliet*
120   Come, bitter conduct, come, unsavoury guide!
Thou desperate pilot, now at once run on
The dashing rocks thy seasick weary bark!
Here's to my love. O true apothecary,   *Drinks*
Thy drugs are quick. Thus with a kiss I die.   *Dies*
Enter Friar Laurence with lantern, crow and spade

---

96 **advancèd** raised   100 **his . . . enemy** i.e. Romeo's own   103 **unsubstantial** bodiless
106 **still** always   110 **true** honest/true to his trade   119 **dateless bargain** eternal contract
engrossing monopolizing/all-consuming (with legal connotations: "to engross" is "to write
in a manner appropriate to legal documents")   120 **conduct** guide (i.e. the poison)
122 **dashing** destructive   124 **quick** speedy/active (with a play on "invigorating/life-giving")

125   FRIAR LAURENCE   Saint Francis be my speed! How oft tonight
      Have my old feet stumbled at graves! Who's there?
    BALTHASAR   Here's one, a friend, and one that knows you well.
    FRIAR LAURENCE   Bliss be upon you! Tell me, good my friend,
      What torch is yon that vainly lends his light
130   To grubs and eyeless skulls? As I discern,
      It burneth in the Capels' monument.
    BALTHASAR   It doth so, holy sir, and there's my master,
      One that you love.
    FRIAR LAURENCE   Who is it?
135   BALTHASAR   Romeo.
    FRIAR LAURENCE   How long hath he been there?
    BALTHASAR   Full half an hour.
    FRIAR LAURENCE   Go with me to the vault.
    BALTHASAR   I dare not, sir.
140   My master knows not but I am gone hence,
      And fearfully did menace me with death
      If I did stay to look on his intents.
    FRIAR LAURENCE   Stay then, I'll go alone. Fear comes upon me:
      O, much I fear some ill unlucky thing.
145   BALTHASAR   As I did sleep under this yew tree here,
      I dreamt my master and another fought,
      And that my master slew him.
    FRIAR LAURENCE   Romeo!
    Alack, alack, what blood is this which stains
150   The stony entrance of this sepulchre?
      What mean these masterless and gory swords
      To lie discoloured by this place of peace?
      Romeo! O, pale! Who else? What, Paris too?
      And steeped in blood? Ah, what an unkind hour
155   Is guilty of this lamentable chance!
      The lady stirs.

---

125 speed protector, aid   **129 vainly** pointlessly   **154 unkind** unnatural/cruel

JULIET   O, comfortable friar, where's my lord?   *Waking*
     I do remember well where I should be,
     And there I am. Where is my Romeo?

160   FRIAR LAURENCE   I hear some noise. Lady, come from that nest
     Of death, contagion and unnatural sleep:
     A greater power than we can contradict
     Hath thwarted our intents. Come, come away.
     Thy husband in thy bosom there lies dead,

165   And Paris too. Come, I'll dispose of thee
     Among a sisterhood of holy nuns.
     Stay not to question, for the watch is coming.
     Come, go, good Juliet, I dare no longer stay.   *Exit*

JULIET   Go, get thee hence, for I will not away.

170   What's here? A cup closed in my true love's hand?
     Poison I see hath been his timeless end.
     O churl, drink all and left no friendly drop
     To help me after? I will kiss thy lips,
     Haply some poison yet doth hang on them,

175   To make me die with a restorative.   *Kisses him*
     Thy lips are warm.

Enter Boy and Watch [Constable and other Watchmen]   *At a distance*

CONSTABLE   Lead, boy, which way?

JULIET   Yea, noise? Then I'll be brief. O happy dagger,
     This is thy sheath: there rust, and let me die.

                         Kills herself

180   PAGE   This is the place, there where the torch doth burn.

CONSTABLE   The ground is bloody, search about the churchyard:
     Go, some of you, whoe'er you find attach.

                     [Exeunt some Watchmen]
     Pitiful sight! Here lies the county slain,
     And Juliet bleeding, warm, and newly dead,

185   Who here hath lain these two days burièd.

---

157 comfortable comforting   **171 timeless** untimely/eternal   **172 churl** miser/villain
174 Haply perhaps/with luck   **178 happy** fortunate/opportune   **182 attach** arrest

Go, tell the prince, run to the Capulets,
Raise up the Montagues, some others search.

[*Exeunt other Watchmen*]

We see the ground whereon these woes do lie,
But the true ground of all these piteous woes
190   We cannot without circumstance descry.

Enter Romeo's man [Balthasar with Watchman]

SECOND WATCHMAN   Here's Romeo's man: we found him in the
churchyard.

CONSTABLE   Hold him in safety, till the prince come hither.

Enter Friar and another Watchman

THIRD WATCHMAN   Here is a friar that trembles, sighs and weeps:
We took this mattock and this spade from him,
195   As he was coming from this churchyard side.

CONSTABLE   A great suspicion: stay the friar too.

Enter the Prince [and Attendants]

PRINCE   What misadventure is so early up,
That calls our person from our morning rest?

Enter Capulet and his Wife [and others]

CAPULET   What should it be that they so shriek abroad?

200   LADY CAPULET   O, the people in the street cry 'Romeo',
Some 'Juliet', and some 'Paris', and all run
With open outcry toward our monument.

PRINCE   What fear is this which startles in your ears?

CONSTABLE   Sovereign, here lies the County Paris slain,
205   And Romeo dead, and Juliet, dead before,
Warm and new killed.

PRINCE   Search, seek, and know how this foul murder comes.

CONSTABLE   Here is a friar, and slaughtered Romeo's man,
With instruments upon them, fit to open
210   These dead men's tombs.

CAPULET   O heaven! O wife, look how our daughter bleeds!
This dagger hath mista'en — for lo his house

---

189 ground cause (quibbles on the literal meaning in the previous line)   **190 circumstance**
details (perhaps with a play on sense of "physical surroundings")   **196 stay** detain
212 mista'en mistaken its rightful **house** (i.e. sheath)

Is empty on the back of Montague —
And is mis-sheathèd in my daughter's bosom!

215 LADY CAPULET   O me, this sight of death is as a bell
That warns my old age to a sepulchre.

Enter Montague

PRINCE   Come, Montague, for thou art early up
To see thy son and heir now early down.

MONTAGUE   Alas, my liege, my wife is dead tonight:
220 Grief of my son's exile hath stopped her breath.
What further woe conspires against my age?

PRINCE   Look and thou shalt see.

MONTAGUE   O, thou untaught, what manners is in this?
To press before thy father to a grave?

225 PRINCE   Seal up the mouth of outrage for awhile,
Till we can clear these ambiguities,   ↓*The tomb may be closed*↓
And know their spring, their head, their true descent,
And then will I be general of your woes,
And lead you even to death. Meantime forbear,
230 And let mischance be slave to patience.—
Bring forth the parties of suspicion.

FRIAR LAURENCE   I am the greatest, able to do least,
Yet most suspected, as the time and place
Doth make against me of this direful murder:
235 And here I stand both to impeach and purge
Myself condemnèd and myself excused.

PRINCE   Then say at once what thou dost know in this.

FRIAR LAURENCE   I will be brief, for my short date of breath
Is not so long as is a tedious tale.
240 Romeo, there dead, was husband to that Juliet,
And she, there dead, that's Romeo's faithful wife:

---

216 **warns** summons   **sepulchre** tomb   219 **is dead tonight** died last night   223 **untaught**
ignorant, unmannerly person (referring to Romeo, whose body he has seen)   225 **mouth of
outrage** may refer to the tomb or to the characters who are reacting to events (or both)
outrage violence/disorder/passionate outcry   227 **spring, their head** source   228 **general**
leader   229 **to death** to the utmost/to death from grief/to securing death as the penalty for
the wrongdoers   230 **slave to** governed by   234 **make against** conspire against, accuse
235 **impeach . . . excused** accuse myself of what I should be condemned for and exonerate
myself where I deserve to be excused   238 **date of breath** amount of remaining life

I married them and their stol'n marriage day
Was Tybalt's doomsday, whose untimely death
Banished the new-made bridegroom from this city,
245   For whom, and not for Tybalt, Juliet pined.
You, to remove that siege of grief from her,
Betrothed and would have married her perforce
To County Paris. Then comes she to me,
And with wild looks bid me devise some means
250   To rid her from this second marriage,
Or in my cell there would she kill herself.
Then gave I her — so tutored by my art—
A sleeping potion, which so took effect
As I intended, for it wrought on her
255   The form of death. Meantime I writ to Romeo
That he should hither come as this dire night
To help to take her from her borrowed grave,
Being the time the potion's force should cease.
But he which bore my letter, Friar John,
260   Was stayed by accident, and yesternight
Returned my letter back. Then all alone,
At the prefixèd hour of her waking,
Came I to take her from her kindred's vault,
Meaning to keep her closely at my cell,
265   Till I conveniently could send to Romeo.
But when I came — some minute ere the time
Of her awaking — here untimely lay
The noble Paris and true Romeo dead.
She wakes, and I entreated her come forth,
270   And bear this work of heaven with patience:
But then a noise did scare me from the tomb,
And she, too desperate, would not go with me,
But, as it seems, did violence on herself.
All this I know, and to the marriage

---

247 perforce by compulsion   **252 art** skill, knowledge   **254 wrought** brought
about/fashioned   **256 as** on   **260 stayed** detained   **264 closely** secretly, concealed
268 true faithful, constant

275   Her nurse is privy: and if aught in this
       Miscarried by my fault, let my old life
       Be sacrificed, some hour before the time,
       Unto the rigour of severest law.

PRINCE   We still have known thee for a holy man.—
280   Where's Romeo's man? What can he say to this?

BALTHASAR   I brought my master news of Juliet's death,
       And then in post he came from Mantua
       To this same place, to this same monument.
       This letter he early bid me give his father,   *Shows letter*
285   And threatened me with death, going in the vault,
       If I departed not and left him there.

PRINCE   Give me the letter, I will look on it.
       Where is the county's page, that raised the watch?—
       Sirrah, what made your master in this place?

290   PAGE   He came with flowers to strew his lady's grave,
       And bid me stand aloof, and so I did:
       Anon comes one with light to ope the tomb,
       And by and by my master drew on him,
       And then I ran away to call the watch.

295   PRINCE   This letter doth make good the friar's words,
       Their course of love, the tidings of her death:
       And here he writes that he did buy a poison
       Of a poor 'pothecary, and therewithal
       Came to this vault to die, and lie with Juliet.

300   Where be these enemies? Capulet, Montague?
       See, what a scourge is laid upon your hate,
       That heaven finds means to kill your joys with love.
       And I for winking at your discords too
       Have lost a brace of kinsmen: all are punished.

---

275 privy aware, in on the secret   **aught** anything   **277 the time** its natural limit   **279 still** always   **282 post** haste   **289 made** did   **293 by and by** immediately   **295 make good** confirm   **298 therewithal** that being accomplished/with the poison   **301 scourge** punishment of divine origin   **302 joys** happiness/children   **303 winking at** shutting my eyes to   **304 brace** pair (i.e. Mercutio and Paris)

305 CAPULET   O brother Montague, give me thy hand:
This is my daughter's jointure, for no more
Can I demand.

MONTAGUE   But I can give thee more,
For I will raise her statue in pure gold,
310 That whiles Verona by that name is known,
There shall no figure at such rate be set
As that of true and faithful Juliet.

CAPULET   As rich shall Romeo by his lady lie,
Poor sacrifices of our enmity!

315 PRINCE   A glooming peace this morning with it brings,
The sun, for sorrow, will not show his head.
Go hence to have more talk of these sad things:
Some shall be pardoned, and some punishèd,
For never was a story of more woe
320 Than this of Juliet and her Romeo.   *Exeunt*

---

306 jointure marriage portion given by the bridegroom's family   **309 raise** have constructed
statue almost certainly a reclining figure that would be set on Juliet's tomb   **311 figure** statue
(plays on the sense of "number")   **rate be set** worth be valued   **313 Romeo** i.e. Romeo's
statue   **314 Poor sacrifices of** pitiful victims of/inadequate atonements for   **315 glooming**
gloomy/darkened/frowning/melancholy

Q1 = First Quarto text of 1597 (of uncertain authority)
Q2 = Second Quarto text of 1599
Q1/Q2 = a reading in which the First Quarto and Second Quarto agree
Q3 = Third Quarto text of 1609
Q4 = Fourth Quarto text of 1622
F = First Folio text of 1623
F2 = a correction introduced in the Second Folio text of 1632
Ed = a correction introduced by a later editor
SD = stage direction
SH = speech heading (i.e. speaker's name)

List of parts = Ed **Prologue . . . mend** = Q2. *Not in* F

1.1.25 in = Q1. *Not in* F **59 swashing** = Q4. F = washing **73 SH LADY
CAPULET** = Ed. F = *Wife (or Mo. or Old La. throughout)* **76 SH LADY
MONTAGUE** = Ed. F = *2. Wife* **97 further** = Q1/Q2. F = Fathers
125 humour = Q2. F = Honour **142 other** = Q2. F = others **175 create**
= Q1. F = created **178 well-seeming** = Q4. F = welseeing **214 bide** =
Q2. F = bid **215 ope** = Q2. F = open
1.2.42 are here = Q2. F = are **48 thy** = Q2. F = the **58 God . . . e'en** *spelled*
Godgigoden *in* F **65 daughters** = Q2. F = *daughter* **99 she . . . show** =
Q1/Q2. F *(uncorrected)* = she shew scant shell. F *(corrected)* = she shall
scant shell **99 seems** = Q2. F = shewes
1.3.32 eleven = Q2. F = a eleuen **40 should** = Q1/Q2. F = shall **41 Jule** =
Q2. F = *Iulet*. Q1 = Juliet **43 SH LADY CAPULET** = Ed. F = *Old La.*
58, 59 honour = Q1. F = houre **91 it** = Q1. *Not in* F **96 SH LADY
CAPULET** = Ed. F = *Mo.*
1.4.18 so = Q2. F = to **43 in** = Q2. F = I **44 light lights** = Ed. F = lights
lights **46 five** = Ed. F = fine **55 O . . . bodes** = *prose in* Q2/F, *verse in* Q
57 an = Q1/Q2. *Not in* F **65 film** = F2. F = Philome **68 maid** = Q1.
F = man **74 curtsies** *spelled* Cursies *in* F **75 dream** = Q2. F = dreamt
81 a = Q1/Q2. *Not in* F **88 ear** = Q2. F = eares **92 elflocks** = Q1.
F = Elk-locks **119 SH CHIEF SERVINGMAN** = Ed. F = *Ser.* **132 SH
CAPULET** = Ed. F = 1. *Capu.* **137 a bout** = Ed. F = about **142 SD** *they* =
Q2. F = *the* **157 SH CAPULET** = Q2 (1. *Capu.*). F = 3. *Cap.* **188 this** =
Q2. F = the **200 my** = Q2. F = the **216 ready** = Q1. F = did ready
259 wedding = Q1/Q2. F = wedded **267 learned** = Q1/Q2. F = learne

2.0.1 SH CHORUS = Ed. *Not in* F
2.1.8 SH MERCUTIO Nay . . . too = Q1. *Line assigned to Benvolio in* F
   11 but = Q2. F = me but **12 pronounce** = Q1. F = Prouant
   12 dove = Q1. F = day **14 heir** = Q1. F = her **18 and I** = Q2. F = I
   27 it there = Q2. F = it **40 open arse and** = Ed. F = open, or. Q1 = open
   Et caetera **65 eye** = F. Q1 = eyes **88 nor any other part** = Q1. *Not in* F
   89 Belonging . . . name = Ed. F = O be some other name / Belonging to
   a man **90 What's . . . name?** = Q1. F = What? in a names **139 love me**
   = Q2. F = Loue **142 laughs** = Q2. F = laught **150 more** = Q1. *Not in* F
   156 blessèd moon = Q2. F = Moone **209 toward** = Q2.
   F = towards **214 mine** = Q1. *Not in* F **220 nyas** = Ed. F = Neece
   239–240 Parting . . . morrow *assigned to Juliet as in* Q1. F *assigns to Romeo*
   241 SH ROMEO Sleep . . . breast! = Q1. F *assigns to Juliet*
2.2.95 households' = Q2. F = houshould
2.3.20 minim rests = Q2. F = minum **26 phantasimes** = Ed. F = phantacies
   41 the = Q2. F = the the **45 good Mercutio** = Q2. F = *Mercutio*
   49 curtsy *spelled* cursie *in* F **61 Switch** *spelled* Swits *in* F **73 then**
   well = Q2. F = well **94 for** = Q1/Q2. F = or **98 good e'en** *spelled* gooden
   in F **104 well said** = Q2. F = said **107 SH ROMEO** = Q1/Q2.
   F = *Nur.* **169 stay** = Q2. F = stay thou **180 man's** = Q2. F = man
   184 see a toad = Q2. F = a see Toade
2.4.11 Is = Q2. F = I **40 leg** = Q2. F = legs **43 gentle as** = Q2. F = gentle
   45 this = Q2. F = this this **52 that** = Q2. F = that that **52 not** = Q2.
   F = so
2.5.23 is his = Q2. F = in his **33 such** = Q2. F = such such **34 sum up sum**
   spelled sum vp some *in* F
3.1.27 ribbon *spelled* Riband *in* F **66 love** = Q2. F = lou'd **71 *stoccado***
   spelled stucatho *in* F **114 Mercutio is** = Q1/Q2. F = *Mercutio's* is
   117 more *spelled* mo *in* F **141 prince's name** = Q2. F = Princes
   names **152 bloody fray** = Q2. F = Fray **159 Tybalt** = Q2. F = *Tybalts*
   167 agile = Q1. F = aged **185 SH MONTAGUE** = Q4. F = *Cap.* **195 out** =
   Q2. F = our **199 but** = Q1/Q2. F = not
3.2.9 By = Q4. F = And by **38 welladay** *spelled* welady *in* F **38 he's**
   dead = Q2. F *omits third repetition* **51 shut** *spelled* shot *in* F **56 corpse**
   spelled Coarse *in* F *throughout* **58 swoonèd** *spelled* sounded *in* F
   62 one *spelled* on *in* F **74 SH NURSE** = Q1. *Assigned to Juliet in* F
   75 SH JULIET = Q1. *Assigned to the Nurse in* F **78 Dove-feathered** = Ed.
   F = Rauenous Doue-feather'd **81 damnèd** = Q4. F = dimne
   99 chide at = Q2. F = chide **112 word** = Q2. F = words **125 with** = Q2.
   F = which
3.3.48 Howling = Q2. F = Howlings **52 a little speak** = Q2. F = speake
   63 dispute = Q1/Q2. F = dispaire **65 I, Juliet thy** = Q2. F = *Iuliet*
   my **78 will?** F *here prints a redundant entry direction for the Nurse*

99 cancelled = Q1/Q2. F = conceal'd **105 deadly** = Q2. F = dead
120 lives = F2. F = lies **144 of** = Q1/Q2. F = or **144 blessings** = Q1/Q2.
F = blessing **146 mishavèd** = Q2. F = mishaped **147 pouts upon** = Q4.
F = puttest vp

3.4.35 very late = Q2. F = late

3.5.21 the = Q1. *Not in* F **35 light it** = Q1/Q2. F = itli ght **36 SD** *Enter*
Nurse = Ed. F = *Enter Madam and Nurse* **66 It is** = Q2. F = Is it
86 him = Q4. *Not in* F **115 that** = Q2. F = this **119 thee there** = Q2. F =
thee **123 woo** = Q2. F = woe **139 thy** = Q2. F = the **151 hate** = Q1/Q2.
F = haue **155 And . . . you?** = Q2. *Line omitted in* F, *probably due to com-*
positorial eyeskip **177 gossips** = Q2. F = gossip **179 SH CAPULET** = Q1.
F = Father *(printed as part of the dialogue)* **180 SH NURSE** = Q4. *Not in* F
182 bowl = Q2. F = bowles **186 tide** = Q2. F = ride **219 Alack** = Q2. F =
Hlacke **248 Is it** = Q1/Q2. F = It is

4.1.35 my face = Q2. F = thy face **41 we** = Q1/Q2. F = you **48 strains** =
Q2. F = streames **55 with this** = Q2. F = with' his **76 from** = Q1/Q2. F =
fro **79 off** *spelled* of *in* F **84 chapless** = Q1. F = chappels
86 tomb = Ed *(Q1 = Or lay me in tombe with one new dead).* F = graue
101 wanny = Ed. F = many **101 thy** = Q2. F = the **102 shuts** = Q2. F =
shut **117–18 and . . . waking** = Q3. *Not in* F, *due to compositorial eyeskip*
123 fear = Q2. F = care

4.3.17 life = Q2. F = fire **50 wake** = Q4. F = walke **58 a** = Q2. F = my

4.4.15 what is = Q2. F = what **16 SH SERVINGMAN** = Q1. F = *Fel.* **20 SH**
ANOTHER SERVINGMAN = Q1 *(Ser:).* F = *Fel.* **106 should** = Q2. F =
shouldst **116 us all** = Q2. F = all us **130 SH FIRST MUSICIAN** = Ed.
F = *Mu.* **138 of woe** = Q4. *Not in* F **138–139 O . . . me** = Q2. *Not in* F,
probably due to compositorial eyeskip **160, 163 Prates** = Q2. F = Pratest

5.1.3 lord *abbreviated* L. *in* F **4 this day** = Q2. F = thisan day **17 SH**
BALTHASAR = Q1. F = *Man. (throughout scene)* **19 lives** = Q2. F = live
34 No = Q2. F = Mo **35 SD** *Exit Man* = *positioned here in* Q1, *two lines*
earlier in F **40 a dwells** = Q2. F = dwells

5.3.1 aloof = Q2. F = aloft **3 yew** = Q1. F = young **19 way** = Q2.
F = wayes **20 rite** *spelled* right *in* F **22 SD** *Balthasar* = Q1. F = *Peter*
40 SH BALTHASAR = Q1. F = *Pet. (throughout scene)* **60 these** = Q2. F
= those **71 SH PAGE** = Q4. F = *Pet.* **94 art** = Q2. F = are
102–103 Shall . . . That = Ed. F = I will beleeue, / Shall I beleeue, that
143 Fear = Q2. F = feares **145 yew** = Ed. F = young **169 not away** = Q2.
F = notuaway **172 left** = Q2. F = lest **177 SH CONSTABLE** = Ed.
F = *Match. (for Watch., but has Con. at 192 and 196)* **179 This is** = Q2. F
= 'Tis in **180 SH PAGE** = Ed. F = *Boy.* **191 SH SECOND WATCHMAN**
= Ed. F = *Watch* **198 morning** = Q2. F = mornings **202 our** = Q2. F =
out **223 is in** = Q1/Q2. F = in is **281 SH BALTHASAR** = Q2.
F = *Boy.* **311 such** = Q2. F = that

SCENE-BY-SCENE ANALYSIS

PROLOGUE

The sonnet structure emphasizes the poetic nature of the play, a high proportion of which is in verse. The themes of love, conflict, and fate are introduced and, in revealing the outcome of the story, the deaths of the "star-crossed lovers' Romeo and Juliet are established as predestined. The meta-theatrical reference to the "two hours' traffic of our stage" establishes the repeated motif of time which gives intensity and pace to events and emphasizes the brevity of the lives and marriage of Romeo and Juliet.

ACT 1 SCENE 1

Lines 1–155: Sampson and Gregory discuss their hatred of the Montagues in a witty, bawdy exchange. They encounter two Montague Servingmen and provoke them to a fight. Benvolio tries to intervene, but Tybalt appears and, declaring that he hates "all Montagues," fights him. Lord and Lady Capulet arrive, followed by Lord and Lady Montague. The heads of the two houses threaten each other while being restrained by their wives, emphasizing the links and tensions between private and public that run throughout the play as the quarrel between the two families spills onto the streets of Verona. Prince Escalus announces that the next person to disturb the peace by fighting will be executed. The Montagues remain, questioning Benvolio about the quarrel, glad that Romeo does not seem to have been involved. Benvolio reveals that Romeo was out "early walking," "an hour before the worshipped sun." The sun is a key image in the play, used to create binary images of light and dark and life and death, as well as helping to evoke the progress of time. Montague describes his concern over his son's recent moods: his "tears" and "deep sighs" and how he "locks fair daylight out" of his chamber, creating "artificial night." Romeo

himself approaches and the Montagues leave Benvolio to speak
to him.

Lines 156–243: Benvolio learns that Romeo is in love, but that his
love is unrequited. With the exaggerated poeticism of a young lover,
Romeo offers to "groan and tell" who it is he loves, but is countered
by Benvolio's prosaic responses. Romeo explains that the girl he loves
has sworn herself to chastity, emphasizing the sexual side of love
that presents a counterpart to the more spiritual, poetic notions of
"romance" throughout the play. In an exchange that raises the
theme of sight and perception, Benvolio argues that Romeo should
"forget to think of her" and "Examine other beauties" instead, but
Romeo claims that "He that is strucken blind cannot forget / The precious treasure of his eyesight lost."

ACT 1 SCENE 2

Lines 1–37: Paris asks for Juliet's hand in marriage, but Montague
argues that she is too young: "She hath not seen the change of fourteen years." Despite Paris' argument that "Younger than she are
happy mothers made," Montague says that he must wait, but gives
him permission to "woo" Juliet and "get her heart," showing that he
favors the suit and that Juliet's husband will be subject to his choice
and approval rather than her own. He invites Paris to a "feast" that
night and sends his Servingman out with a list of invitations.

Lines 38–101: The Servingman cannot read, so appeals to Benvolio and Romeo to help. He thanks them by inviting them to the feast,
as long as they are "not of the house of Montagues." On the list is
Capulet's niece, Rosaline, the object of Romeo's unrequited love,
and Benvolio suggests that they go so that Romeo can compare Rosaline with other women and see that his "swan" is a "crow." His reference to the "crystal scales" of Romeo's eyes in which he can
weigh Rosaline "against some other maid" reinforces the motif of
sight and also raises the concept of opposition and balance which
is sustained throughout the play, as characters, themes, and con-
cepts of light/dark, life/death, male/female, and actions/words are
"weighed" against each other.

ACT 1 SCENE 3

In addition to her own deliberate bawdy humor, the Nurse becomes an unwitting figure of fun through her unconsciously long-winded and vulgar speeches. Lady Capulet tells her to call Juliet and then leave them to speak privately, but changes her mind and asks her to stay, perhaps emphasizing a closeness between the Nurse and Juliet that is lacking in the mother-daughter relationship. Juliet's youth is focused on again as Lady Capulet comments that she is of "a pretty age." The Nurse agrees, relating a lengthy, repetitious anecdote concerning an unwitting sexual innuendo made by the infant Juliet. She is finally silenced by Juliet, and Lady Capulet introduces the idea of marriage. Juliet says that this is "an honour" that she "dream[s] not of." With interruptions from the Nurse, Lady Capulet reveals that "The valiant Paris" seeks Juliet "for his love." Juliet promises that she will "look to like" Paris but, while her words are obedient, they are noncommittal.

ACT 1 SCENE 4

Lines 1–118: Romeo, Benvolio, and Mercutio are dressed as Masquers, a visual representation of the secrecy in the play. Romeo wishes to carry a torch rather than dance, but Mercutio insists that he join in. Their exchange reveals Mercutio's verbal dexterity and, once again, the tensions between "romance" and sex are emphasized as Romeo's declarations of love are given a bawdy twist by Mercutio. Romeo worries that they should not go because of a dream he has had, but Mercutio mocks him, claiming that Romeo has been with "Queen Mab." Mercutio is temporarily consumed by his own imagination and words in a fervent, fantastical description of Mab, which becomes more disturbing in its imagery until Romeo interrupts. Despite Benvolio's practical comments, Romeo insists that there is "Some consequence yet hanging in the stars," an "untimely death," emphasizing the presence of fortune/fate in the events of the play, and creating dramatic irony.

Lines 132–213: Capulet encourages everyone to dance. As he watches the dancers he reminisces about how long it is since he was "in a mask"—"thirty years" ago, establishing another contrast in the play: age and youth. Romeo sees Juliet and, struck by her beauty, declares that he did not "love till now." His description of Juliet reinforces the imagery of light and dark: she is "a snowy dove trooping with crows," but the references to a jewel and his claim that her beauty is "too rich for use," "too dear," also reinforce Juliet's potential status as a commodity within a patriarchal world. Tybalt recognizes Romeo's voice and, outraged at the intrusion, sends a servant for his rapier. Capulet tells him to be "content" and "take no note," as he does not want "a mutiny among [his] guests." The movement in Capulet's speech between reproving Tybalt and talking to his guests emphasizes the tension between public and private in this scene.

Lines 214–232: This tension is heightened as Romeo and Juliet speak, touch, and kiss for the first time: a poignantly intimate moment that takes place within a public space. Their initial exchange is in the form of a sonnet, each contributing a quatrain and then uniting in alternate lines. This echoes traditional expressions of romantic love, but perhaps also serves to remind us of the sonnet prologue and the destiny of the lovers. The pair use religious imagery throughout the exchange and, despite a loverlike wrangling, there is a unity in language, both of structure and imagery, that is in contrast with much of the verbal sparring—comic or aggressive—that has taken place so far in the play. Romeo is initially more forward, being more practiced at flirtation than youthful Juliet, but soon she is urging him to "Give me my sin again."

Lines 233–270: Juliet's Nurse interrupts, sending her to speak with her mother. Romeo takes the opportunity to ask who she is. Learning that she is a Capulet, he laments: "My life is my foe's debt." Juliet calls her Nurse and, seeming to inquire after a number of guests, contrives to find out Romeo's identity. She privately asserts that, if he is married, her "grave is like to be [her] wedding bed," echoing Romeo's earlier speeches that foreshadow their fate. The Nurse reveals that he is "Romeo, and a Montague" and, again echoing Romeo's words, Juliet declares: "My only love sprung from my only hate!"

ACT 2, CHORUS

A sonnet details Romeo's switch in allegiance from Rosaline to Juliet and the difficulties besetting the new lovers.

ACT 2 SCENE 1

Lines 1–45: Romeo hides as Mercutio and Benvolio look for him. When he does not respond, Mercutio (unaware that Romeo is now in love with Juliet) begins to mock him, first as a conventional lover who sighs and speaks in rhyme, and then becoming increasingly more bawdy, saying that Romeo wishes Rosaline "were / An open arse [slang name for the medlar fruit] and [he] a pop'rin pear." Benvolio decides that Romeo "means not to be found," and he and Mercutio leave.

Lines 46–248: Romeo begins to comment, but stops as he sees Juliet above. Using images of light to describe her once more, he claims that "Juliet is the sun," sustaining this celestial imagery (reinforced by their relative positions on the stage). Romeo's tone shifts toward physical desire as he wishes not just to watch but to touch: "O, that I were a glove upon that hand, / That I might touch that cheek." Juliet, believing herself alone, speaks and Romeo forms a dual audience with the one in theater. She declares her love and wishes that Romeo was not a Montague, saying that if he would be "but sworn" her love, she would "no longer be a Capulet." Romeo reveals his presence and declares that he will "be new baptized," reinforcing the religious imagery that runs throughout their exchanges. Shocked, Juliet demands to know who has intruded upon her "counsel" and, when Romeo identifies himself, fears that if her kinsmen find him there, they will kill him. Romeo claims that love helped him to "o'er-perch these walls" and that it will protect him. Juliet worries that Romeo will think her too forward and that their mutual declarations of love are "too rash, too unadvised, too sudden," but she acknowledges her love for him. During a series of "partings," as Juliet responds to calls from her Nurse and then returns to Romeo, Juliet declares that if Romeo's purpose is marriage, he must send word to her the next day "by the hour of nine."

ACT 2 SCENE 2

Friar Laurence is gathering herbs, showing his knowledge of their various properties. Romeo interrupts and the Friar is surprised to see him so early, guessing that "Romeo hath not been in bed tonight." When Romeo confirms this, Friar Laurence assumes that he has been with Rosaline, and is relieved when Romeo claims that he has "forgot that name." However, when Romeo confesses his love for Juliet and asks the Friar to marry them, Friar Laurence is skeptical, reminding Romeo of his all-consuming love for Rosaline and suggesting that "Young men's love then lies / Not truly in their hearts, but in their eyes." Romeo insists that he loves Juliet and, more important, she loves him, which Rosaline did not. Friar Laurence relents, deciding that marriage between Romeo and Juliet may turn their "households' rancor to pure love."

ACT 2 SCENE 3

Mercutio and Benvolio believe Romeo is still pining for "hard-hearted" Rosaline. Benvolio reports that a challenge to Romeo from Tybalt has been delivered at the Montague house. When Romeo arrives, Mercutio continues his usual mockery. Romeo responds and there is a fast-paced, witty exchange that contrasts with the lower comedy that is generated after the arrival of the Nurse. She is looking for "the young Romeo" and, after Mercutio has poked fun at her, he and Benvolio leave. More humor is created by the Nurse's verbosity and Romeo's attempts to get her to listen, but eventually he arranges that she will tell Juliet to go to Friar Laurence's cell that afternoon to be "shrived and married." He also tells her to wait for his man, who will bring a rope ladder for her to let down to him that night.

ACT 2 SCENE 4

Juliet anxiously waits for the Nurse who "promised to return" in "half an hour," but has been gone for three, another of the increasing references to time, creating a growing sense of urgency and transience. The Nurse arrives and teases Juliet with her procrastinating, but eventually tells her to go to Friar Laurence's cell, as "There stays a husband to make you a wife."

ACT 2 SCENE 5

The Friar and Romeo wait for Juliet and, again foreshadowing the tragic conclusion of the play, the Friar cautions against impetuous love, as "These violent delights have violent ends." Juliet arrives and the Friar leads them away to be married.

ACT 3 SCENE 1

In contrast to the privacy of the Friar's cell, and the romantic nature of the last few scenes, the action moves to the public arena of Verona's streets and focuses on violence and issues of male honor. It is hot, and Benvolio tries to persuade Mercutio to "retire," as such heat makes "mad blood" stir and that they "shall not scape a brawl" with the Capulets. Mercutio, somewhat unjustly, retorts that Benvolio is as capable of a quarrel as "any in Italy," and they are interrupted by Tybalt, looking for Romeo. As Mercutio and Tybalt's exchange becomes more heated, Benvolio again urges reason: they are in a "public haunt" and should withdraw to "some private place." Romeo arrives and Tybalt commands him to "turn and draw." Romeo refuses, caught between loyalty to his own household and that of his new wife. Although he cannot explain, he refuses to fight, assuring Tybalt that he has a reason to love him.

Frustrated by what he sees as "dishonourable, vile submission," Mercutio draws his sword on Tybalt. As Romeo and Benvolio try to part them, Tybalt stabs Mercutio and flees. Repeatedly calling down "A plague o'both the houses," Mercutio is led away to his death. Tybalt reappears and Romeo's anger is roused by his "triumph" in Mercutio's death, and they fight until Romeo kills Tybalt. Benvolio urges him to "begone" as he will be executed, and Romeo cries that he is "fortune's fool!" before escaping. Prince Escalus arrives with Montague and Capulet and their wives. Benvolio describes what has happened, emphasizing Romeo's initial refusal to fight. Each family blames the other and demands justice for their dead. Escalus decides to banish Romeo.

ACT 3 SCENE 2

Juliet's language shows an awakened sexual awareness as she impatiently invokes the night, claiming that she has "bought the mansion of a love / But not possessed it." Her Nurse arrives and Juliet demands news of Romeo, but all that the Nurse can repeat is "he's dead." Juliet understands this to mean Romeo and is overcome with grief until the Nurse mentions Tybalt, upon which Juliet believes them both to be dead. When the Nurse finally explains, Juliet finds herself in a position similar to that of Romeo in the previous scene as her loyalties are torn between her family and her husband, but she immediately defends Romeo when the Nurse curses him. Juliet laments Romeo's banishment, fearing that she will "die maiden-widowèd" and declares her intention to kill herself. The Nurse promises to find Romeo and bring him to Juliet, taking a ring to give to him.

ACT 3 SCENE 3

Romeo is hiding in Friar Laurence's cell when the Friar brings him news of his banishment, describing it as a "gentler judgement" than death. Romeo disagrees, arguing that "Heaven is here, / Where Juliet lives." He refuses the Friar's attempts to console him and throws himself to the ground. The Nurse arrives and urges him to "stand up" and "be a man: / For Juliet's sake." This appeal to his masculinity is echoed by the Friar; when Romeo threatens to stab himself he asks "Art thou a man?" and suggests that Romeo's tears are "womanish." He outlines a plan: Romeo will go to Juliet until he must leave for Mantua. Once he is in exile, they will find a way to put things right. The Nurse gives Romeo Juliet's ring, and the Friar promises to send news to Romeo in exile.

ACT 3 SCENE 4

Capulet tells his wife and Paris that Juliet will be "ruled" by him, and that Lady Capulet is to tell her she will be married to Paris on Thursday. The pace of events is emphasized, particularly by Capulet's observation that "It is so very late, / That we may call it early."

ACT 3 SCENE 5

Lines 1–64: Juliet tries to persuade Romeo that it is not yet morning: "It was the nightingale, and not the lark" that he heard. He explains that he must either leave or die, but at her refusal to acknowledge the dawn and their consequent separation, Romeo submits and says that he will face death. Juliet then insists that he leave and the Nurse interrupts to warn them of Lady Capulet's imminent arrival. The lovers say farewell and, in another ironic foreshadowing of their destinies, Juliet observes that Romeo is as pale "As one dead in the bottom of a tomb."

Lines 65–129: Lady Capulet misunderstands Juliet's tears as continued grief for Tybalt, and their subsequent conversation is filled with irony as Lady Capulet assumes that Juliet hates Romeo and Juliet manages to sustain dual meanings in everything that she says, reflecting the theme of concealment and Juliet's separation from her family. Lady Capulet breaks the news that Juliet is to be married to Paris "early next Thursday morn," but Juliet refuses. She is in an impossible situation: she cannot marry Paris but she cannot reveal her reasons to her family.

Lines 130–213: Juliet repeats her refusal to her father, who is furious. His violent rage contrasts with the tenderness of the lovers at the beginning of the scene, and these extremities of mood perhaps reflect Juliet's turmoil at this point. Capulet reiterates his patriarchal authority and his "right" to dispose of her in marriage, threatening to disown her if she refuses: "An you be mine, I'll give you to my friend, / An you be not, hang, beg, starve, die in the streets." Juliet appeals to her mother, but Lady Capulet declares that she has "done" with her daughter.

Lines 214–254: Juliet's final appeal is to her Nurse, but she also urges her to marry Paris, a "betrayal" that breaks the bond that has existed between them until now. After sending the Nurse to tell her mother that she has gone to Friar Laurence, Juliet acknowledges this break with her "counsellor" Nurse, declaring: "Thou and my bosom henceforth shall be twain." She decides that if the Friar cannot help her, she will kill herself.

ACT 4 SCENE 1

The relatively short scenes that make up this act increase the pace of the action and reinforce a sense of the unalterable direction of events.

Lines 1–44: Paris is at Friar Laurence's cell, arranging his marriage to Juliet. The Friar is concerned by how soon the wedding is to be, but Paris explains that he has Capulet's blessing, as they believe that Juliet is grieving "immoderately" for Tybalt and that marriage will "stop the inundation of her tears." Juliet arrives and Paris greets her as "my lady and my wife," but Juliet's responses are reserved. She asks the Friar if he can hear her confession and Paris leaves, giving Juliet a "holy kiss"—an ironic reminder of her first meeting with Romeo.

Lines 45–128: Juliet tells the Friar that unless his wisdom can prevent her marriage, she will kill herself, showing him a knife. He replies that his solution is as "desperate" as the event they are trying to prevent: Juliet is to "consent / To marry Paris," but on the night before her wedding she must drink the "distilling liquor" that he will give her. This will make her appear to be dead for "two-and-forty hours." Friar Laurence will get word to Romeo and, once Juliet has been placed in the Capulet vault, Romeo will come and take her away to Mantua. Juliet agrees.

ACT 4 SCENE 2

Juliet tells her father that she has repented. Capulet declares that the marriage will take place the next day.

ACT 4 SCENE 3

Having selected her wedding clothes, Juliet says good night to her Nurse and her mother. Her soliloquy begins with a series of questions, revealing her uncertainty and concerns that the potion will not work, or that it will kill her in a "subtle" plan by Friar Laurence to prevent her telling of his role in the secret marriage. Her imagination conjures up the horrors of the tomb, including the body of

Tybalt "fest'ring in his shroud," but she resolves to take the potion, drinking to Romeo as she does so.

ACT 4 SCENE 4

Lines 1–129: Preparations are under way for the wedding and Capulet sends the Nurse to wake Juliet. The Nurse duly finds her "dead" and calls for her parents. The Friar and Paris arrive to take Juliet to church and are told the news. The Capulets, Paris, and the Nurse indulge in violent grief until the Friar offers reasoned, spiritual advice, arguing that Juliet "is advanced / Above the clouds, as high as heaven itself." Capulet orders that the wedding preparations become those for a funeral.

Lines 130–172: In contrast with the rest of the scene, there is a comic exchange between the Servingman, Peter, and the Musicians.

ACT 5 SCENE 1

Romeo is in Mantua, recounting a dream in which Juliet found him dead but revived him with kisses. Balthasar interrupts and gives him the news of Juliet's death. Romeo declares: "I deny you stars," and announces his intention to return to Verona. After Balthasar leaves, Romeo calls on an Apothecary, knowing that the man is so poor that he will willingly sell him poison. Romeo leaves with a poison so strong that, if he "had the strength / Of twenty men," it would kill him "straight."

ACT 5 SCENE 2

Friar Laurence learns from Friar John that his message never reached Romeo, and he hurries to the Capulet tomb for Juliet's waking.

ACT 5 SCENE 3

Lines 1–124: Paris lays flowers at the tomb. His Page signals that someone is approaching and Paris withdraws to watch, again creating a dual audience to the action and establishing a series of observers and intruders on Romeo and Juliet's final moments, so that their deaths, like their first meeting, become a public rather than a private event. Romeo takes a "mattock and wrenching iron" from Balthasar, gives him a letter to Lord Montague and tells him to leave. Balthasar, however, conceals himself nearby as he doubts Romeo's "intents." Paris recognizes Romeo and, believing that he intends "some villainous scheme / To the dead bodies," challenges him. Romeo, not recognizing Paris, warns him to "tempt not a desp'rate man." They fight and Romeo kills Paris, whose last request is to be laid beside Juliet. Romeo recognizes the man he has killed and declares that he will bury him in a "triumphant grave," opening the tomb. He marvels at the beauty of Juliet and comments ironically that she does not seem dead. He says farewell, takes the poison, and, "with a kiss," he dies.

Lines 125–179: Friar Laurence hurries to the tomb and sees Balthasar. He learns that Romeo has already entered, and when he goes in, he finds the bodies of Romeo and Paris. As he does so, Juliet awakes and asks for Romeo. The Friar is forced to tell her that he is dead, and urges her to come "from that nest / Of death" quickly, as the Watch is coming. He leaves, and Juliet finds the empty poison bottle, observing that Romeo has "left no friendly drop" to help her die. She kisses Romeo, and, hearing the Watch, she stabs herself.

Lines 180–320: While some Watchmen discover the bodies and send for the Capulets and the Montagues, others enter holding Balthasar and then the Friar. Prince Escalus and the families arrive, although Montague is alone: his wife has died from grief at Romeo's banishment. Friar Laurence reveals the events that have led to this point in a statement that will both "condemn" and "purge" him. Capulet and Montague make peace, but this resolution has come at a high price.

ROMEO AND JULIET IN PERFORMANCE: THE RSC AND BEYOND

The best way to understand a Shakespeare play is to see it or ideally to participate in it. By examining a range of productions, we may gain a sense of the extraordinary variety of approaches and interpretations that are possible—a variety that gives Shakespeare his unique capacity to be reinvented and made "our contemporary" four centuries after his death.

We begin with a brief overview of the play's theatrical and cinematic life, offering historical perspectives on how it has been performed. We then analyze in more detail a series of productions staged over the last half century by the Royal Shakespeare Company. The sense of dialogue between productions that can only occur when a company is dedicated to the revival and investigation of the Shakespeare canon over a long period, together with the uniquely comprehensive archival resource of promptbooks, program notes, reviews, and interviews held on behalf of the RSC at the Shakespeare Birthplace Trust in Stratford-upon-Avon, allows an "RSC stage history" to become a crucible in which the chemistry of the play can be explored.

We then go to the horse's mouth. Modern theater is dominated by the figure of the director. He or she must hold together the whole play, whereas the actor must concentrate on his or her part. The director's viewpoint is therefore especially valuable. And finally, we offer the actor's perspective: a view of the play through the eyes of Romeo and Juliet.

FOUR CENTURIES OF ROMEO AND JULIET: AN OVERVIEW

Romeo and Juliet is one of Shakespeare's most popular plays, written around 1595–96, although there is no direct evidence of specific performance dates before the Restoration. Nevertheless, the early printed texts suggest that it was popular from the start; the First Quarto of 1597 claims that "it hath been often (with great applause) played publicly, by the right Honorable the Lord of Hunsdon his Servants"; the Second Quarto, two years later, says it is "Newly corrected, augmented and amended as it hath been sundry times publicly acted by the right Honourable the Lord Chamberlain his servants," while the Third Quarto, after the accession of James I, when the Lord Chamberlain's Men became the King's Men, repeats the claim that "it hath been sundry times publicly acted by the King's Majesty's Servants." We know that the company comedian Will Kempe played Peter, since "Kemp" appears in places instead of the speech prefix. The stage directions also tell us something about how the play must have been staged, requiring an upper staging, a bed and a discovery space, and the stage properties required. There is good evidence that the company's leading actor, Richard Burbage, played the part of Romeo.

The first recorded performance after the Restoration was by Sir William Davenant's Duke's Company at Lincoln's Inn Fields in 1662. Samuel Pepys attended the opening on 1 March:

> and thence to the Opera and there saw *Romeo and Julett*, the first time it was acted. But it is the play of itself the worst that ever I heard in my life, and the worst acted that ever I saw these people do; and I am resolved to go no more to see the first time of acting, for they were all of them out more or less.[1]

In his *Roscius Anglicanus*, the bookkeeper of Davenant's company, John Downes, mentions a tragicomic adaptation by James Howard in which the lovers survive, which may have been the play that Pepys saw. Downes' cast list names Henry Harris as Romeo, Mary Saunderson as Juliet (the first female to play the part), and Thomas Betterton as Mercutio. In a later revival, Shakespeare's and Howard's plays were alternated. Downes also mentions the occasion on which,

> there being a fight and scuffle in this play, between the House of Capulet, and House of Paris; Mrs Holden acting his wife,

entered in a hurry, crying 'O my dear Count!' She inadver-
tently left out 'O' in the pronunciation of the word 'Count!' giving it a vehement accent, put the house into such laughter,
that London Bridge at low-water was silence to it.[2]

Howard's version set a precedent for cutting, adapting, and rewriting
the play. Shakespeare's text, with its mix of comedy and tragedy and
bawdy language, was out of tune with Restoration sensibility and
was not performed again until Theophilus Cibber's 1744 production.

In 1677 Davenant's company staged Thomas Otway's adaptation
The History and Fall of Caius Marius, in which the plot of *Romeo and
Juliet* is transposed to ancient Rome and given a contemporary political slant, being set against the background of civil war. Otway introduced other changes, including a scene in Juliet's garden where the
lovers, Marius and Lavinia, played by Thomas Betterton and Elizabeth Barry, say their farewells. In the final act, Lavinia wakes before
Marius dies, a variation retained by Cibber and Garrick. The most
popular performances, though, were Cave Underhill as Sulpitius
(Mercutio) and James Nokes' comic turn as the Nurse.

Cibber's 1744 revival advertised itself as Shakespeare's play "not
acted once these 100 years," but was in fact an amalgamation of
Romeo and Juliet and *The Two Gentlemen of Verona*, with elements from
Otway's play plus his own additions. Cibber cast himself as Romeo
and his fourteen-year-old daughter, Jennie, as Juliet. Two years later,
Thomas Sheridan mounted a successful production at Smock Alley
in Dublin. In 1748 Garrick staged the play at Drury Lane with
Spranger Barry and Susannah Cibber as the leads. When they left for
Covent Garden, Garrick took over the part of Romeo himself, with
George Anne Bellamy as Juliet. They were thus in direct competition
and critics were undecided as to which they preferred. This was one
anonymous female spectator's verdict:

Had I been Juliet to Garrick's Romeo,—so ardent and impas-
sioned was he, I should have expected that he would *come up* to
me in the balcony; but had I been Juliet to Barry's Romeo, so
tender, so eloquent, and so seductive was he, I should certainly
have *gone down* to him![3]

The critic Arthur Murphy however, under his pseudonym "Theatricus," objected that all four leading actors "seem to want what no actor can truly feign, no spectator can thoroughly be deceived in; I mean that degree of puberty, which is but just distinguished from childhood."[4] Moreover, playgoers objected to the limited choice which the same play in both licensed theaters offered, and an anonymous contributor to the London Magazine complained:

> Well—what to night? Says angry Ned,
>   As up from bed he rouses:
> Romeo again!—and shakes his head,
>   Ah! Pox on both your houses.[5]

Garrick's adaptation, used in both productions and designed to clarify plot, focused on the lovers, eliminated Rosaline and all other extraneous elements including, according to Garrick's advertisement, its "jingle and quibble" (rhyming and punning), and included a "new duologue for the lovers in which they go successively mad";[6] it was phenomenally successful, holding the stage for almost a century.

John Philip Kemble, using Garrick's text practically unaltered, played Romeo in a handful of performances, and Sarah Siddons played Juliet only once. Edmund Kean's Romeo was equally uninspired; according to the normally enthusiastic William Hazlitt, "Mr Kean . . . stood like a statue of lead."[7] William Charles Macready rarely performed the play, and although Charles Kemble's Romeo had been well received, he was better known for his Mercutio, the role he played when his daughter Fanny made her theatrical debut to great acclaim as Juliet in 1829. There were notable nineteenth-century Juliets, such as Adelaide Neilson and Helen Faucit, but the part of Romeo was coming to be perceived as problematic for leading tragic actors.

In the event, the role and Shakespeare's play was restored to the repertory by a woman, the great American actress Charlotte Cushman, playing Romeo as a breeches part in her production at the Haymarket in 1845, with her sister, Susan, playing Juliet. Cushman excised most of Garrick's additions and restored Rosaline, but not Shakespeare's wordplay; her textual cuts served on the whole to enhance Romeo's role still further. It was a theatrical triumph and critics were unanimous in their praise:

> It is enough to say that the Romeo of Miss Cushman is far superior to any Romeo that has been seen for years. The distinction is not one of degree, it is one of kind. For a long time Romeo has been a convention. Miss Cushman's Romeo is a creative, a living, breathing, animated, ardent, human being. The memory of play-goers will call up Romeo as a collection of speeches delivered with more or less eloquence, not as an individual. Miss Cushman has given the vivifying spark, whereby the fragments are knit together, and become an organized entirety.[8]

A number of productions followed Cushman's success. Edwin Booth's for the 1869 opening night of Booth's Theater, New York, proved a great popular success with its spectacular decor:

> Picturesque Italian streets, luxurious gardens, gay and bright interiors, and the solemn, cypress-shaded precincts of the tomb unite in the ever-changing picture, and create such an absorbing illusion that the spectator of the loves, happiness, sorrow, and wretched fate of Romeo and Juliet may follow them with a sense of their reality and nearness as if he were indeed living in a remote past, walking about the streets and partaking of the current experience of Verona and Mantua three hundred years ago.[9]

Henry Irving's production at the Lyceum in 1882 was similarly magnificent:

> This was the market-place place at Verona, busy with its buying and selling. Donkeys, children, a picturesque conduit on the centre stage, a sloping bridge in the background, life, animation, and color, groupings all admirably arranged and studied, presented themselves to the expectant gaze.[10]

Henry James was less complimentary about the acting: "Mr Irving is not a Romeo; Miss Terry is not a Juliet; and no one else save Mrs Stirling [playing the Nurse], is anything in particular."[11] George Bernard Shaw was no more enthusiastic about Johnston Forbes-Robertson's 1895 revival at the Lyceum with Mrs. Patrick Campbell as Juliet in which he found the actors miscast and the production tame: "Mr Forbes Robertson has evidently no sympathy for Shakespeare's love of a shindy: you see his love of law and order coming out in his stage management of the fighting scenes."[12]

Reaction against visually spectacular productions came with William Poel and the Elizabethan Stage Society, dedicated to producing Shakespeare's plays, employing full texts and original staging conditions as far as possible. The venture was not a financial success, but its influence on a new generation of directors was long-lasting and profound. *Romeo and Juliet* was the Society's final production in 1905 and Poel cast two teenage unknowns, Esmé Percy and Dorothy Minto, in the lead roles. The production lasted only four performances and not everyone was convinced—the *Academy*'s reviewer adverted to the Romantic notion that Shakespeare can never adequately translate from study to stage[13]—but the critic J. C. Trewin recognized its significance and found that "for the first time it became endurable. I sat at it with Granville Barker* . . . the lovers, instead of cold technique, brought the ardour of extreme youth."[14]

John Gielgud brought many of Poel's ideas on simple staging, fast-moving action, and simple verse-speaking to his productions of the play at the Oxford University Dramatic Society in 1932 and the Old Vic in 1935. In the Oxford production, Gielgud cast male students against Peggy Ashcroft as Juliet and Edith Evans as the Nurse. These two reprised their roles in the Old Vic production in which Gielgud and Laurence Olivier alternated the roles of Romeo and Mercutio. The critic James Agate recognized that "The difficulty of producing plays written for the Elizabethan and transferred to the picture stage must always be resolved by compromise, which means that good and bad must go hand in hand." In his view, the good in this production was that "it enabled that fiery-footed steed which is

---

*Harley Granville Barker was a leading member of the Elizabethan Stage Society who had played the lead in Poel's 1899 *Richard II*. He went on to become a successful director, critic, and playwright.

this tragedy to gallop sufficiently apace"; the bad was that the permanent set, designed to avoid scene changes, was cumbersome, so that "the action seemed to take place not so much in Verona as in a corner of it." He also found fault with the lighting—"gone were the sun and warmth of Italy and the whole thing happened at night, the tomb scene being the cheerfullest of all!" while "The costumes were charming, even if the football jerseys of the rival factions reminded us less of Montague and Capulet than of Wanderers and Wolves."[15]

Critics expressed reservation concerning individual performances, but most were agreed that, overall, Gielgud's production "brings out to the full the cruelty of the lovers' fate."[16] *The Times* thought the production's "principal fascination" lay in "Miss Peggy Ashcroft's Juliet [in which] art and temperament perpetually seem to be moving hand in hand. Her performance is memorable for the exquisite naturalness with which it holds the character to the plane of poetry."[17] Edith Evans' Nurse was similarly admired: "Miss Edith Evans, as the Nurse, is a grand piece of nature to the fingertips; . . . Her performance alone would make it imperative to see this revival."[18] Odious as comparisons might be, in this case they were inevitable, and most agreed with Agate: "Mr Olivier's Romeo showed himself very much in love but rather butchered the poetry, whereas Mr Gielgud carves the verse . . . exquisitely . . . Yet is this Romeo ever really in love with anybody except himself?"[19]

Peter Brook's 1947 production at the Shakespeare Memorial theatre in Stratford was described in *The Times* as a "recklessly spectacular version . . . which sacrifices poetry, acting, and even the story itself, to pictorial splendour."[20] However, individual performances were praised:

Paul Scofield's magnetic Mercutio and Myles Eason's superbly feline Tybalt were outstanding . . . Beatrix Lehmann's Nurse was a striking performance, sufficiently vulgar and sentimental to provide a proper background for Juliet without stealing her scenes. Laurence Payne's Romeo was virile, even violent, but it lacked subtlety and variety . . . Daphne Slater's Juliet was young and fresh, and she was successful in conveying the

1. Peter Brook's 1947 production: Paul Scofield as Mercutio, Laurence Payne as Romeo, and John Harrison as Benvolio.

pathos of the role, but she has not yet the resources for the highest moments, and her big scenes lacked variety.[21]

The problem, as ever, was finding leading actors who looked sufficiently young to be credible in the parts while experienced enough to do them justice.

In 1960 Franco Zeffirelli, the anglophile Italian designer and director who had established his reputation in critically acclaimed productions of Italian opera at Covent Garden in the late 1950s, was invited to direct *Romeo and Juliet* for the Old Vic Company. His shows were characterized by "naturalism," narrative simplicity, and beautiful sets. This was his first Shakespeare play. He wanted to appeal to a young audience and to bring out the passion of the play. He cut everything that he regarded as extraneous, which didn't add to the play's narrative drive, including Servants, Musicians, Petrarchan exchanges early in the play, narrative accounts of events that the audience had seen, Friar Laurence's advice, as well as numerous individual lines, and much of the last two acts. In total he cut about a thousand lines, roughly one third of the text, and concentrated on delivering a romantic, fast-paced production.[22] The production introduced Judi Dench as Juliet and John Stride as Romeo. Critics were struck by its freshness and vitality: "Last Tuesday at the Old Vic a foreign director approached Shakespeare with fresh eyes, quick wits and no stylistic preconceptions; and what he worked was a miracle." Kenneth Tynan goes on to detail the features which produced its success and to rebut critics nostalgic for a more traditional approach:

> The characters were neither larger nor smaller than life; they were precisely life-size, and we watched them living, spontaneously and unpredictably. The director had taken the simple and startling course of treating them as if they were real people in a real situation; and of asking himself just how those people, in that situation would behave. It sounds obvious enough; yet the result . . . is a revelation, even perhaps a revolution. Nobody on stage seems to be aware that he is appearing in an immortal tragedy, or indeed in a tragedy of any kind; instead, the actors behave like ordinary human beings, trapped in a quandary whose outcome they cannot foretell. Handled thus realistically, it is sometimes said, Shakespeare's essential quality gets lost. I passionately demur. What gets lost is not Shakespeare but the formal, dehumanized stereotype that we have so often made of him.[23]

"Meaning and character were wedded," he concludes, "and out of their interaction poetry arose. The production evoked a whole town, a whole riotous manner of living, so abundant and compelling was the life on stage that I could not wait to find out what happened next. The Vic has done nothing better for a decade."[24] The production was a huge box-office success and went on to tour the world. Zeffirelli drew on his experience of staging this production when making his popular and influential 1968 film version.

Numbers of productions of *Romeo and Juliet* have increased dramatically in recent years—the RSC alone has mounted fifteen at

Stratford since Brook's in 1947, which are discussed in detail below. The play's continuing popularity is due to the archetypal appeal of its stark, tragic plot and youthful protagonists, which educationalists believe likely to engage the sympathies of a young audience, and hence to its frequent inclusion in school syllabuses. The nature of the plot has also made it ideal for updating and adapting to a range of different cultural scenarios, from Prague in 1963, to East Berlin in 1981 and Canada in Robert LePage's 1991 bilingual *Roméo et Juliette* with francophone Capulets and anglophone Montagues.[25]

While capitalizing on inherent dramatic possibilities, setting the play in politically explosive situations can skew the text, as Katherine Duncan-Jones points out in her review of Tim Supple's 2000 production at the National Theatre in which Montagues were black and Capulets white:

> The racial differentiation of the Capulets and Montagues turns out to throw this well constructed play badly off balance. Their "ancient grudge" no longer looks like pointless prolonged feuding between families whose culture and ambitions are identical, for it appears to derive from antagonisms between races that are all too recognizable, and recognizably intransigent.[26]

Nevertheless, she concludes, in practice, "different-race casting has surprisingly little effect."

Over the course of four centuries, the play has undergone translation and transformation not only to new settings but across different languages and media, including "[m]ore than thirty operas . . . ranging from Benda's and Schwanenberger's (both dated 1776) to . . . Gounod's *Roméo et Juliette* (1867)."[27] The best known and most popular is Leonard Bernstein's *West Side Story*, which locates the story in late twentieth-century New York. Famous ballets were choreographed to the music of Tchaikovsky and Prokofiev. Douglas Lanier lists film and television adaptations from Merchant Ivory's *Shakespeare Wallah* (1965), set in India, to the Marvel Comics' *Uncanny X-Men volume 5: She Lies with Angels* (2004).[28]

Romeo and Juliet has been one of the most frequently filmed of Shakespeare's plays. A number of silent versions were shot between

1902 and 1926 and several sound versions before Irving Thalberg and George Cukor's 1936 Hollywood production with Norma Shearer and Leslie Howard in the title roles, and Renato Castellani's Anglo-Italian version of 1954. The best known, most successful, and most widely available films are Franco Zeffirelli's 1968 version and Baz Luhrmann's of 1996. Zeffirelli's film was a logical extension of his 1960 stage production. His determination to popularize Shakespeare had resulted in the immensely successful 1966 film version of *The Taming of the Shrew* with Richard Burton and Elizabeth Taylor. Two years later he filmed *Romeo and Juliet* and, as Jill Levenson explains, "Conceptualising the film, Zeffirelli repeated his earlier methods in theory and practice. This time, of course, he was able to carry many cinematic ideas to their logical conclusions."[29] Both Zeffirelli's and Luhrmann's films are visually brilliant but quite different in setting and filmic approach. Zeffirelli re-creates medieval Verona, whereas Luhrmann transports the scene to Verona Beach, a suburb in modern-day America:

> [Zeffirelli's] film is melodramatic and linear, highlighting the role of fate and the sense that the story of Romeo and Juliet could not have ended differently. Luhrmann's interpretation of Shakespeare's text, on the other hand, pays homage not only to the primary source, but also to filmic versions that came before. However, Luhrmann's depiction of the two young lovers, Leonardo DiCaprio and Claire Danes, marks a definitive departure from Zeffirelli's in that his two young lovers are more grounded and reflective and show more of an inner maturity and strength of character; his depiction of adolescence through these two characters is more worldly. Luhrmann's *Romeo and Juliet* makes much use of flashback and flashforward to add to the drama of the script. His style suggests irony and downplays the role of fate in the story.[30]

Both films have attracted much critical attention, not all of it favorable. Luhrmann's in particular has raised critical hackles: "Can Shakespeare's tragedy withstand the shock of the modern and the playful inventiveness of such postmodern tomfoolery as this movie

2. Gangs in a modern "Verona Beach": Mercutio (Harold Perrineau) reaches for Romeo's (Leonardo DiCaprio) gun (trademark "Sword") in Baz Luhrmann's 1996 movie *William Shakespeare's Romeo + Juliet*.

employs? It's a judgment call at best."[31] For others, though, it was a brilliant opening up of Shakespeare to a young audience.

AT THE RSC

Often the search for a socially relevant context for the story of two young lovers caught in the crossfire of their parents rivalry leads directors to try and find a motive for their ancient grudge, whether it's race, religion or color. I've seen black Montagues and white Capulets, protestant and catholic, Israeli and Arab and famously the Jets and the Puerto Rican Sharks in West Side New York . . . However many times the play is done, whatever slant is put upon it, whether enlightening or obstructive, the play itself, the text, will always be there.[32]

The frequency with which *Romeo and Juliet* has been performed has led to problems, which critics, who brace themselves for another retread of the famous tragedy, are quick to pick up on. How to make it different, how to give it a new relevance when a production is put on every few years, challenges every director and actor coming to the play. It is interesting when reading interviews with actors that they usually claim never to have seen a production of *Romeo and Juliet* before taking it on. How is this possible, one wonders! The baggage that comes with the play, the past "definitive" productions, performances, and film versions obviously weigh heavily. In 2004 Matthew Rhys, who played Romeo, worried that the audience would be "disappointed when they see I don't look like Leonardo DiCaprio!"[33]

Productions since the 1960s have taken a definite shift toward seeking out an emotional and psychological truth behind the characters. Performances of Romeo are often referred to as "Hamlet in love,"[34] the excitement and passion of love mixed with a deep melancholy fatalism. Juliets have become more sexually aware, and have been portrayed as the more dominant of the couple, driving the relationship forward. Mercutio's scathing words about love and his rash actions are sometimes attributed to an unrequited homosexual desire for Romeo. Directors have focused on darker elements in the play: violence, hate, and fatalism. Due to the very nature of the story, directors wish to make the play fresh and accessible. A play which appeals to, and is still amazingly relevant for young people, it is often a chosen text for schools, and a first introduction to Shakespeare on the stage. And this, too, one senses, is at the back of every director's mind.

> In terms of theatrical interpretation since the middle of the twentieth century, Verona has become more of a living city and less of a Renaissance ideal, the bawdy humor has been given freer expression, and the lovers are now measured by the standards of modern young people rather than a poetic and artistic ideal . . . However, the situations and behavior of the protagonists can seem to echo modern preoccupations in ways that enliven and fuel performances and engage young audiences.[35]

In Fair Verona We Set Our Scene?

Directors have not often chosen to make reference to an Italianate setting, despite the very specific locale of the play. Creating a coherent community and appropriate atmosphere for the play's action has become more important when representing the play for a modern audience. This less specific attention to Italian references demonstrates an emphasis on the accessibility of the play. Some productions have made very clear distinctions in the hierarchical structure of the Veronese society, whereas others have done away with this altogether. The importance of the society in shaping the destiny of Romeo and Juliet, however, cannot be overestimated. A modern setting obviously makes the play more immediate, but does lead to questions as to why a young woman like Juliet would not run off with her lover and settle down in Mantua with him, when she has already defied her parents by marrying him. To contemporary audiences and theater critics since the 1960s, this has proved a continual stumbling block in the credibility of the plot. The setting is therefore extremely important in any production of this play in making the plight of the lovers believable.

Michael Boyd's 1999 production, staged in the Royal Shakespeare Theatre and designed by Tom Piper, avoided specific place and time by having an abstract set which fulfilled a symbolic purpose:

> It was a non-specific design, basically two curving walls, facing each other, that could represent different things throughout the evening—whether they were the orchard walls that Romeo climbs, the wall under Juliet's balcony, or, more symbolically, a simple representation of the two families, ever present and immovably solid.[36]

The simple but effective bleakness of the set was criticized by some critics who referred to it as a "hostile, inner-city multi-storey car-park." However, the intensity of love was thrown into sharp relief in this threatening, violent and barren world: "Boyd placed the tragedy of love in a hostile environment, a bare platform with a runway down through the auditorium and two walls of plain wood curving into a 'blind' exit at the back of the stage."[37] As well as symbolically representing the fissure in which the hate of the feuding families festers and Romeo and Juliet's love flourishes, the immovable curved walls appeared to symbolize tragic fate and the inevitability of

tragedy for two people whose love could have brought harmony out
of anarchy and violence.

Michael Attenborough's 1997 production staged in the Swan
Theatre stripped the play of any pomp and the traditional class defi-
nitions associated with the socially powerful Montagues and
Capulets. Attenborough believed:

> it is a domestic play . . . not a play of grand scale. I've got rid of
> the economic scale of the play in order to allow the scale of the
> emotions to come to the centre of the stage. I've stripped it of
> its grandeur in social and economic terms; there are no ser-
> vants; it is simply about two families in a humble town in
> Northern Italy. I want to home in on the passionate centre of
> the play, create passion in the form of human love, and
> destructive passion in the social violence . . . The most impor-
> tant thing about that world for us is its earthiness, its sensual-
> ity, its beauty, the simmering passion underneath the skin of
> the play, which sometimes is contained and at other times
> erupts. It can erupt in love, between Romeo and Juliet, or it can
> erupt in hate, between the Montagues and the Capulets.[38]

Attenborough's focus on the play was as a domestic tragedy. Juliet
was seen cooking for the ball, scrubbing clothes and beating carpets.
The emphasis was on the sense of community and the way people
interacted with each other in a constricted and intense environment. Designer Robert Jones explained:

> We didn't want to do the play in Elizabethan period. Mike
> [Attenborough] referred a lot to the film of The Godfather and the
> early scenes of Bertolucci's film 1900 . . . And that's where we
> got this strong sense of community, people who worked on the
> land and the landowners. All the boys worked on the land. The
> first thing you see is them with scythes. Sharpening knives . . .
> their tools later become weapons. It's very much set in a small
> community—tightly knit, houses opposite one another, and a
> general village square which everyone gravitates toward, like a
> market town . . . The space has to be used as a bedroom, a

kitchen, a square, a tomb, a church, Mantua. So it has to be multi-purpose . . . The floor is a very strong anchor—red bricks, cobbles, drains. We decided that there would be a natural focus in the set—a low, brick rostrum . . . It can be a bed, a table, a place to dance on. People fight on it and die on it . . . I'm trying to get the feeling of heat. In the outdoor scenes the lighting is from very strong angles that catch the texture of the walls so you get the feeling of sunlight coming through alleyways. There's a tap where people fill buckets all the time. The boys throw water over themselves to cool off. It's quite an earthy production . . . The boys are all in vests, braces, very high waist trousers, belts. Juliet is very much a village girl; barefoot and in long vest shaped dresses. All the fabrics are natural colors as they come from vegetable dyes.[39]

The critic David Benedict recognized the production's intentions: "Robert Jones creates a wonderfully warm atmosphere . . . Attenborough is at pains to point out the youthful physicality at the play's heart and uses the heat of the Verona sun to bring out sweat and sexuality. That in turn emphasizes the macho violence which shimmers like a heat haze about the characters."[40]

Michael Bogdanov's influential modern-dress production in 1986 gave a highly politicized reading of the play in which children were used as commodities in a capitalist society gone mad. The tragedy of the couple stemmed from a community that placed its values on wealth and status ahead of love. A direct critique of Thatcherite philosophy, and the impact it can have on the souls of both parents and children, Bogdanov used *Romeo and Juliet* to show what life is reduced to when the people with power believe, in the words of Margaret Thatcher, that "there's no such thing as society. There are individual men and women and there are families. And no government can do anything except through people, and people must look after themselves first."[41] It was, as scholar and academic Russell Jackson described,

Set in "a modern north Italian city, all brass and marble, sports cars, motor bikes, cycling clerics and hard-faced, swanky teenagers." Capulet (Richard Moore) had become a self-made tycoon . . . It was implied that political and financial corruption were rife . . . With the Montagues and Capulets locked in a Mafia-style rivalry, their children were at once privileged and confined in a manner that suits the play: ten years later Baz Luhrmann's film would use a similar social framework.[42]

This air of corruption was carried on into Mantua, where "Romeo tangles with a city carnival and buys the poison under the comic-sinister gaze of huge masks of world leaders [Thatcher and Reagan]."[43]

The production took a satirical view of the 1980s "yuppie" lifestyle:

As we enter the Stratford theatre, a rock group is playing mood-indigo music, a black guy is cruising round the marble-smooth stage on roller-skates and there is a pervasive whiff of black leather . . . And, as Benvolio arrives on a motorbike and Tybalt turns up in the Veronese square in a low-slung red sports car, it becomes impossible not to dub this the Alfa *Romeo and Juliet*. Michael Bogdanov, in short, has set the play unequivocally in Verona 1986. The result is hip, cool, clever and witty . . . he creates a complete society in which everyone has a defined place. Montagues and Capulets are rival families living under a Mafia prince with Capulet himself an urban predator working from a green-marble desk and staggeringly indifferent to his daughter's welfare and his wife's affair with cousin Tybalt. Capulet also throws some spectacular thrashes: at the big one, Tybalt essays [Andrew Lloyd Webber's] *Memory* on the saxophone (thus becoming the Prince of "Cats") and Mercutio, the original Gucci loafer, jives headlong into the pool with his partner.[44]

The set had a cold angularity and rigid structure which, as Romeo and Juliet became aware of their entrapment in their society, resembled a gilded cage:

3. Sean Bean (right) as Romeo in Michael Bogdanov's modern-dress ("yuppie") production of 1986.

Chris Dyer's Cubist-inspired set, a revolving central unity of white staircase and landings, is backed by changing photographic blow-ups, huge and grainy, of Sloanes, clones, copes and bits of architecture.[45]

In the 1976 and 1989 RSC productions, the set design for Verona was minimalist and without the detail that builds up a visual world of the play. Closer to Shakespeare's stage, it is the performances of the lead characters that will dominate or create the necessary atmosphere in which the play functions. In 1989, the bare structure of the Swan Theatre acted as the set for the play. Gregory Doran, Assistant Director on this production, explained:

We decided to adopt a version of Shakespeare's open stage for *Romeo and Juliet*. The actors would have to rely on the spoken word to create the scenery. Terry Hands began rehearsals by emphasizing how important words were to the Elizabethans. Nowadays, perhaps, the currency of words has been devalued by TV and film which relies on images not words for effect.[46]

Surprising critics and audience, in 1976 the main stage of the Royal Shakespeare Theatre was adapted into the nearest approximation of an Elizabethan theater that could be met within the structural limits of the existing auditorium:

> A shock awaits one as one enters the RST. At the back of the stage is a timbered, two-tiered balcony for spectators, below there is an inner recess and the stage itself thrust further into the auditorium than ever. It marks Stratford's most radical attempt yet to return to an Elizabethan model.[47]

In this production, many critics mentioned John Woodvine's excellent performance as Capulet, in which he indicated that the violence of Veronese society emanated from the head of a feudal household, and from twisted parental control:

> What also gave the end its strength was the emergence of Capulet, thanks to John Woodvine, as the source and fountain of the hate and violence that runs through the play. Hearing of Juliet's refusal to wed Paris, he hurls her intemperately to the floor; and even in the family vault he can't resist kicking Romeo's corpse and taking a dagger to the bungling Friar.[48]

Stars Shine Darkly Over Me[49]

The feel of a production is often dependent on the director's reading of how fated the lovers actually are. Many modern productions play heavily on the idea that the lovers are on an inescapable journey, hurtling toward their fate with a gothic sense of dread. In 1967, director Karolos Koun seized avidly on the word "fate":

> Whether Shakespeare believed in fate or not, he used it theatrically. There's a current of hate that runs right through Verona that has to be got rid of. It's the old Greek theme of a sacrifice having to be made as an atonement. Out of the loins of these

4. Trevor Nunn's 1976 production: John Woodvine as Capulet, furious in the face of his daughter's refusal to marry the man he has chosen for her, with Francesca Annis as Juliet, Marie Kean as her Nurse, and Barbara Shelley as her mother.

fatal enemies spring what the Chorus calls "death-marked lovers." They are made to love each other so that the city may be cleansed of blood. It's a very beautiful and moving pattern.[50]

In the play, Romeo expresses an almost supernatural awareness of his own destiny. In Koun's production, Ian Holm played Romeo as intensely aware of the ominous nature of his uncontrollable love:

The lovers' tragedy is complicated by differences in temperament—Romeo "a man of uncertain responsibility" . . . and Juliet, practical, far-seeing, committed. And it is further complicated by Romeo's sense of a tragic destiny hanging over him in the stars: "I am sure he's got a feeling that it is not going to work out right," Holm says.[51]

As one critic described:

In the last agonising moments of the balcony scene—when Juliet asks: "Thinkest thou we shall meet again?" Ian Holm, short, vigorous, modern, the very antithesis of the traditional swooning Romeo, replies: "I doubt it." There is a pause before he completes the line to reassure Juliet, and adds the word "not." So Shakespeare's line "I doubt it not" with its following words "And all those woes shall serve for sweet discourses in our times to come," is subtly rearranged. For this Romeo is a pessimistic fellow, torn apart and troubled deeply in his soul. He has no confidence in any future for their love. In the last scenes of the play, as all his fears are confirmed, he rushes gladly toward death with a sort of elation, delivering his last words "I die" with a relief that is oddly anti-climactic. The destructive and bitter violence of Verona's continuing feud between the Capulets and the Montagues is certainly a likely source of Romeo's revulsion with life, with the "death wish" suggested in Ian Holm's moving and at times powerful performance.[52]

Similarly, in 1989:

Mark Rylance's excellent Romeo . . . seems death-haunted from the start. This is not just a moody Petrarchan dreamer but a man "whipped and tormented" by his love for Rosaline and given to a shy, nervous stammer. Even his passion for Juliet has a doomed intensity: at one poignant moment they simply stare at each other in wordless rapture and Friar Laurence virtually has to prise them apart with a crowbar to get them to the altar. Mr Rylance delivers all the lines hinting at the operation of fate ("O, I am Fortune's fool") with the quiet certainty of someone aware that happiness is a frail and perilous affair. It adds up to a pensively intelligent study of a man "wedded to calamity."[53]

When they meet at the ball . . . time seems to stand still. The other guests are freeze-framed in a rich amber radiance, while the two lovers converse and take their first kiss under a cone of harder, whitish light. Both romantic and oddly premonitory, this stage picture gives a subtle hint that the two youngsters have been picked out (or on) by Fate.[54]

Michael Boyd's production in 2000 brought to life this sense of gothic and numinous dread that underpins the play. Helped by David Tennant's strong performance as the ill-fated Romeo, the production worked effectively as a ghostly retread of the events of the tragedy. Trapped in a state of limbo, the lovers, with the play's other victims, are doomed to relive their tale, observers and yet participants in an apparently never-ending tragic cycle:

It struck me very early on that Romeo had a fairly well developed sense of the world of fate and destiny. He talks of his dreams and makes numerous references to the stars and what lies in them . . . The first explicit reference I found was his justification for not going to the Capulet ball by saying "I dreamt a dream tonight" . . . I began to wonder what this dream he had had could be, and the answer came from an idea of Michael Boyd's to have Romeo speak the Prologue.

Two households, both alike in dignity
In fair Verona, where we lay our scene . . .

is one of those bits of Shakespeare that the audience can practically chant along with you . . . Michael's idea was to have the Prologue spoken midway through the first scene, so that it would cut through the street-fight and suspend the action; and he also wanted it to be spoken by Romeo. This wouldn't be the same Romeo that we would meet for the first time a few minutes later, however; this would be Romeo after his death, a spectre who could speak the Prologue with all the despair, resignation and even bitterness, of hindsight. As the action on stage was suspended, I could even address some of it to other characters in the play, so the lines

And the continuance of the parents' rage,
Which, but their children's end, naught could remove

could be said directly to my father, who was even then in the midst of a sword fight with Capulet . . . It helped, I think, to confound audience expectation early on—something we'd always been keen to do . . . This became Romeo's dream, this vision of himself walking through an all-too-familiar battle-field as a ghost of himself telling a story that would only make partial sense, but warned of a tragedy that would take his life. Indeed, as his story unfolded it would seem that this portent of doom was only becoming ever more inescapable.[55]

In this production, the worlds of the living and the dead mingled. As characters died, their spirits emerged above the left-hand wall of the set, watching down upon and even influencing the action. For example, Mercutio handed down the poison to the Apothecary—an act of revenge fulfilling the "curse on both your houses" that will see the deaths of Romeo, Juliet, and the future hopes of the Montagues and Capulets. As Juliet contemplated the horrors of the tomb, building to a state of self-induced frenzy, Tybalt's ghost ran past her, on the lines "O look! Methinks I see my cousin's ghost / Seeking out Romeo that did spit his body / Upon a rapier's point. Stay, Tybalt, stay!" In this spine-tingling moment he emerged from the "blind" entrance at the back of the stage and exited through the auditorium, sprinting with a death's-head stare focused ahead on some unknown sight and purpose.

A sense of doom was also evoked by the dance at Capulet's ball, reminiscent of a dance of death, "an erotic dance in which the men simulate strangling their partners . . . These lovers are not just star-crossed, they are positively cursed."[56] As theater historian James N. Loehlin described:

> many of Boyd's images were vivid and compelling. He depicted the violence depopulating Verona as literal plague, so that by the end of the play all the characters were wearing surgical masks to try and avoid infection. The presiding spirit of this Verona was not the Prince, an enervated old man hobbling on two canes, but rather Paris, a strapping, black-clad sadist, always accompanied by a band of armed retainers, who nearly raped Juliet in the Friar's cell. The final attempt to establish a "glooming peace" was a hollow one. While the families wallowed in self-pity and made futile gestures of reconciliation, Romeo and Juliet emerged eerily from the tomb and walked out through the audience, noticed only by Friar Laurence. The diseased world of Verona was far from ready to receive or even

understand them, and the play ended on a note of fatalism and despair.[57]

Other devices and pieces of stage business not inherent in the text have been used by directors in order to indicate the inescapable hand of fate. In Terry Hands's 1973 production, the figure of the Apothecary took on an extra significance, very much in keeping with the play:

> Hands's motto for the production was "these violent delights have violent ends"; he emphasized the speed and impulsiveness with which the lovers fling themselves into tragedy, as well as the cruel tricks of fate that hasten their doom. The Apothecary, a sinister embodiment of Destiny, brooded over crucial points of the action from a metal catwalk high over the stage.[58]

> A hooded figure takes up a position on [the] high bridge whenever ancient grudges break to new mutiny below. Presumably he is there to suggest Death brooding over the star-crossed lovers but his final identification as the Apothecary, though not exactly inappropriate, introduces a sharp touch of bathos.[59]

Juliet's bed, often center stage, acts as an important symbol of birth, marriage, and death. The bed will often anticipate the furnishings of the family vault, so that the lovers will be seen lying together in the same position here and in the play's final sequence. In 1980, 1984, and 1997, the inclusion of Juliet's funeral reinforced the effect foreshadowed in Juliet's line just after meeting Romeo: "If he be marrièd, / My grave is like to be my wedding bed."[60]

Ever Fallen in Love with Someone (You Shouldn't've . . .)[61]

The casting of the two central characters is essential to the success of the production. For the 1986 production Michael Bogdanov sensibly held auditions for the two leads on the same day so that it was evident from the start that the actors had the essential spark that could make the production work. However, many productions have been criticized for a lack of magnetism between the two leads. In 2004, the leads, "while admirable individually, are less exciting when together; and never suggest that they are overborne by sexual passion."[62] And, in 1995 critic Michael Billington suggested the pair radiated "about as much sexual intensity as a couple in a Sunday school Bible class."[63] Regardless of the merits of a production, without a couple that can communicate, the nature of the lovers' relationship in the production will fail to engage the audience emotionally and convey their tragedy.

A sharp distinction is made in the play between the different attitudes to love expressed by individual characters: the pure love of Romeo and Juliet; Mercutio's view that relationships between the sexes are for sexual gratification only; and marriage as a means to social position and standing in the community, as made clear by the Capulets' hopes for their daughter.

The Capulets, in Michael Bogdanov's production, saw Paris as a financial bargain, with Juliet as a tool to social standing and wealth:

Shakespeare ends *Romeo and Juliet* with the pious thought that the lovers' deaths have patched up the family feud. That is not how Michael Bogdanov sees the events, which he presents as an irreconcilable clash between the forces of affection and property. The key line is the friar's reproof to Juliet's parents: "The most you sought was her promotion." From the start the overbearing elders treat their young like walking investments; when disaster strikes it is as though their shares have taken a tumble.[64]

Niamh Cusack, who played Juliet, realized:

What makes Romeo and Juliet's love so vivid . . . is the contrast with the hatred between the families. Juliet is not so much rebelling against her parents as discovering her own values. They don't include "making a good match," love as a business transaction to increase the power of her family.[65]

This is a world of rich kids, fixed marriages and tough deals where, when two people meet, it's business at first sight; and for once Bogdanov creates a real sense that, by falling in love, Romeo and Juliet are defying the local customs . . . But all this Bogdanovian invention builds to a point which is that young love is as vulnerable as it ever was to parental exploitation and cruelty: more so since Richard Moore's crude tycoon of a Capulet is ready to slap his daughter around to get his way. And after the two lovers are safely dead (Romeo, incidentally, expires by shooting up after a peculiarly creepy encounter with a Mantuan fixer), they are instantly transformed into gold statues before which the survivors smilingly pose for the paparazzi. Renaissance tragedy is transformed into social critique.[66]

Significantly, James N. Loehlin pointed out how:

In the latter half of the twentieth century, *Romeo and Juliet* was transformed, in production and perception, from a play about love into a play about hate. Modern productions have tended to emphasize the feud over the love story, and have used it to comment on a variety of social ills.[67]

However, it is the very nature of the society and the feud which often throws the lovers' emotional life into sharp relief. This was especially true in Michael Boyd's production in 2000, in which "the idea seems to be to show the violence and morbidity endemic in Shakespeare's world and thereby intensify the romance which takes place in a deathward-bound *vale of tears*".[68]

Zoë Waites played Juliet to much acclaim in Michael Attenborough's 1997 production. In this Verona, where "emotions are raw and likely to run amok,"[69] she emphasized the sexual awakening which comes with Juliet's experience of true love:

I think it should be incredibly sexy, that they're completely desperate for one another. Juliet hasn't had a sexual relationship before so there's all the fear of that. Fear and excitement. Wanting but not knowing.[70]

In this production, the audience were

reminded constantly that this is a play about the connection between sexuality and death. Both are pursued with orgasmic intensity in this hot, passionate world, and the link is made most evident in Zoë Waites's remarkable Juliet. This is a girl who, judging by the lascivious way she dances with Paris or the manner in which she rolls round her bed saying she is "possessed but not yet enjoyed," is carnally desperate.[71]

Juliet dances a tango with Paris to non-tango music; but the production makes a virtue of this as she sees Romeo, because the music is suddenly peeled away into a quiet hum, and we watch Juliet still dancing this elaborate tango (a real Argentino one, not the campy ballroom version, with heavenly sensuous details of footwork) as if suspended in time, as if the only music for her now is her new interest in Romeo, whom she keeps trying to regard, this way or that, over Paris's shoulder.[72]

Likewise, her Romeo, Ray Fearon, was "an intense, muscular Romeo, totally at the mercy of his hormonal overload, careering from one impetuous deed to the next."[73] In this earthy interpretation, Romeo and Juliet were not portrayed as "romantic" ideals but real, vital, and passionate people. Fearon interpreted Romeo's feelings as those usually experienced in adolescence, and gave full credence to the fact that these two characters are in love—not a doomed love, but a love which could have lasted, as many relationships between many childhood sweethearts do:

It's that point when you're about sixteen—I remember it myself—and you start thinking about the universe and yourself and your existence and the thing that's triggered that off could be a relationship, someone you've broken up with. And that happened to me and you don't understand fully what's going on. . . . The love is real for Romeo. It's that point in his life that is special, when you make that transition, when you just go, "right, this is it." Everything else stops. You've fallen in love and you try to talk to people about it and they don't want to, or they make fun of you . . . Some people play the tragedy before the tragedy happens but I think what we should aim for is to make the audience believe that this relationship is going to work. You have to play the scenes as they are, be in the moment all the time, believe you're not going to die.[74]

The common conception of "soppiness" in the lovers' wooing is a fallacy which directors have been keen to remedy. The words of Romeo and Juliet ring out true and strong, often in perfect poetry, contrasting strongly with the language of those around them. As Gregory Doran pointed out: "When Romeo and Juliet first meet they are so delighted, they create a perfect sonnet between them, sharing the lines and matching each other's rhymes."[75]

The possibility of harmony and peace in Verona is glimpsed in the very language that the couple use. The importance of having actors who express the strength of true love cannot be underestimated. There is a tendency for reviewers to believe that any emotions felt in adolescence cannot be genuine, lasting or significant, and reductively ascribe the tragedy to the vagaries of a dodgy postal system. For all its lighter moments, what Shakespeare presents us with is a disturbed society in which love cannot function. All relationships are twisted in subtle and insidious ways, except one, and it is this that elevates this couple above their parents and peers. Regardless of setting, when the casting is right, *Romeo and Juliet* remains one of Shakespeare's most heart-wrenching and poignant tragedies; when done badly, as reviewers point out, it can make for a very long night in the theater.

THE DIRECTOR'S CUT: INTERVIEW WITH MICHAEL ATTENBOROUGH

Michael Attenborough, born in 1950 to a distinguished theatrical family, graduated from Sussex University in 1972 and worked as associate director at the Mercury Theatre, Colchester, from 1972 to 1974. He was artistic director of the Leeds (now West Yorkshire) Playhouse from 1974 to 1979, associate director of the

Young Vic from 1979 to 1980, artistic director of the Palace Theatre Watford from 1980 to 1983, and director of the Hampstead Theatre from 1984 to 1989, which won twenty-three awards during his tenure. In 1989 he was appointed artistic director of the Turnstyle Group in the West End, and then, in 1990, Resident director and executive producer of the Royal Shakespeare Company, becoming principal associate director in 1996. In July 2002 he was appointed artistic director of London's Almeida Theater. He is also joint vice-chairman of the Royal Academy of Dramatic Art and an honorary associate artist of the RSC. Originally seen as specializing in directing new writing, he rapidly established himself as a sensual, non-flashy director of Shakespeare's plays. He directed *Romeo and Juliet* for the RSC in 1997 with Ray Fearon as Romeo and Zoë Waites as Juliet.

How do you deal with the fact that this is such a famous love story, and get around the many preconceptions that the audience are bound to bring to the play?

I had something very particular that I wanted to investigate in the play and, interestingly, you put your finger on it in the question: I don't think it's a love story. Theirs is hardly a profound, romantic, explored relationship. These are two kids who are as horny as hell and who can't wait to get their hands on each other. So I think it's a play about passion, not a play about love. That may not sound like a huge shift, but I think it *is* quite big. I think it's a play about both the positive and creative elements of passion *and* its destructive and violent elements. I had to find a world in which the dividing line between brawling and knifing somebody and having an illicit sexual relationship was almost invisible; one in which I could move from one to the other almost seamlessly. So I needed an environment in which heat—in some sense metaphorical, in some sense literal—was at the center of the event. We were not particularly interested in romance or love. Love of course emerges out of it, but what should sweep the audience away is the passion within the society. Again and again in the play, death is expressed in sexual terms and sex is expressed in terms of death. Sex and death are terribly close; in fact, "dying" is the slang term for having an orgasm, so you have in that one juxtaposition the positive and negative elements of passion sitting right next to each other.

I wanted a society that was not nearly so hierarchical as is conventionally portrayed and I wanted it very elemental, very earthy, very simple. I set it in a Tuscan peasant village about ten years into the twentieth century. If you've ever been to any of those French, Italian or Spanish villages in the hills in the heat of the day there's always two or three old folk sitting around, a man in a beret and a woman all in black, probably with a basket of flowers or fruit, just nodding off, a little kid playing around, some lads on motorcycles. That was the feel we had. The crickets chirping around the old folk, and then slowly the lads drift on and a fight starts. The lads were in those quite thick rural trousers, collarless shirts, braces, big boots that would withstand a lot of agricultural work. The girls were in long skirts, but right down off the shoulders, cleavages to the fore. Other than Escalus, nobody had any money, so the line at the end of the play "I will raise her statue in pure gold" wasn't taken literally; it meant "this will be the most precious thing in the village." The atmosphere was very machismo, hot, flash, quick-tempered.

I actually started the production with their funeral. They were carried on in a very heavy, Catholic funeral and laid down on slabs in exactly the positions they would be in at the end of the play. Escalus spoke the Prologue over their dead bodies. It seemed to me that in effect Shakespeare was saying that these kids were so driven that their inevitable destiny was death, self-destruction. I wanted that sense of predestination, which Shakespeare clearly intended.

What did you do about the Chorus? An actor with no other lines? A doubled role?

I gave the Chorus to the actor that played Escalus. Actually, in effect he wasn't a chorus. He was Escalus doing a soliloquy. When Escalus arrives he's almost like a *deus ex machina*: he walks in and takes control of events, or attempts to. So his authority socially was reflected in his authority theatrically.

Did you have a particular way of distinguishing between Montagues and Capulets—visually, stylistically?

No. The play makes it so clear that you grasped who was who very quickly. And in our production they were people who couldn't afford much, so they didn't have the choice of, say, wearing distinctive clothing.

They don't call each other "Lady" Capulet or "Lady" Montague in the play, only in the cast list. They don't have to be Ladies and Gentlemen. So the only hierarchy was the enmity which existed between the Montagues and the Capulets. In a funny kind of a way, that age-old vendetta, where no one really understands why it began, is very believable in a village context amongst the peasantry, in a way more so than in aristocratic families. They are hemmed in together, rubbing shoulder to shoulder, can't avoid bumping into each other in streets and alleyways. The fights were done with farming implements: machetes, scythes. There was a wonderful fight that Terry King [Fight Director] put together, and when Mercutio got involved he was clearly much cleverer than Tybalt or any of the others, and all he fought with was a broom. Tybalt was slashing away with a vicious-looking machete, and because Mercutio is just that little bit quicker and sharper, suddenly he'd be behind Tybalt, poking him with the broom! There was no social etiquette, it was about passion and people who would encounter it very quickly.

Several of the characters, most notably the Nurse, are often played as a particular stereotype (Nurse usually quite old, garrulous, often a cheerful fat lady)—did you try to get away from this?

She was cheerful, and, if Sandra [Voe] will allow me, very sexy! I wanted her to be like a great mate of the Capulets. They were not people who could lord it over the Nurse. She was dressed all in black, clearly a widow who'd lost her husband early, she maybe lived two doors down; they've got a child and she doesn't have kids so she comes in and helps. She's much earthier, free from any responsibility of being a parent. She was completely bananas about Juliet, but she wasn't the inappropriate, slightly eccentric servant, she was really like a neighbor. In a sense, we upped her status and made her a much more ordinary human being. In different ways we did that with Friar Laurence as well: rather than him being the rather bumbling, well-intentioned fellow he is often presented as, we made him a real rustic priest. When we encountered him in that first speech, he wasn't wandering along with a posy, he'd got his sleeves rolled up—he'd been out in an allotment growing things. And when, in the second half, Romeo's bemoaning his banishment in a rather self-pitying, indulgent way, Friar Laurence hit him, just beat him about to wake him up, in a way that an urban priest would never do. They [Nurse and Friar] were both ordinary people. One had the status of being a very good mum, the other had the status of being a very good priest. But they were part of a community who knew each other extremely well.

Do you see the play as a battle of the generations as much as a battle between rival households?

You see, in all walks of life, different demands and energies separate different generations. We were teenagers once, we were like that, now our job is to be grown-ups and to preach the benefits of some order and control. The sense of difference between generations is that the younger generation are out of control, and the elders frantically try and bring them under control. I do think that the Capulet/Juliet scene is wonderful because he's clearly panicking: he's suddenly realized that this is no longer a little girl, this is a woman with her own feelings (in my view, Juliet is a lot tougher than Romeo) and she stands up to him, and he's *shocked* and he goes way over the top. It's as if the younger generation, because of their passions and because of their sudden maturity, are out of control and the older generation are powerless to help them. It wasn't a generational battle so much as the endless cycle of life.

The play seems to subvert the age-old idea of the boy as the sexual desiring figure, the girl as the one who is desired. Were you and your Juliet surprised by how active and sexually energized she is?

It was certainly one of the keys in rehearsals, which is why I cast Zoë [Waites], because she's a very spunky, earthy actress. Temperamentally, Zoë's not particularly English: there's nothing dainty about Zoë, she's a middle-class girl but her instincts are toward the earth as opposed to the intellect, although she's ferociously bright. So she was the perfect Juliet for me. She had a fantastic feel for the language, which reflects the character who paints her world incredibly vividly. You get the sense very quickly of a girl with tremendous emotional strength and, perhaps even more important, imagination. I think Romeo's imagination is much more stilted and limited. She tends to see the cup half-full and he doesn't always. There's no question one of the joys of Juliet is that there's nothing passive or ladylike about her and it makes her very attractive. When the play starts and Romeo's already in love with Rosaline you see him shift from an idealized, romanticized, unrequited love, which was in lots of ways the literary tradition that Shakespeare had inherited, to something that just swept him off his feet. It was like he was being gravitationally pulled into Juliet's world. He changes, I think, in the play. She forces him to grow up.

How did you approach the ages of the lovers? The text doesn't give Romeo a particular age, but it's very explicit about Juliet being thirteen (and that's a problem in our time, isn't it?).

It's pretty explicit. Ray [Fearon] and Zoë were still young: in their twenties. I didn't in any way try to get Zoë to pretend to be fourteen because you end up with something rather twee and not very helpful to the actor. What's exciting theatrically is seeing people discover things for the first time. If you can get that to be real—that they were encountering things for the very first time—that made them young. Of course, one of the great things that we get from two passionate actors like Ray and Zoë is huge energy and emotional and linguistic power, so you have to excite the audience's imagination through the character rather than try and make the actor look younger.

How did you stage the ball and the first meeting of Romeo and Juliet? It must be quite a challenge to provide intense focus on just the two of them when they are on a crowded stage in the midst of a noisy dance.

5. Ray Fearon as Romeo and Zoë Waites as Juliet in Michael Attenborough's 1997 production.

In terms of the story of the play, right from the word go I wanted the sense that we were building toward this party. It took place in what was in effect the village square. In the middle of the square there was a rectangular platform which was used as the place where the bodies were laid at the end of the play, as the bed when they were in bed together, and as a fountain-cum-stand where the boys would lounge around. In the middle of it we had a section which pulled out and revealed a fire, and you could hang a bowl above it to cook pasta. So the Nurse is actually preparing, with Lady Capulet, the meal for the big party that is going to happen in the square, with rows of colored bulbs around. She was literally rolling fresh pasta, and when she did the speech about carrying the baby in her arms she'd just pick up this load of pasta and hold it in her arms as the baby. When Juliet entered, she was running in from the fields where she'd been picking herbs, which she put into the pot, and you could actually smell the pasta being cooked. So it was again very earthy: no social pretension, social graces, middle-class manners. There was a lot of dancing— flamboyant, sexy, great fun, everybody getting drunk quite quickly: a real sense of a village community.

It is a challenge to stage their meeting. I did something very simple, which is that when Romeo and Juliet were either looking at or speaking to each other, I went into an almost entire freeze with everybody else, took their lights down to 20 per cent, pushed Romeo and Juliet's up to 100 per cent, and played their scene. I've watched productions before where, suddenly, by some strange coincidence, everybody exits on a conga, conveniently leaving the stage for just the length of their dialogue! Surely the point is that it is not that easy? They have to talk to each other in a certain way because people could be watching.

The other thing I did in that scene was to foreground the notion that the whole thing is happening in order to pair Juliet off with Paris. Paris is nearly often cast as wet, which always strikes me as a bit daft; it's actually much more interesting if you've got a really good-looking man playing Paris, but she wants the other guy. It becomes really interesting then. I did get a very handsome young Paris [Oliver Fox], and he and Juliet did this sexy, passionate period dance, which we choreographed in such a way that although their bodies were incredibly close together her eyes never left Romeo. This was before either of them had said two words to each other. There's something sexy about that. It's one of those strange things about a quite stern Catholic environment in which sexual mores are very particularly mapped out, and young girls aren't allowed out without a chaperone, that when you see them dancing it always seems terribly erotic. We made use of that, and Juliet and Paris were very good dancers, so everybody thought that they fancied each other, but in fact the erotic charge going through her body was for the man she saw standing on the side of the dance floor.

Juliet at her window—or balcony, as it became in David Garrick's eighteenth-century production—and Romeo below, then climbing up, is one of the most famous scenes in the history of world theater. How did you set about making it new, making it your own?

In the context of our setting, it was rather simple. There were no grand, high buildings, barely even a balcony. Somehow, because they could virtually touch each other by leaning over, clawing to try to get hold of each other, it took on its own power.

Because the set was all faded terra-cotta plasterwork and vines rotting in the sun, there was nothing grand or operatic about it, which I think is when it gets silly and clichéd and young kids start to giggle. If it's about two kids who can't wait to get into each other's arms, it takes on a different sensual atmosphere. I think a huge amount is down to Romeo in that scene, and you can't get much earthier than Ray Fearon. He's a muscular, instinctive hunk of a black actor, brilliant with the language! It wasn't difficult. The location and context helped us so much to get rid of the clichés of the balcony scene.

The reconciliation of the households at the end: lasting peace or temporary union?

We went for a lasting peace. A lasting peace that was partly out of shame and partly out of exhaustion. Shakespeare's very clever in actually making a point in the first speech, of saying that nobody knows where this enmity has come from: "From ancient grudge break to new mutiny." So by the end they're going, "Does anybody remember why we are fighting?" I'm sure other directors have wanted to make it temporary, but I think it belittles the story because what you then say is that the death of their children is not worth much. Now, in my experience that's the most devastating thing that can ever happen. When things emerge to the parents that they never knew about, they think "How did we go so seriously wrong that we're only now, so many years later, discovering things about our children that they felt they had to keep from us?" But it doesn't nec- essarily mean the parents are bad parents, it's the younger genera- tion wanting to assert their independence: "No, I run my own life, I don't need to run it by you." We wanted to play it as profoundly shocking that all these things had happened behind their backs. But there's also a curious feeling in the play, as if the intensity of their relationship has burnt them out, almost a self-destruct mechanism. In a funny kind of way, I think if there was something that was never going to last, it was Romeo and Juliet, and not necessarily the even- tual peace between the two families.

There are certain human structures at the beginning of the play which get burst apart. I was fascinated by the relationship between Romeo, Benvolio, and Mercutio. There were two things I wanted to play on. One, that I think Mercutio and Romeo are flip-sides of the same coin: scratch a romantic and you'll find a cynic; scratch a cynic, you'll find a romantic. I think Romeo and Mercutio adore each other because of their unity of opposites. And those two, like a lot of very volatile, combustible relationships, need a third person that glues them together that they can play off; somehow, if that person wasn't there, they'd end up fighting. It's not a dramaturgical accident that Benvolio disappears after Mercutio dies. It's because he's lost his function; he can't just tag around after Romeo—that threesome's broken. In our show he was the last person to leave the stage after the big fight, he was completely wasted. Benvolio is very sweet, very loyal, but finally not as complete and interesting a human being as Mercutio and Romeo. But he was a vital part of the dynamic between the three of them. And that gets broken apart by Mercutio's death. Yet another character defined by passion.

DAVID TENNANT ON PLAYING ROMEO

David Tennant was born in 1971 and brought up in Scotland. He attended the Royal Scottish Academy of Music and Drama. His earliest theater work was with agitprop 7:84 Theatre Company, but he soon went on to establish his career in British theater, playing Touchstone in *As You Like It*, Antipholus of Syracuse in *The Comedy of Errors*, and Jack Absolute in *The Rivals*, as well as Romeo in Michael Boyd's production of *Romeo and Juliet* in 2000 for the Royal Shakespeare Company and Nicholas Beckett in Joe Orton's *What the Butler Saw* for the National Theatre. He has also made a successful television career and is best known today for his incarnation as the tenth Doctor Who in the long-running and enormously popular BBC television series. He has also made numerous film appearances, notably as Barty Crouch Jr. in *Harry Potter and the Goblet of Fire*. He returned to the RSC in 2007 to play the prince in *Hamlet* and Berowne in *Love's Labour's Lost*.

How old did you imagine your Romeo to be?

I think Alex [Gilbreath, who played Juliet] and I both felt we were at the far end of being able to get away with it, but it's more difficult for Juliet because her age is stated so explicitly. Strictly speaking, Romeo could be any age, in that there's no textual evidence to suggest exactly how old he is, but of course there's something in the character which suggests teenage angst and perhaps hotheadedness. I didn't focus too specifically on an age because I was twenty-nine when I did it, and I didn't want to spend the whole production feeling like I was trying to play a teenager. I didn't want that to be my focus. So I kept it, even to myself, slightly vague. I suppose I thought of him as a young man, and beyond that I didn't spend too much time worrying about exactly how old he was. I think as human beings we tend not to focus on what age we are when we're having whatever experiences it is that we're having. So I tried not to make it too big an issue, which was perhaps partly my own fear of being slightly too old to be playing it.

How did you set about conveying to the audience the difference between Romeo's love for Rosaline and his love for Juliet?

Well, we never see Rosaline. Michael Boyd [the director] was always determined that Rosaline was a novitiate nun, and he encouraged me to think that from the off; the idea being that Rosaline was the ultimate unachievable goal, and that part of what Romeo was doing to himself was that especially (although not exclusively) adolescent thing where people fall in love with the unattainable. Whereas Juliet is certainly very real. I think the relationship with Juliet is a much more mature relationship, within the terms of the whole relationship itself being very young. Rosaline is unattainable and really more of a crush, whereas we have to believe that he falls for Juliet. He believes his life has found its meaning when he finds her. With Rosaline, he is in love with the idea of being in love; with Juliet, he's in love with Juliet. I think that's probably the biggest difference. The love for Rosaline is a kind of melodramatic exhibition of his self-perceived complicated maturity, which by definition proves that he isn't very complicated or mature. When he meets Juliet he genuinely falls in love with another human being, rather than the concept of love itself.

To what degree does he change in the course of the play? Does he go from being one of the lads to isolated lover, or has he always stood apart from the rest?

There's certainly something of the self-dramatist in Romeo. I think that's how he likes to cast himself, even within his group of friends. He likes to see himself, and for them to see him, as the slightly complicated, Byronic tortured soul, and what I think happens is that he genuinely becomes that. Rather than it being a part he plays, it becomes his life. So I think by the end of the play he has found the purpose that he pretends to have found at the start of the play.

And does Romeo's language seem to grow to maturity in the course of the play?

It's not something I remember noticing at the time, but that's not to say that it doesn't. I try not to be too objective about things like that because then you get into a self-consciousness which is, dare I say, an old-fashioned way of approaching Shakespeare and one which I try to avoid. I think you've got to try to focus directly and solely on the text that a character is speaking in that moment if you're trying to interpret the character for a stage experience. You have to try to get within it, and not be too aware of anything going on "without" it, which might be relevant to somebody studying the text for a thesis (and I'm not saying that it's not there and those points aren't there to be made). So I don't remember noticing that in the rehearsal rooms, but I suppose what I'm saying is that maybe I was trying *not* to.

It's about the most famous fictional love affair of all time, and the window/balcony scene is one of the most celebrated ever written, so how do you get past the clichés, the historical inheritance? Did you have any special tricks for making the part and the play your own?

The fact that they come with that baggage and expectation is possibly the most difficult thing about doing those famous roles, and

Romeo and Juliet more than most, because everybody's got an opinion on it and everyone has an expectation of what it is. Even people who have never read or seen the play think they know what *Romeo and Juliet* is. And actually I think most of the time they're wrong! What I remember particularly about *Romeo and Juliet* is that people expect a chocolate-box love story. I think that's what people imagine that story is, even though they know it's tragic and it doesn't end happily. They're expecting some great essay on love. I don't think that's what the play is. Romeo and Juliet spend remarkably little time onstage together and, when they are onstage together, the longest chunk of time you see them interacting with each other is the balcony scene, where the very definition is that they can't touch, they can't be together, there's a physical and emotional barrier between them. I think the play is about all sorts of things, but I don't know really that it is about love. That's one of the things that you have to get over when playing Romeo, because if you come to the play thinking "I've come to play a great lover," that's not a very helpful place to start. Certainly our production was set in a quite bitter, tough environment. The play is as much about society and the politics of the world they're in as it is the meditation on love which people expect.

But to answer your question, no, I don't have any particular tricks. I'm always feeling the need to discover those tricks, but I don't know that I've quite done it yet. Having just finished doing *Hamlet*, which is another one that comes with all those expectations and preconditions, I still don't know what the answer is. You just have to try and see past it. You have to breathe a bit in the rehearsal room and try to see the scene that you're playing and the text that you're playing, rather than the weight of history—easier said than done, of course! I think another way of doing that is to try not to approach it as an English Literature exercise, which is always very tempting with Shakespeare and something that you clearly can do; there is so much to be said about every line. If I do have a "trick" or a way of approaching it, it's to just see each line for what it immediately is, in a dramatic truth and emotional context, rather than to see it in the context of what one might be looking for if you were writing a book about it.

Do you see the play as a battle between the young and the old, parents and children? Or are there some important bonds between the lovers and older mentors (the Friar for Romeo, the Nurse for Juliet)?

We probably get to understand the relationship between Romeo and the Friar more clearly than we get to understand the relationship between Romeo and Juliet, just in terms of stage time. It's more immediately explicable. It's not immediately clear why Romeo and Juliet fall for each other, a bit like how, when people fall in love in real life, it's not immediately clear why they do. The relationship with the Friar is easier to unpack; it's very important to who Romeo is, more so than his parents because we don't get to know Romeo's parents at all in the play, in the way that we do with Juliet's. I suppose there is a battle. There is a generation gap in the play and a conflict between the idealism of youth, who believe that love can conquer all, as opposed to the pragmatic, cynical older characters who can see the woods from the trees and know that it's not going to be that simple. I think there is an interesting debate in the play as to whether love can conquer all or not. It was explored in our production in terms of the older characters; there were design nods toward them being from a different world—the older the character, the more traditional their dress was. I was in quite a modern leather bomber jacket, whereas at the other end of the scale you had Alfred Burke [Escalus] wearing the full Elizabethan doublet and hose, and then all the other characters in between. Michael Boyd was clearly interested in that, and that was something we explored, yes.

In the seventeenth-century theater, there was a rumor that Shakespeare decided to kill Mercutio off halfway through the play because he was upstaging Romeo. Is the sheer brilliance of Mercutio's language a problem for Romeo?

I don't think it's a problem for Romeo. I suppose if that rumor is true, it may be a problem for the audience. I think Romeo has a genuine love for Mercutio. I think his brilliance, his energy, and mercurial wit is something that Romeo clearly cherishes. There are all sorts of questions as to quite what their relationship is, and I think there are decisions that you have to make about that in performance: about how close they are, about whether Mercutio might need Romeo more than Romeo needs Mercutio. Whether he got killed off because he was upstaging Romeo we will of course never know, but it's certainly a well-worn theatrical device: to create a character that you invest in and become fascinated by, and then kill him off for shock value.

6. David Tennant as Romeo and Des McAleer as Friar Laurence in Michael Boyd's 2000 production.

Of course it takes the play in a completely new direction. I think it's unlikely Shakespeare didn't see that coming, and just made it up because he was writing a part that was too good! I can't imagine that's the way he went about things! I imagine if he was really that entranced by that character he would have written a play called *Mercutio* and we would get to see more of him. I'm not really sure that Mercutio's language is a problem for Romeo because I don't think Mercutio is a problem for Romeo. I think Romeo is a problem for Mercutio.

The critic William Hazlitt said that "Romeo is Hamlet in love"—do you agree?

Hamlet is a more grown-up version of Romeo in that he is more aware of himself. I think Romeo has the capacity for introspection and self-knowledge, but it's a bit raw, and again with Hamlet you get someone who is beginning to understand himself and is tussling with that. Romeo believes he understands himself, but I don't think he quite does. The way he is with Rosaline is clearly a fairly immature way of interpreting what it is to be in love. Of course, he comes to understand what it is to be in love and to grow when he meets Juliet, but yet we never quite get to see Romeo grow up. It's quite possible that Hamlet could have been a bit like Romeo when he was younger. They certainly share a gift for language. I think we get to see Hamlet in love actually, because, albeit briefly, I think Hamlet is in love with Ophelia, and I don't think it's quite the same as for Romeo. So I don't think they're the same person, but I suppose there are certainly similarities and echoes between the two.

What do you think Romeo would like his epitaph to be?

I suppose what seems to be important to Romeo is that he is true to himself, as far as he knows what that "self" is. The very fact that he kills himself because he can't live without Juliet is the mark of an idealism backed up with a pure hedonism and a certainty: certainty about who he is and what is important. I think he would like to be remembered as someone who has purity of purpose. That's important to him: the fact that he doesn't give in to the pressures of what we see as the adult world, although he wouldn't see it that way. I suppose he'd like to be remembered as somebody clear-headed and true. I think he'd probably see the world around him as quite morally and emotionally bankrupt, so he would like his epitaph to be something that recognized he was the opposite of that. It's not exactly pithy, that answer, is it?! I think you were after a sound bite that I haven't quite been able to provide!

ALEXANDRA GILBREATH ON PLAYING JULIET

Alexandra Gilbreath was born in Chalfont St. Giles in 1969 and attended the London Academy of Music and Dramatic Art. She has established her career both in the theater and on screen. In 1996 she won the Ian Charleson Award for her performance in English Touring Theatre's production of *Hedda Gabler*. Apart from playing Juliet in Michael Boyd's 2000 production of *Romeo and Juliet* to David Tennant's Romeo, she has played Kate in the Royal Shakespeare Company's *The Taming of the Shrew* and Maria in John Fletcher's sequel *The Tamer Tamed*, as well as Rosalind in *As You Like It*, Hermione in *The Winter's Tale*, and Mistress Ford in the musical version of *The Merry Wives of Windsor*. Her best-known television role is as Stella Moon in the BBC series *The Monarch of the Glen*.

The text is explicit that Juliet is not quite fourteen years old. Did you play her as a thirteen-year-old, or is that inappropriate nowadays?

I was thirty-one, and so, honestly, was a bit long in the tooth to play her. But I'm of the belief that when you're young enough to play Juliet, you're not old enough to play her, and when you're old enough to play Juliet, you're too old! Of all the Shakespearean roles I've played, I found her, in terms of her personality, the toughest. Hers are not the actions of an innocent pre-teen. I found her brutally honest and very, very single-minded. She sees something and she goes out to get it, with no wavering. Mike [Michael Boyd, the director] said right at the beginning that he wanted the overall feeling of the play to lack sentimentality. He was very keen that Juliet, especially when played by someone who's a bit older (he used to call me the "geriatric Juliet"!), was not too romantic and full of whimsy. I certainly didn't find anything flowery about her.

I think some thirteen-year-olds actually appear tougher and a bit more brutal than sixteen- or seventeen-year-olds because, although they're still children, they're playing at being something else and they haven't quite recognized their limits. Also, these plays were written at a time when you were betrothed and married at thirteen, had your children and were quite likely dead by your thirties, so maybe when we talk about her innocence, that's imposing too modern a perspective. I didn't and couldn't at thirty-one go out to play a thirteen-year-old, but I could tell the story of someone who single-mindedly does something very specific and very dangerous. It sometimes manifested itself in the feeling that you were playing someone incredibly innocent who suddenly has this *overwhelming* feeling, and that desire takes over everything. "Gallop apace, you fiery-footed steeds" (Act 3 Scene 2) is not an innocent saying. It's someone saying "Come *on* sun, move on! I need this man to come at night because I need to sleep with him! I want to have sex with him!" That's not an innocent thirteen-year-old! I think that when you're a little bit older you can perhaps understand that better. I think you have to be a bit more experienced and a bit more self-aware, because I think she's incredibly self-aware.

To what degree does she change in the course of the play? Is it a case of some very rapid growing up?

I don't think she's in a mature position when the play begins. She's single-minded and has a very powerful personality, but with the speed at which the play develops, yes, she does change. She grows up immediately. She experiences something in her early life that is quite overwhelming: would you love anyone enough to actually put a knife to your own throat? That's why sometimes when it is played a bit sentimental, a bit flowery, you don't quite believe it. I don't know if I myself have such overwhelming conviction to be able to have the courage to do that. That's why I was surprised by her strength. When you play someone like Rosalind or Hermione they don't necessarily take you by surprise, but playing Juliet really did surprise me.

And does Juliet's language seem to grow to maturity in the course of the play?

It wasn't something that I noticed, because you would therefore become too self-conscious. It seemed to me that she creates language in the moment: "This is what I want and this is how I'm going to get it." I didn't feel that it was pre-planned: she's just creating, right in the middle of it. And the words that she chooses and how she expresses herself are not those of someone who matches the conventional innocent.

Both poetically and sexually, she in many ways takes the lead in the relationship, doesn't she? Was the sense of her as an active partner, as opposed to a passive love object, a big part of the excitement of playing the role?

That's why the play took me by surprise. It's like *Titanic*; we know the boat's going to sink, so why go and see the movie? It's the same with *Romeo and Juliet*. We know what's going to happen. That play in particular is very much in the public domain and everyone has got an opinion, an instinct, a feeling about it. What I love about presenting Shakespeare now, four hundred-odd years after it was written, is readdressing some issues. If people think "I like my Juliets to be sweet and innocent," you think, "What happens if they're not? How does that make you feel?" That seems to me to be the point of doing them now: not to rework them for the sake of it, but because you have an idea. Mike kept saying, "No, it's too sentimental. I don't want any sentimentality. It's much more brutal. Every single step of the way is like a car crash in your head." It's monumental what they go through, and you have to tell that story to a group of people who know what's going to happen. So you are continually reworking or readdressing exactly what, for example, "Gallop apace, you fiery-footed steeds" *really* means to someone who is desperate for the day to pass and the night to come. And when the night comes, what's she going to do? We found that she isn't some sweet and innocent child, she is someone who is on the front foot the whole time, and I found that fascinating.

It's about the most famous fictional love affair of all time, and the window/balcony scene is one of the most celebrated ever written, so how do you get past the clichés, the historical inheritance? Did you have any special tricks for making the part and the play your own?

It is very hard to play a scene with David Tennant [who played Romeo] without finding it funny! There were these little moments that we would find that made us laugh. I think Mike relished that: that the two of us found things that not only made us laugh, but made the audience laugh too. So instead of the balcony scene being this very famous, intimidating scene, we did it in our own way and it turned out to be quite funny.

There are scenes in certain Shakespeare plays where you think "Okay, how are we going to deal with this one?" The final speech at the end of *The Taming of the Shrew* is one. To find ways of making it work and making it fresh and interesting—for you and the audience—you sometimes have to start from a point of ignorance. As a result you let your instincts take over and then you're not necessarily thinking "I'm treading in *these* footsteps." Then hopefully everything develops organically, because you're responding to the other actors onstage as opposed to thinking, "Well, I know that Vivien Leigh, or whoever, played it this way."

Sometimes you do these great plays, and they were only done two or three years ago, and you've got the pressure of a great production that was in the repertoire recently, and you think "Bloody hell!" So you strap the play on your back and think, "What am I going to do?" And sometimes you do find things, because it's *you*, it's no one else playing it. It's you playing with the other actors and the director. Some people hated the fact that our production was unsentimental. Often the audience project their own ideas of what they want to see. What I find a much more interesting and appealing way of doing Shakespeare is to try to surprise people. Instead of making the audience feel comfortable, why don't we make them feel uncomfortable?

That's the point of it, isn't it? Otherwise we just do the same old thing over and over again. But if it's something completely different, then people talk about it, and if they're talking about it, then they're engaging with a play that was written four hundred years ago—what a thrill is that?!

Do you see the play as a battle between the young and the old, parents and children? Or are there some important bonds between the lovers and older mentors (for Juliet, the Nurse)?

Not necessarily a battle between young and old, but there is a battle between ideas. Juliet battles with her father, but not necessarily with the Nurse. For me when playing it, it wasn't so much about young and old, more about "This is what I want and you are the obstacle in my way." It just so happened that Romeo and Juliet are very young and they happen to be part of two warring families.

Juliet's apparent death is a big part of the final act. Some technical questions about playing it: first, what's the trick of keeping so still for so long?

Keeping still for so long wasn't necessarily a problem—you kind of get into a little zone. Although, in *The Winter's Tale*, playing Hermione as the statue used to panic me! I'd think, "What happens if I sneeze?"! But because you're concentrating on listening to what Romeo is saying, your mind is on other things. The problem with that final scene is not making it melodramatic. It is brutal and horrific, and yet you've somehow got to try and make it believable.

And when she does awake, how do you set about immediately conveying Juliet's fear and horror on finding herself in the family tomb? And was it especially difficult to move in so few lines from awakening to seeing the dead Romeo to suicide?

I found that scene very hard, every single night, because you really want to make it believable. What you want to do is make the audience think, "She's going to wake up. It'll be fine in the end." But because they know it isn't, I found it very hard to do every time we did it. You

7. The "balcony" scene: Alexandra Gilbreath as Juliet and David Tennant as Romeo in Michael Boyd's 2000 production.

have to put in everything, all your concentration, all your emotional self, to try and make that scene believable, because the audience know what's going to happen; they're pretty much waiting for it. What you want to do is get them on the edge of their seat, so although they know what's going to happen, they can't bear the thought that it actually will. That is the challenge of doing *Romeo and Juliet*. That's what great productions of all those classic plays do, be they Ibsen or Chekhov: they retell them in such a way that people are on the edge of their seats going, "I know what's going to happen, but . . ."

What do you think Juliet would like her epitaph to be?

"It is better to have loved and lost than never to have loved at all." Because the extremity of her emotion and her feelings for this one person are such that she is prepared to stick a knife in her gut, and if you actually stop to think about that, it is overwhelming. What happens in the moments before? How do you get to that stage when you're so overwhelmed by something you are prepared to take your own life? In that respect, I think if she had her time again, she'd say: "I wouldn't change a thing."

I don't think Juliet is capable of compromise. We have to get used to that in everyday life. As you get older and you have children, you compromise. Juliet, in her innocence, has no space for compromise. That's why I think there's nothing innocent, nothing flowery and sentimental about her.

SHAKESPEARE'S CAREER IN THE THEATER

BEGINNINGS

William Shakespeare was an extraordinarily intelligent man who was born and died in an ordinary market town in the English Midlands. He lived an uneventful life in an eventful age. Born in April 1564, he was the eldest son of John Shakespeare, a glove-maker who was prominent on the town council until he fell into financial difficulties. Young William was educated at the local grammar in Stratford-upon-Avon, Warwickshire, where he gained a thorough grounding in the Latin language, the art of rhetoric, and classical poetry. He married Ann Hathaway and had three children (Susanna, then the twins Hamnet and Judith) before his twenty-first birthday: an exceptionally young age for the period. We do not know how he supported his family in the mid-1580s.

Like many clever country boys, he moved to the city in order to make his way in the world. Like many creative people, he found a career in the entertainment business. Public playhouses and professional full-time acting companies reliant on the market for their income were born in Shakespeare's childhood. When he arrived in London as a man, sometime in the late 1580s, a new phenomenon was in the making: the actor who is so successful that he becomes a "star." The word did not exist in its modern sense, but the pattern is recognizable: audiences went to the theater not so much to see a particular show as to witness the comedian Richard Tarlton or the dramatic actor Edward Alleyn.

Shakespeare was an actor before he was a writer. It appears not to have been long before he realized that he was never going to grow into a great comedian like Tarlton or a great tragedian like Alleyn. Instead, he found a role within his company as the man who patched up old plays, breathing new life, new dramatic twists, into tired repertory pieces. He paid close attention to the work of the university-educated dramatists who were writing history plays and tragedies for the public stage in a style more ambitious, sweeping, and poetically grand than anything which had been seen before. But he may also have noted that what his friend and rival Ben Jonson would call "Marlowe's mighty line" sometimes faltered in the mode of comedy. Going to university, as Christopher Marlowe did, was all well and good for honing the arts of rhetorical elaboration and classical allusion, but it could lead to a loss of the common touch. To stay close to a large segment of the potential audience for public theater, it was necessary to write for clowns as well as kings and to intersperse the flights of poetry with the humor of the tavern, the privy, and the brothel: Shakespeare was the first to establish himself early in his career as an equal master of tragedy, comedy, and history. He realized that theater could be the medium to make the national past available to a wider audience than the elite who could afford to read large history books: his signature early works include not only the classical tragedy *Titus Andronicus* but also the sequence of English historical plays on the Wars of the Roses.

He also invented a new role for himself, that of in-house company dramatist. Where his peers and predecessors had to sell their plays to the theater managers on a poorly paid piecework basis, Shakespeare took a percentage of the box-office income. The Lord Chamberlain's Men constituted themselves in 1594 as a joint stock company, with the profits being distributed among the core actors who had invested as sharers. Shakespeare acted himself—he appears in the cast lists of some of Ben Jonson's plays as well as the list of actors' names at the beginning of his own collected works—but his principal duty was to write two or three plays a year for the company. By holding shares, he was effectively earning himself a royalty on his work, something no author had ever done before in England. When the Lord Chamberlain's Men collected their fee for performance at court in the Christmas season of 1594, three of them went along to the Treasurer of the Chamber: not just Richard Burbage the tragedian and Will Kempe the clown, but also Shakespeare the scriptwriter. That was something new.

The next four years were the golden period in Shakespeare's career, though overshadowed by the death of his only son, Hamnet, aged eleven, in 1596. In his early thirties and in full command of both his poetic and his theatrical medium, he perfected his art of comedy, while also developing his tragic and historical writing in new ways. In 1598, Francis Meres, a Cambridge University graduate with his finger on the pulse of the London literary world, praised Shakespeare for his excellence across the genres:

> As Plautus and Seneca are accounted the best for comedy and tragedy among the Latins, so Shakespeare among the English is the most excellent in both kinds for the stage; for comedy, witness his *Gentlemen of Verona*, his *Errors*, his *Love Labours Lost*, his *Love Labours Won*, his *Midsummer Night Dream* and his *Merchant of Venice*: for tragedy his *Richard the 2*, *Richard the 3*, *Henry the 4*, *King John*, *Titus Andronicus* and his *Romeo and Juliet*.

For Meres, as for the many writers who praised the "honey-flowing vein" of *Venus and Adonis* and *Lucrece*, narrative poems written when the theaters were closed due to plague in 1593–94, Shakespeare was marked above all by his linguistic skill, by the gift of turning elegant poetic phrases.

PLAYHOUSES

Elizabethan playhouses were "thrust" or "one-room" theaters. To understand Shakespeare's original theatrical life, we have to forget about the indoor theater of later times, with its proscenium arch and curtain that would be opened at the beginning and closed at the end of each act. In the proscenium arch theater, stage and auditorium are effectively two separate rooms: the audience looks from one world into another as if through the imaginary "fourth wall" framed by the proscenium. The picture-frame stage, together with the elaborate scenic effects and backdrops beyond it, created the illusion of a self-contained world—especially once nineteenth-century developments in the control of artificial lighting meant that the auditorium could be darkened and the spectators made to focus on the lighted stage. Shakespeare, by contrast, wrote for a bare platform stage with a standing audience gathered around it in a courtyard in full daylight. The audience were always conscious of themselves and their fellow spectators, and they shared the same "room" as the actors. A sense of immediate presence and the creation of rapport with the audience were all-important. The actor could not afford to imagine he was in a closed world, with silent witnesses dutifully observing him from the darkness.

Shakespeare's theatrical career began at the Rose Theater in Southwark. The stage was wide and shallow, trapezoid in shape, like a lozenge. This design had a great deal of potential for the theatrical equivalent of cinematic split-screen effects, whereby one group of characters would enter at the door at one end of the tiring-house wall at the back of the stage and another group through the door at the other end, thus creating two rival tableaux. Many of the battle-heavy and faction-filled plays that premiered at the Rose have scenes of just this sort.

At the rear of the Rose stage, there were three capacious exits, each over ten feet wide. Unfortunately, the very limited excavation of a fragmentary portion of the original Globe site, in 1989, revealed nothing about the stage. The first Globe was built in 1599 with similar proportions to those of another theater, the Fortune, albeit that the former was polygonal and looked circular, whereas the latter was rectangular. The building contract for the Fortune survives and allows us to infer that the stage of the Globe was probably substantially wider than it was deep (perhaps forty-three feet wide and twenty-seven feet deep). It may well have been tapered at the front, like that of the Rose.

The capacity of the Globe was said to have been enormous, perhaps in excess of three thousand. It has been conjectured that about eight hundred people may have stood in the yard, with two thousand or more in the three layers of covered galleries. The other "public" playhouses were also of large capacity, whereas the indoor Blackfriars theater that Shakespeare's company began using in 1608—the former refectory of a monastery—had overall internal dimensions of a mere forty-six by sixty feet. It would have made for a much more intimate theatrical experience and had a much smaller capacity, probably of about six hundred people. Since they paid at least six-pence a head, the Blackfriars attracted a more select or "private" audience. The atmosphere would have been closer to that of an indoor performance before the court in the Whitehall Palace or at Richmond. That Shakespeare always wrote for indoor production at court as well as outdoor performance in the public theater should make us cautious about inferring, as some scholars have, that the opportunity provided by the intimacy of the Blackfriars led to a significant change toward a "chamber" style in his last plays—which, besides, were performed at both the Globe and the Blackfriars. After the occupation of the Blackfriars a five-act structure seems to have become more important to Shakespeare. That was because of artificial lighting: there were musical interludes between the acts, while the candles were trimmed and replaced. Again, though, something similar must have been necessary for indoor court performances throughout his career.

Front of house there were the "gatherers" who collected the money from audience members: a penny to stand in the open-air yard, another penny for a place in the covered galleries, sixpence for the prominent "lord's rooms" to the side of the stage. In the indoor "private" theaters, gallants from the audience who fancied making themselves part of the spectacle sat on stools on the edge of the stage itself. Scholars debate as to how widespread this practice was in the public theaters such as the Globe. Once the audience were in place and the money counted, the gatherers were available to be extras onstage. That is one reason why battles and crowd scenes often come later rather than early in Shakespeare's plays. There was no formal prohibition upon performance by women, and there certainly were women among the gatherers, so it is not beyond the bounds of possibility that female crowd members were played by females.

The play began at two o'clock in the afternoon and the theater had to be cleared by five. After the main show, there would be a jig—which consisted not only of dancing, but also of knockabout comedy (it is the origin of the farcical "afterpiece" in the eighteenth-century theater). So the time available for a Shakespeare play was about two and a half hours, somewhere between the "two hours' traffic" mentioned in the prologue to *Romeo and Juliet* and the "three hours' spectacle" referred to in the preface to the 1647 Folio of Beaumont and Fletcher's plays. The prologue to a play by Thomas Middleton refers to a thousand lines as "one hour's words," so the likelihood is that about two and a half thousand, or a maximum of three thousand lines made up the performed text. This is indeed the length of most of Shakespeare's comedies, whereas many of his tragedies and histories are much longer, raising the possibility that he wrote full scripts, possibly with eventual publication in mind, in the full knowledge that the stage version would be heavily cut. The short Quarto texts published in his lifetime—they used to be called "Bad" Quartos—provide fascinating evidence as to the kind of cutting that probably took place. So, for instance, the First Quarto of *Hamlet* neatly merges two occasions when Hamlet is overheard, the "Fishmonger" and the "nunnery" scenes.

The social composition of the audience was mixed. The poet Sir John Davies wrote of "A thousand townsmen, gentlemen and whores, / Porters and servingmen" who would "together throng" at the public playhouses. Though moralists associated female playgoing with adultery and the sex trade, many perfectly respectable citizens' wives were regular attendees. Some, no doubt, resembled the modern groupie: a story attested in two different sources has one citizen's wife making a post-show assignation with Richard Burbage and ending up in bed with Shakespeare—supposedly eliciting from the latter the quip that William the Conqueror was before Richard III. Defenders of theater liked to say that by witnessing the comeuppance of villains on the stage, audience members would repent of their own wrongdoings, but the reality is that most people went to the theater then, as they do now, for entertainment more than moral edification. Besides, it would be foolish to suppose that audiences behaved in a homogeneous way: a pamphlet of the 1630s tells of how two men went to see *Pericles* and one of them laughed while the other wept. Bishop John Hall complained that people went to church for the same reasons that they went to the theater: "for company, for custom, for recreation . . . to feed his eyes or his ears . . . or perhaps for sleep."

Men-about-town and clever young lawyers went to be seen as much as to see. In the modern popular imagination, shaped not least by *Shakespeare in Love* and the opening sequence of Laurence Olivier's *Henry V* film, the penny-paying groundlings stand in the yard hurling abuse or encouragement and hazelnuts or orange peel at the actors, while the sophisticates in the covered galleries appreciate Shakespeare's soaring poetry. The reality was probably the other way round. A "groundling" was a kind of fish, so the nickname suggests the penny audience standing below the level of the stage and gazing in silent open-mouthed wonder at the spectacle unfolding above them. The more difficult audience members, who kept up a running commentary of clever remarks on the performance and who occasionally got into quarrels with players, were the gallants. Like Hollywood movies in modern times, Elizabethan and Jacobean plays exercised a powerful influence on the fashion and behavior of the young. John Marston mocks the lawyers who would open their lips, perhaps to court a girl, and out would "flow / Naught but pure Juliet and Romeo."

THE ENSEMBLE AT WORK

In the absence of typewriters and photocopying machines, reading aloud would have been the means by which the company got to know a new play. The tradition of the playwright reading his complete script to the assembled company endured for generations. A copy would then have been taken to the Master of the Revels for licensing. The theater book-holder or prompter would then have copied the parts for distribution to the actors. A partbook consisted of the character's lines, with each speech preceded by the last three or four words of the speech before, the so-called "cue." These would have been taken away and studied or "conned." During this period of learning the parts, an actor might have had some one-to-one instruction, perhaps from the dramatist, perhaps from a senior actor who had played the same part before, and, in the case of an apprentice, from his master. A high percentage of Desdemona's lines occur in dialogue with Othello, of Lady Macbeth's with Macbeth, Cleopatra's with Antony, and Volumnia's with Coriolanus. The roles would almost certainly have been taken by the apprentice of the lead actor, usually Burbage, who delivers the majority of the cues. Given that apprentices lodged with their masters, there would have been ample opportunity for personal instruction, which may be what made it possible for young men to play such demanding parts.

8. Hypothetical reconstruction of the interior of an Elizabethan playhouse during a performance.

After the parts were learned, there may have been no more than a single rehearsal before the first performance. With six different plays to be put on every week, there was no time for more. Actors, then, would go into a show with a very limited sense of the whole. The notion of a collective rehearsal process that is itself a process of discovery for the actors is wholly modern and would have been incomprehensible to Shakespeare and his original ensemble. Given the number of parts an actor had to hold in his memory, the forgetting of lines was probably more frequent than in the modern theater. The book-holder was on hand to prompt.

Backstage personnel included the property man, the tire-man who oversaw the costumes, call-boys, attendants, and the musicians, who might play at various times from the main stage, the rooms above, and within the tiring-house. Scriptwriters sometimes made a nuisance of themselves backstage. There was often tension between the acting companies and the freelance playwrights from whom they purchased scripts: it was a smart move on the part of Shakespeare and the Lord Chamberlain's Men to bring the writing process in-house.

Scenery was limited, though sometimes set pieces were brought on (a bank of flowers, a bed, the mouth of hell). The trapdoor from below, the gallery stage above, and the curtained discovery space at the back allowed for an array of special effects: the rising of ghosts and apparitions, the descent of gods, dialogue between a character at a window and another at ground level, the revelation of a statue or a pair of lovers playing at chess. Ingenious use could be made of props, as with the ass's head in *A Midsummer Night's Dream*. In a theater that does not clutter the stage with the material paraphernalia of everyday life, those objects that are deployed may take on powerful symbolic weight, as when Shylock bears his weighing scales in one hand and a knife in the other, thus becoming a parody of the figure of Justice who traditionally bears a sword and a balance. Among the more significant items in the property cupboard of Shakespeare's company, there would have been a throne (the "chair of state"), joint stools, books, bottles, coins, purses, letters (which are brought onstage, read or referred to on about eighty occasions in the complete works), maps, gloves, a set of stocks (in which Kent is put in *King Lear*), rings, rapiers, daggers, broadswords, staves, pistols, masks and vizards, heads and skulls, torches and tapers and lanterns which served to signal night scenes on the daylit stage, a buck's head, an ass's head, animal costumes. Live animals also put in appearances, most notably the dog Crab in *The Two Gentlemen of Verona* and possibly a young polar bear in *The Winter's Tale*.

The costumes were the most important visual dimension of the play. Playwrights were paid between £2 and £6 per script, whereas Alleyn was not averse to paying £20 for "a black velvet cloak with sleeves embroidered all with silver and gold." No matter the period of the play, actors always wore contemporary costume. The excitement for the audience came not from any impression of historical accuracy, but from the richness of the attire and perhaps the transgressive thrill of the knowledge that here were commoners like themselves strutting in the costumes of courtiers in effective defiance of the strict sumptuary laws whereby in real life people had to wear the clothes that befitted their social station.

To an even greater degree than props, costumes could carry symbolic importance. Racial characteristics could be suggested: a breastplate and helmet for a Roman soldier, a turban for a Turk, long robes for exotic characters such as Moors, a gabardine for a Jew. The figure of Time, as in *The Winter's Tale*, would be equipped with hourglass, scythe, and wings; Rumour, who speaks the prologue of *2 Henry IV*, wore a costume adorned with a thousand tongues. The wardrobe in the tiring-house of the Globe would have contained much of the same stock as that of rival manager Philip Henslowe at the Rose: green gowns for outlaws and foresters, black for melancholy men such as Jaques and people in mourning such as the Countess in *All's Well that Ends Well* (at the beginning of *Hamlet*, the prince is still in mourning black when everyone else is in festive garb for the wedding of the new king), a gown and hood for a friar (or a feigned friar like the duke in *Measure for Measure*), blue coats and tawny to distinguish the followers of rival factions, a leather apron and ruler for a carpenter (as in the opening scene of *Julius Caesar*—and in *A Midsummer Night's Dream*, where this is the only sign that Peter Quince is a carpenter), a cockle hat with staff and a pair of sandals for a pilgrim or palmer (the disguise assumed by Helen in *All's Well*), bodices and kirtles with farthingales beneath for the boys who are to be dressed as girls. A gender switch such as that of Rosalind or Jessica seems to have taken between fifty and eighty lines of dialogue—Viola does not resume her "maiden weeds," but remains in her boy's costume to the end of *Twelfth Night* because a change would have slowed down the action at just the moment it was speeding to a climax. Henslowe's inventory also included "a robe for to go invisible": Oberon, Puck, and Ariel must have had something similar.

As the costumes appealed to the eyes, so there was music for the ears. Comedies included many songs. Desdemona's willow song, perhaps a late addition to the text, is a rare and thus exceptionally poignant example from tragedy. Trumpets and tuckets sounded for ceremonial entrances, drums denoted an army on the march. Background music could create atmosphere, as at the beginning of *Twelfth Night*, during the lovers' dialogue near the end of *The Merchant of Venice*, when the statue seemingly comes to life in *The Winter's Tale*, and for the revival of *Pericles* and of *Lear* (in the Quarto text, but not the Folio). The haunting sound of the hautboy suggested a realm beyond the human, as when the god Hercules is imagined deserting Mark Antony. Dances symbolized the harmony of the end of a comedy—though in Shakespeare's world of mingled joy and sorrow, someone is usually left out of the circle.

The most important resource was, of course, the actors themselves. They needed many skills: in the words of one contemporary commentator, "dancing, activity, music, song, elocution, ability of body, memory, skill of weapon, pregnancy of wit." Their bodies were as significant as their voices. Hamlet tells the player to "suit the action to the word, the word to the action": moments of strong emotion, known as "passions," relied on a repertoire of dramatic gestures as well as a modulation of the voice. When Titus Andronicus has had his hand chopped off, he asks "How can I grace my talk, / Wanting a hand to give it action?" A pen portrait of "The Character of an Excellent Actor" by the dramatist John Webster is almost certainly based on his impression of Shakespeare's leading man, Richard Burbage: "By a full and significant action of body, he charms our attention: sit in a full theatre, and you will think you see so many lines drawn from the circumference of so many ears, whiles the actor is the centre . . . ."

Though Burbage was admired above all others, praise was also heaped upon the apprentice players whose alto voices fitted them for the parts of women. A spectator at Oxford in 1610 records how the audience were reduced to tears by the pathos of Desdemona's death. The puritans who fumed about the biblical prohibition upon cross-dressing and the encouragement to sodomy constituted by the sight of an adult male kissing a teenage boy onstage were a small minority. Little is known, however, about the characteristics of the leading apprentices in Shakespeare's company. It may perhaps be inferred that one was a lot taller than the other, since Shakespeare often wrote for a pair of female friends, one tall and fair, the other short and dark (Helena and Hermia, Rosalind and Celia, Beatrice and Hero).

We know little about Shakespeare's own acting roles—an early allusion indicates that he often took royal parts, and a venerable tradition gives him old Adam in *As You Like It* and the ghost of old King Hamlet. Save for Burbage's lead roles and the generic part of the clown, all such castings are mere speculation. We do not even know for sure whether the original Falstaff was Will Kempe or another actor who specialized in comic roles, Thomas Pope.

Kempe left the company in early 1599. Tradition has it that he fell out with Shakespeare over the matter of excessive improvisation. He was replaced by Robert Armin, who was less of a clown and more of a cerebral wit: this explains the difference between such parts as Lancelet Gobbo and Dogberry, which were written for Kempe, and the more verbally sophisticated Feste and Lear's Fool, which were written for Armin.

One thing that is clear from surviving "plots" or storyboards of plays from the period is that a degree of doubling was necessary. *2 Henry VI* has over sixty speaking parts, but more than half of the characters only appear in a single scene and most scenes have only six to eight speakers. At a stretch, the play could be performed by thirteen actors. When Thomas Platter saw *Julius Caesar* at the Globe in 1599, he noted that there were about fifteen. Why doesn't Paris go to the Capulet ball in *Romeo and Juliet?* Perhaps because he was doubled with Mercutio, who does. In *The Winter's Tale*, Mamillius might have come back as Perdita and Antigonus been doubled by Camillo, making the partnership with Paulina at the end a very neat touch. Titania and Oberon are often played by the same pair as Hippolyta and Theseus, suggesting a symbolic matching of the rulers of the worlds of night and day, but it is questionable whether there would have been time for the necessary costume changes. As so often, one is left in a realm of tantalizing speculation.

THE KING'S MAN

On Queen Elizabeth's death in 1603, the new king, James I, who had held the Scottish throne as James VI since he had been an infant, immediately took the Lord Chamberlain's Men under his direct patronage. Henceforth they would be the King's Men, and for the rest of Shakespeare's career they were favored with far more court performances than any of their rivals. There even seem to have been rumors early in the reign that Shakespeare and Burbage were being considered for knighthoods, an unprecedented honor for mere actors—and one that in the event was not accorded to a member of the profession for nearly three hundred years, when the title was bestowed upon Henry Irving, the leading Shakespearean actor of Queen Victoria's reign.

Shakespeare's productivity rate slowed in the Jacobean years, not because of age or some personal trauma, but because there were frequent outbreaks of plague, causing the theaters to be closed for long periods. The King's Men were forced to spend many months on the road. Between November 1603 and 1608, they were to be found at various towns in the south and Midlands, though Shakespeare probably did not tour with them by this time. He had bought a large house back home in Stratford and was accumulating other property. He may indeed have stopped acting soon after the new king took the throne. With the London theaters closed so much of the time and a large repertoire on the stocks, Shakespeare seems to have focused his energies on writing a few long and complex tragedies that could have been played on demand at court: *Othello*, *King Lear*, *Antony and Cleopatra*, *Coriolanus*, and *Cymbeline* are among his longest and poetically grandest plays. *Macbeth* only survives in a shorter text, which shows signs of adaptation after Shakespeare's death. The bitterly satirical *Timon of Athens*, apparently a collaboration with Thomas Middleton that may have failed on the stage, also belongs to this period. In comedy, too, he wrote longer and morally darker works than in the Elizabethan period, pushing at the very bounds of the form in *Measure for Measure* and *All's Well That Ends Well*.

From 1608 onward, when the King's Men began occupying the indoor Blackfriars playhouse (as a winter house, meaning that they only used the outdoor Globe in summer?), Shakespeare turned to a more romantic style. His company had a great success with a revived and altered version of an old pastoral play called *Mucedorus*. It even featured a bear. The younger dramatist John Fletcher, meanwhile, sometimes working in collaboration with Francis Beaumont, was pioneering a new style of tragicomedy, a mix of romance and royalism laced with intrigue and pastoral excursions. Shakespeare experimented with this idiom in *Cymbeline* and it was presumably with his blessing that Fletcher eventually took over as the King's Men's company dramatist. The two writers apparently collaborated on three plays in the years 1612–14: a lost romance called *Cardenio* (based on the love-madness of a character in Cervantes' *Don Quixote*), *Henry VIII* (originally staged with the title "All Is True"), and *The Two Noble Kinsmen*, a dramatization of Chaucer's "Knight's Tale." These were written after Shakespeare's two final solo-authored plays, *The Winter's Tale*, a self-consciously old-fashioned work dramatizing the pastoral romance of his old enemy Robert Greene, and *The Tempest*, which at one and the same time drew together multiple theatrical traditions, diverse reading, and contemporary interest in the fate of a ship that had been wrecked on the way to the New World.

The collaborations with Fletcher suggest that Shakespeare's career ended with a slow fade rather than the sudden retirement supposed by the nineteenth-century Romantic critics who read Prospero's epilogue to *The Tempest* as Shakespeare's personal farewell to his art. In the last few years of his life Shakespeare certainly spent more of his time in Stratford-upon-Avon, where he became further involved in property dealing and litigation. But his London life also continued. In 1613 he made his first major London property purchase: a freehold house in the Blackfriars district, close to his company's indoor theater. *The Two Noble Kinsmen* may have been written as late as 1614, and Shakespeare was in London on business a little over a year before he died of an unknown cause at home in Stratford-upon-Avon in 1616, probably on his fifty-second birthday.

About half the sum of his works were published in his lifetime, in texts of variable quality. A few years after his death, his fellow actors began putting together an authorized edition of his complete *Comedies, Histories and Tragedies*. It appeared in 1623, in large "Folio" format. This collection of thirty-six plays gave Shakespeare his immortality. In the words of his fellow dramatist Ben Jonson, who contributed two poems of praise at the start of the Folio, the body of his work made him "a monument without a tomb":

And art alive still while thy book doth live
And we have wits to read and praise to give . . .
He was not of an age, but for all time!

SHAKESPEARE'S WORKS: A CHRONOLOGY

1589–91	*? Arden of Faversham* (possible part authorship)
1589–92	*The Taming of the Shrew*
1589–92	*? Edward the Third* (possible part authorship)
1591	*The Second Part of Henry the Sixth*, originally called *The First Part of the Contention Betwixt the Two Famous Houses of York and Lancaster* (element of coauthorship possible)
1591	*The Third Part of Henry the Sixth*, originally called *The True Tragedy of Richard Duke of York* (element of co-authorship probable)
1591–92	*The Two Gentlemen of Verona*
1591–92; perhaps revised 1594	*The Lamentable Tragedy of Titus Andronicus* (probably cowritten with, or revising an earlier version by, George Peele)
1592	*The First Part of Henry the Sixth*, probably with Thomas Nashe and others
1592/94	*King Richard the Third*
1593	*Venus and Adonis* (poem)
1593–94	*The Rape of Lucrece* (poem)
1593–1608	*Sonnets* (154 poems, published 1609 with *A Lover's Complaint*, a poem of disputed authorship)
1592–94/ 1600–03	*Sir Thomas More* (a single scene for a play originally by Anthony Munday, with other revisions by Henry Chettle, Thomas Dekker, and Thomas Heywood)
1594	*The Comedy of Errors*
1595	*Love's Labour's Lost*

1595–97	*Love's Labour's Won* (a lost play, unless the original title for another comedy)
1595–96	*A Midsummer Night's Dream*
1595–96	*The Tragedy of Romeo and Juliet*
1595–96	*King Richard the Second*
1595–97	*The Life and Death of King John* (possibly earlier)
1596–97	*The Merchant of Venice*
1596–97	*The First Part of Henry the Fourth*
1597–98	*The Second Part of Henry the Fourth*
1598	*Much Ado About Nothing*
1598–99	*The Passionate Pilgrim* (20 poems, some not by Shakespeare)
1599	*The Life of Henry the Fifth*
1599	"To the Queen" (epilogue for a court performance)
1599	*As You Like It*
1599	*The Tragedy of Julius Caesar*
1600–01	*The Tragedy of Hamlet, Prince of Denmark* (perhaps revising an earlier version)
1600–01	*The Merry Wives of Windsor* (perhaps revising version of 1597–99)
1601	"Let the Bird of Loudest Lay" (poem, known since 1807 as "The Phoenix and Turtle" [turtle-dove])
1601	*Twelfth Night, or What You Will*
1601–02	*The Tragedy of Troilus and Cressida*
1604	*The Tragedy of Othello, the Moor of Venice*
1604	*Measure for Measure*
1605	*All's Well That Ends Well*
1605	*The Life of Timon of Athens*, with Thomas Middleton
1605–06	*The Tragedy of King Lear*
1605–08	? contribution to *The Four Plays in One* (lost, except for *A Yorkshire Tragedy*, mostly by Thomas Middleton)

1606	*The Tragedy of Macbeth* (surviving text has additional scenes by Thomas Middleton)
1606–07	*The Tragedy of Antony and Cleopatra*
1608	*The Tragedy of Coriolanus*
1608	*Pericles, Prince of Tyre*, with George Wilkins
1610	*The Tragedy of Cymbeline*
1611	*The Winter's Tale*
1611	*The Tempest*
1612–13	*Cardenio*, with John Fletcher (survives only in later adaptation called *Double Falsehood* by Lewis Theobald)
1613	*Henry VIII (All Is True)*, with John Fletcher
1613–14	*The Two Noble Kinsmen*, with John Fletcher

FURTHER READING AND VIEWING

CRITICAL APPROACHES

Andrews, John F., ed., *Romeo and Juliet: Critical Essays* (1993). Excellent collection of essays covering language, performance, and social context.

Colie, Rosalie L., *Shakespeare's Living Art* (1974). Extremely sensitive reading, attentive to language and rhetoric.

Frye, Northrop, *Northrop Frye on Shakespeare*, ed. Robert Sandler (1986), pp. 15–33. Introductory lecture by a master critic.

Halio, Jay L., ed., *Shakespeare's Romeo and Juliet: Texts, Contexts, and Interpretations* (1995). Interesting and varied collection of essays.

Halio, Jay L., *Romeo and Juliet: A Guide to the Play* (1998). Sound introduction.

Kahn, Coppélia, "Coming of Age in Verona," in *The Woman's Part: Feminist Criticism of Shakespeare*, ed. Carolyn Ruth Swift Lenz, Gayle Greene, and Carol Thomas Neely (1983), pp. 171–93. Strong feminist reading.

Roberts, Sasha, *William Shakespeare: Romeo and Juliet* (1998). Very useful introduction offering a wide-ranging, theoretically informed account of the play.

Snyder, Susan, "*Romeo and Juliet*: Comedy into Tragedy," *Essays in Criticism*, 20 (1970), pp. 391–402. Exemplary close reading, with attention to genre.

Watts, Cedric, *Harvester New Critical Introductions to Shakespeare: Romeo and Juliet* (1991). Useful introduction to the play and discussion of various textual and interpretive problems.

White, R. S., ed., *New Casebooks: Romeo and Juliet* (2001). Wide-ranging, sophisticated collection of essays.

THE PLAY IN PERFORMANCE

Holding, Peter, *Text and Performance: Romeo and Juliet* (1992). Part 2 discusses five important twentieth-century productions in detail.

Jackson, Russell, *Shakespeare at Stratford: Romeo and Juliet* (2002). Excellent, very detailed account of performances at Stratford from 1947 to 2000.

Levenson, Jill, *Shakespeare in Performance: Romeo and Juliet* (1987). Excellent introduction of play in performance up to Zeffirelli's 1968 film.

Loehlin, James N., ed., *Romeo and Juliet: Shakespeare in Production* (2002). Edition of play with detailed theatrical commentary and useful stage history in introduction.

Smallwood, Robert, ed., *Players of Shakespeare 4* (1998). Includes Julian Glover on playing Friar Laurence.

Smallwood, Robert, ed., *Players of Shakespeare 5* (2003). David Tennant discusses playing Romeo.

Sourcebooks Shakespeare, *Romeo and Juliet: Shakespeare in Performance* (2007). Lively, useful student guide with accompanying CD.

Wright, Katherine L., *Shakespeare's Romeo and Juliet in Performance: Traditions and Departures* (1997). Thoughtful, detailed analysis of four centuries of interpretation of performances of Romeo, Juliet, and Mercutio.

AVAILABLE ON DVD

Romeo and Juliet, directed by George Cukor (1936, DVD 2007). With Norma Shearer and Leslie Howard. Multi-Oscar-nominated, but not popular with critics or audiences. Black and white, well-spoken but definitely dated.

Romeo and Juliet, directed by Renato Castellani (1954, DVD 2000). With Laurence Harvey and Susan Shentall. Won the Grand Prix at the Venice Film Festival.

West Side Story, directed by Robert Wise and Jerome Robbins (1961, DVD 2000). With Leonard Bernstein's brilliant music and lyrics by Stephen Sondheim. The play is updated to contemporary New York and competing gangs of Jets and Sharks, starring Natalie Wood and Richard Beymer. Deservedly won ten Oscars.

Romeo and Juliet, directed by Paul Czinner (1966, DVD 1999). Royal Ballet version of Prokofiev's ballet music, with Margot Fonteyn and Rudolf Nureyev.

Romeo and Juliet, directed by Franco Zeffirelli (1968, DVD 1996). Cast the very young Leonard Whiting and Olivia Hussey. Beautiful to look at, with its re-creation of medieval Verona; popular and appealing.

Romeo and Juliet, directed by Alvin Lakoff (1978, DVD 2005). Part of BBC television's Complete Shakespeare, with Patrick Ryecart and Rebecca Saire as leads in a cast which includes John Gielgud, Michael Hordern, Alan Rickman, and Celia Johnson.

William Shakespeare's Romeo + Juliet, directed by Baz Luhrmann (1996, DVD 2002). For the MTV generation with Leonardo DiCaprio and Claire Danes. Set in modern-day America—inventive and fast-paced, visually stunning, as if edited on acid.

Shakespeare in Love, directed by John Madden (1998, DVD 1999). With screenplay by Tom Stoppard. This dramatized Shakespeare's writing of *Romeo and Juliet*. Clever and funny, it won four Oscars, including Best Picture.

High School Musical, directed by Kenny Ortega for America's Disney Television Channel (2006, DVD 2006). Described by its makers as a modern-day *Romeo and Juliet*: set in an American high school, immensely popular, Emmy Award–winning. There have since been two sequels.

REFERENCES

1. Samuel Pepys, *The Diary of Samuel Pepys*, ed. Robert Latham and William Matthews, Volume 3 (1970), p. 39.
2. John Downes, *Roscius Anglicanus*, ed. Montague Summers (1929, repr. 1969), p. 22.
3. John Doran, *"Their Majesties' Servants," or Annals of the English Stage* (1897), Volume 1, pp. 187–8.
4. Arthur Murphy, *The Student*, 20 October 1750, reprinted in *Shakespeare: The Critical Heritage, 1733–1752*, ed. Brian Vickers, Volume 3 (1975), pp. 374–9.
5. *London Magazine*, October 1750.
6. David Garrick, *The Plays of David Garrick*, ed. with commentary and notes by Harry William Pedicord and Fredrick Louis Bergmann, Volume 3: *Garrick's Adaptations of Shakespeare, 1744–1756* (1981).
7. William Hazlitt, *Champion*, 8 January 1815.
8. *The Times*, London, 30 December 1845.
9. William Winter, "Opening Night at the Booth Theater," *New York Daily Tribune*, 4 February 1869.
10. Clement Scott, *"The Bells" to "King Arthur": A Critical Record of the First-Night Productions at the Lyceum Theatre from 1871 to 1895* (1896), pp. 229–44.
11. Henry James, "London Pictures and London Plays," *Atlantic Monthly*, L, no. CCX–CVIII, August 1882, pp. 253–63.
12. George Bernard Shaw, *Saturday Review*, London, LXXX, 28 September 1895, pp. 409–10.
13. "Romeo and Juliet at the Royalty Theatre," *The Academy*, 68, no. 1723, 13 May 1905, p. 522.
14. J. C. Trewin, "Full Dress, 1900–1914: In Town and Out, 1905–1906," in his *Shakespeare on the English Stage, 1900–1964: A Survey of Productions* (1964), pp. 34–7.
15. James Agate, *Sunday Times*, London, 20 October 1935.
16. Peter Fleming, *Spectator*, 25 October 1935.
17. *The Times*, London, 18 October 1935.
18. Ivor Brown, *Observer*, 20 October 1935.
19. James Agate, *Sunday Times*, 1 December 1935, reprinted in his *More First Nights* (1937), pp. 182–88, 203–8.

20. *The Times*, London, 7 April 1947.
21. H. S. Bennett and George Rylands, *Shakespeare Survey 1* (1948), pp. 107–11.
22. Jill Levenson gives an excellent account of this production in chapter V of her *Shakespeare in Performance: Romeo and Juliet* (1987).
23. Kenneth Tynan, *Observer*, 10 October 1960.
24. Tynan, *Observer*, 10 October 1960.
25. See Dennis Kennedy, ed., *Foreign Shakespeare: Contemporary Performance* (1993) and *A Directory of Shakespeare in Performance, 1970–2005*, Volume I, *Great Britain*, ed. John O'Connor and Katharine Goodland (2007).
26. Katherine Duncan-Jones, *Times Literary Supplement*, 20 October 2000, p. 19.
27. Cedric Watts, *New Critical Introductions to Shakespeare: Romeo and Juliet* (1991), p. xxi.
28. Douglas Lanier, " 'What's in a Name?': *Romeo and Juliet* and Pop Culture," in Sourcebooks Shakespeare, *Romeo and Juliet: Shakespeare in Performance* (2005), pp. 19–25.
29. Levenson, *Romeo and Juliet*, p. 105.
30. Jennifer L. Martin, "Tights vs Tattoos: Filmic Interpretations of *Romeo and Juliet*," *English Journal* 92, no. 1 (September 2002), pp. 41–6. More detailed discussions of Luhrmann's film can be found in Barbara Hodgdon, "*William Shakespeare's Romeo + Juliet*: Everything's Nice in America?," *Shakespeare Survey* 52 (1999), pp. 88–98; James Loehlin, " 'These Violent Delights Have Violent Ends': Baz Luhrmann's Millenial Shakespeare," in *Shakespeare, Film, Fin de Siècle*, ed. Marc Thornton Burnett and Ramona Wray (2000), pp. 121–36, p. 124; Michael Anderegg, *Cinematic Shakespeare* (2004), pp. 73–4.
31. Jim Welsh, "Postmodern Shakespeare: Strictly Romeo," *Literature-Film Quarterly* 25, no. 2 (April 1997), pp. 152–3.
32. Gregory Doran, *Romeo and Juliet*, RSC Education Pack, 1989.
33. *Romeo and Juliet*, RSC Online Playguide, 2004.
34. Originally coined by William Hazlitt in his essay on *Characters of Shakespear's Plays* (1817): "Romeo is Hamlet in love. There is the same rich exuberance of passion and sentiment in the one, that there is of thought and sentiment in the other. Both are absent and self-involved, both live out of themselves in a world of imagination. Hamlet is abstracted from every thing; Romeo is abstracted from every thing but his love, and lost in it."
35. Russell Jackson, *Romeo and Juliet*, Shakespeare at Stratford (2003).

36. David Tennant, "Romeo," in Robert Smallwood (ed.), *Players of Shakespeare 5* (2003).

37. Russell Jackson, *Romeo and Juliet*, Shakespeare at Stratford (2003).

38. *Romeo and Juliet*, RSC Education Pack, 1997.

39. *Romeo and Juliet*, RSC Education Pack, 1997.

40. David Benedict, *Independent*, 8 November 1997.

41. Margaret Thatcher, from an interview on 23 September 1987 to *Woman's Own*, published 31 October 1987.

42. Russell Jackson, *Romeo and Juliet*, including a quotation from the *Sunday Times* Review (*Shakespeare at Stratford*, 2003).

43. Irving Wardle, *The Times*, London, 10 April 1986.

44. Michael Billington, *Guardian*, 10 April 1986.

45. Martin Hoyle, *Financial Times*, 10 April 1986.

46. Gregory Doran, Assistant Director, *Romeo and Juliet*, RSC Education Pack, 1989.

47. Michael Billington, *Guardian*, 2 April 1976.

48. Billington, *Guardian*, 2 April 1976.

49. Sebastian, in Shakespeare's *Twelfth Night* (Act 2 scene 1).

50. Michael Billington, interview with Karolos Koun, *The Times*, 9 September 1967.

51. Keith Brace interview with Ian Holm, *Birmingham Post*, 9 September 1967.

52. Jack Sutherland, *Morning Star*, 15 September 1967.

53. Michael Billington, *Guardian*, 7 April 1989.

54. Paul Taylor, *Independent*, 7 April 1989.

55. David Tennant, "Romeo."

56. Richard Williamson, *Sunday Mercury*, 9 July 2000.

57. James N. Loehlin, *Romeo and Juliet*, Shakespeare in Production (2002).

58. Loehlin, *Romeo and Juliet*.

59. Jeremy Kingston, *Punch*, 4 April 1973.

60. Russell Jackson, *Romeo and Juliet*.

61. The Buzzcocks, "Ever Fallen In Love With Someone (You Shouldn't've Fallen In Love With)?" from the album *Love Bites* (1978).

62. Michael Billington, *Guardian*, 8 April 2004.

63. Michael Billington, *Guardian*, 6 April 1995.

64. Wardle, *The Times*, London, 10 April 1986.

65. Niamh Cusack, interview with Lesley Thornton, *Observer Colour Supplement*, 6 April 1986.

66. Michael Billington, *Guardian*, 10 April 1986.

67. *Romeo and Juliet*, Shakespeare in Production (2002).

68. Patrick Marmion, *Evening Standard*, 6 July 2000.
69. Benedict Nightingale, *The Times*, London, 7 November 1997.
70. *Romeo and Juliet*, RSC Education Pack, 1997.
71. Michael Billington, *Guardian*, 6 November 1997.
72. Alastair Macaulay, *Financial Times*, 10 November 1997.
73. Jane Edwardes, *Time Out*, 12 November 1997.
74. Ray Fearon, *Romeo and Juliet*, RSC Education Pack, 1997.
75. *Romeo and Juliet*, RSC Education Pack, 1989 (Doran was Assistant Director in Terry Hands' production).

ACKNOWLEDGMENTS AND PICTURE CREDITS

Preparation of "*Romeo and Juliet* in Performance" was assisted by a generous grant from the CAPITAL Centre (Creativity and Performance in Teaching and Learning) of the University of Warwick for research in the RSC archive at the Shakespeare Birthplace Trust. The Arts and Humanities Research Council (AHRC) funded a term's research leave that enabled Jonathan Bate to work on "The Director's Cut."

Picture research by Michelle Morton. Grateful acknowledgement is made to the Shakespeare Birthplace Trust for assistance with picture research (special thanks to Helen Hargest) and reproduction fees.

Images of RSC productions are supplied by the Shakespeare Centre Library and Archive, Stratford-upon-Avon. This Library, maintained by the Shakespeare Birthplace Trust, holds the most important collection of Shakespeare material in the UK, including the Royal Shakespeare Company's official archive. It is open to the public free of charge.

For more information see www.shakespeare.org.uk.

1. Directed by Peter Brook (1947) Angus McBean © Royal Shakespeare Company
2. Directed by Baz Luhrmann (1996) © Bazmark/RGA
3. Directed by Michael Bogdanov (1986) Joe Cocks Studio Collection © Shakespeare Birthplace Trust
4. Directed by Trevor Nunn (1976) Joe Cocks Studio Collection © Shakespeare Birthplace Trust
5. Directed by Michael Attenborough (1997) Malcolm Davies © Shakespeare Birthplace Trust
6. Directed by Michael Boyd (2000) Robert Workman © Royal Shakespeare Company
7. Directed by Michael Boyd (2000) Robert Workman © Royal Shakespeare Company
8. Reconstructed Elizabethan playhouse © Charcoalblue

With new commentary, as well as definitive
text and cutting-edge notes from the RSC's
William Shakespeare: Complete Works,
the first authoritative, modernized edition of
Shakespeare's First Folio in more than 300 years.

Hamlet

Love's Labour's
Lost

A Midsummer
Night's Dream

Richard III

The Tempest

Also available in hardcover
William Shakespeare: Complete Works

MODERN LIBRARY IS ONLINE AT WWW.MODERNLIBRARY.COM

MODERN LIBRARY ONLINE IS YOUR GUIDE TO CLASSIC LITERATURE ON THE WEB

THE MODERN LIBRARY E-NEWSLETTER

Our free e-mail newsletter is sent to subscribers, and features sample chapters, interviews with and essays by our authors, upcoming books, special promotions, announcements, and news. To subscribe to the Modern Library e-newsletter, visit **www.modernlibrary.com**

THE MODERN LIBRARY WEBSITE

Check out the Modern Library website at **www.modernlibrary.com** for:

- The Modern Library e-newsletter
- A list of our current and upcoming titles and series
- Reading Group Guides and exclusive author spotlights
- Special features with information on the classics and other paperback series
- Excerpts from new releases and other titles
- A list of our e-books and information on where to buy them
- The Modern Library Editorial Board's 100 Best Novels and 100 Best Nonfiction Books of the Twentieth Century written in the English language
- News and announcements

Questions? E-mail us at **modernlibrary@randomhouse.com**. For questions about examination or desk copies, please visit the Random House Academic Resources site at **www.randomhouse.com/academic**